Psychopharmacology and Aging

ADVANCES IN BEHAVIORAL BIOLOGY

Psychopharmacology and Aging

Edited by

Carl Eisdorfer, Ph.D., M.D.

Professor and Chairman
Department of Psychiatry and Behavioral Sciences
University of Washington Medical School
Seattle, Washington

and

William E. Fann, M.D.

Assistant Professor
Departments of Psychiatry and Pharmacology
Scientific Associate
Center for The Study of Aging and Human Development

Duke University Medical School
Durham, North Carolina

and

Staff Psychiatrist
Veterans Administration Hospital
Durham, North Carolina

PLENUM PRESS • **NEW YORK-LONDON**

Library of Congress Cataloging in Publication Data

Symposium on Psychopharmacology and the Aging Patient,
    Duke University, 1972.
    Psychopharmacology and aging.

    (Advances in behavioral biology, v. 6)
    Sponsored by the Center for the Study of Aging and Human Development and
the Department of Psychiatry at Duke.
    Includes bibliographies.
    1. Psychopharmacology–Congresses. 2. Geriatrics–Congresses. I. Eisdorfer,
Carl, ed. II. Fann, William E., ed. III. Duke University, Durham, N.C. Center for the
Study of Aging and Human Development. IV. Duke University, Durham, N.C. Dept.
of Psychiatry. V. Title. [DNLM: 1. Aging–Congresses. 2. Psychopharmacology–
Congresses. W3 AD215 v. 6 1972 / QV77 S9895p 1972]
RM315.S97   1972   615′.78   73-9995
ISBN 0-306-37906-6

The proceedings of a symposium held at Duke University, May 29-31, 1972

© 1973 Plenum Press, New York
A Division of Plenum Publishing Corporation
227 West 17th Street, New York, N.Y. 10011

United Kingdom edition published by Plenum Press, London
A Division of Plenum Publishing Company, Ltd.
Davis House (4th Floor), 8 Scrubs Lane, Harlesden, London, NW10 6SE, England

Printed in the United States of America

*To the elderly
and to our colleagues
who share our concern
for their well-being*

Acknowledgements

The editors wish to express their sincerest appreciation to Mrs. Dorothy Heyman, Executive Secretary, Center for Aging and Human Development, Duke University Medical Center, for her inestimable work in making the program possible. Also, Jeanine Carver who labored so diligently in editing and proof-reading the manuscripts and especially to Bruce Richman who worked as our special Editorial Assistant for this book.

Contents

Introduction

Section I: Bases of a Psychopharmacology for Aging

Section II: Complications of Drug Use

Section III: Issues in Clinical Management of Drugs

Foreword

This volume represents the proceedings of a Symposium on Psychopharmacology and the Aging Patient, held at Duke University, May 29-31, 1972. The conference was jointly sponsored by the Center for the Study of Aging and Human Development and the Department of Psychiatry at Duke. This Symposium was the first in a series of conferences which will be devoted variously to preclinical and clinical pharmacology of the different groups of psychotropic drugs, especially as they relate to the problems of the elderly patient and to the special considerations that must be given in theory and in practice to changes brought about by the process of aging.

The idea behind this particular symposium was to bring basic and clinical scientists together with practicing clinicians and other mental health professionals for an exchange of ideas and interests through formal didactic and informal small sessions. The major interest, of course, was to disseminate current information on the clinical use and indication for psychoactive agents, particularly as they related to the elderly patient. Recognition and management of psychiatric syndromes of the elderly were included as they were pertinent to psychopharmacology of aging to indicate the direction of ongoing work and to stimulate further research in this area.

The editors wish to gratefully acknowledge the generous financial support of the Symposium granted by the following pharmaceutical firms:

Smith-Kline-French Laboratories
Pfizer Laboratories
and
Abbott Laboratories
Burroughs-Wellcome Company
CIBA — Geigy Corporation
Lakeside Laboratories
McNeil Laboratories, Inc.
Merck, Sharp and Dohme
Roche Laboratories
Sandoz Pharmaceuticals
Schering Corporation

Special thanks are due:

Stanley H. Appel, M.D.
Ewald W. Busse, M.D.
Jonathan O. Cole, M.D.
Morris Lipton, M.D.
Hans Lowenbach, M.D.
Eugene A. Stead, Jr., M.D.
Barnes Woodhall, M.D.

for their contributions as speakers and as guest section chairmen.

Additionally we would like to thank Mary Lee Brehm, Ph.D.; Daniel T. Gianturco, M.D.; John D. Griffith, M.D.; Albert Heyman, M.D.; Marcel Kinsbourne, M.D.; Walter D. Obrist, Ph.D.; Joseph B. Parker, Jr., M.D.; Saul M. Schanberg, M.D., Ph.D.; Virginia Stone, R.N., Ph.D.; Larry W. Thompson, Ph.D.; Hsioh-Shan Wang, M.D.; and Frances L. Wilkie, M.A., for their participation in the conference.

C. Eisdorfer, Ph.D., M.D.
W.E. Fann, M.D.

Contributors

1. Robert J. Barrett, Ph.D., Assistant Professor of Psychology, Department of Psychology, Vanderbilt University, Nashville, Tennessee.

2. H. Keith Brodie, M.D., Assistant Professor of Psychiatry, Stanford University Medical Center, Palo Alto, California.

3. John M. Davis, M.D., Professor of Psychiatry; Associate Professor of Pharmacology, Vanderbilt University Medical School, Nashville, Tennessee.

4. W. Donner Denckla, M.D., Assistant Member, Roche Institute of Molecular Biology, Nutley, New Jersey.

5. Carl Eisdorfer, Ph.D., M.D., Professor and Chairman, Department of Psychiatry, University of Washington Medical Center, Seattle, Washington.

6. M. Khaled El-Yousef, M.D., Instructor in Psychiatry, Vanderbilt University Medical School, Nashville, Tennessee.

7. William E. Fann, M.D., Assistant Professor of Psychiatry; Assistant Professor of Pharmacology, Duke University Medical Center, Durham, N.C.

8. Robert O. Friedel, M.D., Assistant Professor of Psychiatry; Assistant Professor of Pharmacology, Duke University Medical Center, Durham, N.C.

9. Samuel Gershon, M.D., Chief of Neuropsychopharmacology, New York University Medical Center, New York, New York.

10. Robert L. Green, Jr., M.D., Chief of Staff, Veterans Administration Hospital; Professor of Psychiatry, Duke University Medical Center, Durham, N.C.

11. David S. Janowsky, M.D., Associate Professor of Psychiatry and Pharmacology, Vanderbilt University Medical School, Nashville, Tennessee.

12. Lissy F. Jarvik, M.D., Ph.D., Director, Psychogenetic Unit, Veterans Administration Resocialization Center at Sawtelle, Wilshire and Sawtelle Boulevards, Los Angeles, California; Professor of Psychiatry, University of California at Los Angeles, Los Angeles, California.

13. Murray Jarvik, Ph.D., M.D., Professor of Psychiatry and Pharmacology, University of California at Los Angeles, Los Angeles, California.

14. Donald R. Jasinski, M.D., Assistant Professor of Pharmacology, University of Kentucky; Chief, Clinical Pharmacology Section, N.I.M.H., Addiction Research Center, Lexington, Kentucky.

15. C. Raymond Lake, M.D., Ph.D., Resident in Psychiatry, Department of Psychiatry, Duke University Medical Center, Durham, N.C.

16. L. Frank Major, M.D., Resident in Psychiatry, Department of Psychiatry, Duke University Medical Center, Durham, N.C.

17. Alexander Nies, M.D., Professor of Psychiatry, Dartmouth University Medical School, Hanover, New Hampshire; Chief, Psychiatry Service, White River Veterans Administration Hospital.

18. G.C. Palmer, Ph.D., Post-Doctoral Fellow, Department of Pharmacology, Vanderbilt University Medical School, Nashville, Tennessee.

19. George W. Paulson, M.D., Clinical Associate Professor of Neurology, Ohio State University School of Medicine; Private Practice in Medical Neurology; Neurologic Association, Inc., Columbus, Ohio.

20. Daniel T. Peak, M.D., Assistant Professor of Psychiatry, Head of Unit I, Older American Resources and Services (OARS), Duke University Medical Center, Durham, N.C.

21. Eric A. Pfeiffer, M.D., Project Director, Older Americans Resources and Services (OARS); Professor of Psychiatry, Duke University Medical Center, Durham, N.C.

22. Arthur J. Prange, Jr., M.D., Professor of Psychiatry, Head, Section of Psychiatry Research, Department of Psychiatry, University of North Carolina Medical School, Chapel Hill, N.C.

23. C. Lewis Ravaris, Ph.D., M.D., Associate Professor of Psychiatry, University of Vermont College of Medicine, Burlington, Vermont.

24. Oakley S. Ray, Ph.D., Professor of Psychology; Associate Professor of Pharmacology, Vanderbilt University Medical School, Nashville, Tennessee.

25. Donald S. Robinson, M.D., Associate Professor of Medicine and Pharmacology, University of Vermont College of Medicine, Burlington, Vermont.

26. G. Alan Robison, Ph.D., Associate Professor of Pharmacology, Vanderbilt University Medical School, Nashville, Tennessee.

27. Carl Salzman, M.D., Assistant Professor of Psychiatry; Harvard Medical School, Boston, Massachusetts.

28. M.J. Schmidt, Ph.D., Post-Doctoral Fellow, Department of Pharmacology, Vanderbilt University Medical School, Nashville, Tennessee.

29. Richard Shader, M.D., Associate Professor of Psychiatry, Harvard Medical School, Boston, Massachusetts.

30. Bernard Stotsky, Ph.D., M.D., Professor of Psychology, Boston State University; Consultant in Geriatric Psychiatry, Boston State Hospital, Boston, Massachusetts.

31. Adriaan Verwoerdt, M.D., Professor of Psychiatry; Director of Geriatric Psychiatry Training Program, Duke University Medical Center, Durham, N.C.

32. Alan D. Whanger, M.D., Assistant Professor of Psychiatry, Duke University Medical Center, Durham, N.C.

33. Ian C. Wilson, M.D., Research Psychiatrist, North Carolina State Department of Mental Health, The Dorothea Dix Hospital, Raleigh, N.C.

34. William P. Wilson, M.D., Professor and Head, Division of Clinical Neurophysiology; Professor of Psychiatry, Duke University Medical Center, Durham, N.C.

35. William W.K. Zung, M.D., Professor of Psychiatry, Duke University Medical Center, Durham, N.C.

Preface

A perusal of several recent issues of the *Journal of the American Medical Association* revealed some interesting advertising trends. As a limited number of issues were utilized and only full-page advertisements were counted, no definite conclusions are justified, but some speculations are in order. Approximately 25% of the full-page advertisements were devoted to the broad spectrum of psychopharmacological agents. Another 25% were devoted to drugs that influence metabolic and endocrine functions. Twenty per cent were aimed at promoting analgesic agents, many of them not requiring prescriptions. Ten per cent related to antibiotics; and the remainder, a broad variety of pharmacological agents including drugs utilized in cardiovascular disease and those affecting the gastrointestinal tract. Therefore, I believe it is reasonably safe to say that the manufacturers of drugs do recognize the considerable importance of psychopharmacological agents in the modern practice of medicine. However, of the advertisements concerned with alleviating mental and emotional signs and symptoms, very few, i.e., less than 10% of the 25%, made any mention of the specific drug's application or its limitations when applied to mental problems of the elderly. This is indeed unfortunate as too many physicians do not appreciate how the aging process alters the interaction between pharmacological agents and the physiological systems of the patient. In addition, they all too often do not understand that there is a third factor which must always be considered and that is that the simultaneous administration of two or more drugs may result in dangerous toxic reactions and may seriously influence the efficiency of one or all of the medications. For example, the interaction that occurs between hypnotic and sedative drugs on one hand and oral anticoagulants is of extreme importance. Oral anticoagulant potentiation or antagonism has been reported with almost every class of hypnotic and sedative agent. Therefore, the physician, and particularly the psychiatrists, must carefully weigh such possibilities before prescribing these drugs for any patient already receiving anticoagulant therapy.

Obviously, I believe that the need for continuing education in psychopharmacology and the aging is essential to maintaining the skills of the practitioner. The editors and the contributors to this particular volume have skillfully put together much of the knowledge that is needed by the practitioner. It is hoped that all participants responsible for this volume will see fit to periodically update this vitally needed information.

This volume will be a source of stimulation for those interested in investigation.

Ewald W. Busse, M.D., Sc. D.
J.P. Gibbons Professor of Psychiatry
  and Chairman of the Department
Chairman, Council of Aging and Human Development
Duke University

Introduction

Issues in the Psychopharmacology of the Aged

Carl Eisdorfer, Ph.D., M.D.

Aging is a familiar phenomenon. Subsequent to a period of development, all complex biologic systems appear to undergo a process of change leading to the loss of adaptability of that system. In this context, it is surprising that aging in humans has attracted so little attention to the biologist and clinician until recent years. It is interesting to note that the Gerontological Society, that is, the organization of scientists interested in aging, has existed as an entity for only approximately 25 years and the American Geriatrics Society, a group of physicians interested in the aged, is approximately the same age, in contrast to the American Psychiatry Association which dates back well over a century. I suspect that there are many issues underlying this relatively belated interest in careful, scientific, and clinical scrutiny of the aged. Perhaps three reasons of particular interest may help to explain this phenomenon. They include the poor visibility of numbers of aged persons, the questionable efficacy of intervention, and the personal reactions of many people to older persons, old age, and the problem of facing death.

To a certain extent there have been important changes in these factors. The aged population has exhibited a very significant growth in the past several decades. While the population of the United States has grown by a factor of 2½ times since the turn of the century, the aged population has grown 7 fold. Persons over 65 years of age now comprise approximately 10% of the population, about 20 million Americans. Recent trends show that the older part of this population (that is, those 75 and older) is growing at a more rapid rate than the total aged population, and that this rate of growth of the aged, led by the older cohort, will continue to escalate until about the year 2000.

Another factor of some consequence is that while, for the moment, most of the population growth cited exists because of health measures affecting infancy and childhood, we are beginning to see movement toward increased life expectancy in older years. With vigorous approaches to cancer and cardiovascular disease, we may anticipate that the next set of medical advances will influence the extension of life in our older rather than our younger population. This potential carries with it some clear problems.

The aged are a population at risk. In a number of ways they manifest more psychological, medical, and social difficulties than are exhibited in the adult population at large. Not only are the aged economically deprived, receiving as they do only about 50% of their pre-retirement income, but approximately 1/5 are living at income levels below the poverty line. The aged have medical care needs which appear to increase. From 2/3 to 3/4 of older persons have at least one chronic disease and about half the aged population have two. The data show that older persons utilize medical outpatient facilities half again as frequently as do adults aged 17-44, (and that short and long term hospital bed care is even more proportionately used by the aged in comparison with their number in population). Of the approximately one million nursing home patients in the United States, more than 85% are 65 years and older. The rates of suicide are highest among aged adult men and first psychiatric admissions are heightened in persons over 65. All of this and much more suggests that the aged are a vulnerable group. There are also data to suggest that even beyond the heightened rate of utilization of medical care facilities, the needs of the aged may still be greater. Thus, Osfelt and his colleagues (1) in their study of older persons in the Chicago area have demonstrated that although half were seen as needing medical care, on the basis of medical examination only 25% of the group did in fact recognize this need and identify themselves as ill, the remaining proportion feeling that their condition was due to being old. Indeed, a recent report indicates that 46% of our older population suffers from some disability which compromises their work or recreational activities in daily life.

Psychiatric care and the prevention of mental disorder in the aged is hardly known for its advanced state. Until fairly recently, approximately 25% to 30% of all new state hospital admissions were aged patients. It is impressive that during the same period, only 2% of the outpatient visits to mental health professionals in both public and private facilities were made by aged patients. That 2% figure has remained constant. Currently, state hospital inpatient admission for the aged dropped off. This reduction is not due to any particular improvement in the prevention or treatment of those conditions requiring hospitalization by older persons, but rather has been the result of a series of administrative decisions in many of our larger states which divert the aged from state hospitalization to nursing home care. The study by Epstein and Simon (2) tracing the long term outcome to patients in one such state indicates that on most parameters, state hospital patients do better after a year than do nursing home patients. Thus the data must lead us to question seriously whether the use of "nursing homes" as an operational approach to treating people in "the community" does not, in fact, do the patient more harm than good. It does appear, on the face of it, that the care of emotionally and cognitively disturbed aged patients in the nursing home setting, with limited resources, without psychiatric consultation, and often without an adequately trained staff of aides, would lead to considerable difficulties in the treatment of the aged patient. Indeed, serious problems do occur and abuses do appear in the professional and lay literature. It is of some interest, however, that relatively little scientific investigation has been made of the nursing home setting and its effectiveness – a remarkable fact given the hundreds of millions of bed days spent in nursing homes at this time.

One possible area of drug abuse which has come under particularly heavy attack in the lay press has been in the use of psychopharmacologic agents among the nursing home population. Accusations have been levelled that "pharmacologic straitjackets" are used in many institutions to facilitate staff care. These involve large doses of psychotropic agents presumably prescribed to reduce agitation, but actually placing the patient in an almost incapacitated state so that he is more amendable to nursing staff ministrations. The Subcommittee on Long Term Care of the Senate Special Committee on Aging has heard repeated testimony on the overuse and misuse of psychotropic drugs by attendants, aides, and even nurses who will administer one patient's drugs to another or use a supply of drugs ad lib to control a patient's behavior. There are reports of totally untrained, inexperienced aides administering drugs, and one such instance reports a person dispensing drugs within 45 minutes of being hired despite the fact that he reported absolutely no experience in any of the health fields, and presented himself as a derelict looking for any sort of position.

Such anecdotal reports and the expressed concerns of many Americans, including those involved in providing long term care, must lead us to be concerned about the use and abuse of psychoactive drugs.

Lennard and his associates (3) report that more than 202 million prescriptions for psychotropic medication were filled in the United States by persons who saw physicians during the year 1970 alone, and this number is escalating. Among the key issues in the psychopharmacology of the aged are the social impacts of drug utilization of all persons. We see ethical drug companies which devote considerable effort to the education of physicians on broadening the use of psychopharmacologic agents. Professional journals are the sites of advertisements suggesting that adjunctive tranquilizers are valuable in helping individuals hurdle the anticipated difficulties of going into new situations which formerly they had to cope with on the basis of their own personality strengths. We are told that the fears of going to college, going to the dentist and everyday classroom anxieties of the child, among other events, should be modified with tranquilizers of one or another sort. In a sense, the implication is that all potential anxiety provoking situations should be mediated or medicated out of existence by the use of an appropriate psychotropic drug. Of course, the potential long term consequences to personality structure which might occur from the widespread use of this approach are never discussed and indeed are really unknown. Certainly the impact of introducing children and their parents to the control of all situational stresses with medicinal help is frighteningly reminiscent of the pattern portrayed by George Orwell in *1984.* In the balance, however, it must also be pointed out that psychotropic drugs can be tremendously beneficial. The reversal in the need for state hospitalization use by schizophrenics, our ability to reach patients formerly noncommunicative, and the valuable role of reversing such disorders or symptoms as depression, hallucination, and agitation, among others, cannot be ignored. Indeed, it would be unethical and irrational to dismiss all psychotropic drug prescribing or ingestion as evil or worthless. What is clearly indicated however, is a more rational approach to what constitutes the legitimate role of psychoactive agents in human behavior.

As I indicated earlier, in the case of the aged, this need is particularly acute. With approximately 4% of all older persons in full custodial care institutions and the vast majority of all older persons under medical care and, therefore, at the relative mercy of health professionals, most aged persons are typically not in a position to determine for themselves whether they should or should not take drugs. Indeed, in the case of patients in the hospital or nursing home, their wishes typically play a very small role in their treatment.

The role of the health care specialist becomes particularly significant, and the trade off between drug effectiveness for the patients' needs — as opposed to easier management by the staff — becomes a serious issue. In this introduction, I have ignored many of the salient aspects of the aging process. A variety of physical illnesses and metabolic changes involving lungs, kidneys, heart circulation, and the rest, represent significant clinical challenges to the physician so far as effective drug use is concerned. The physician in practice is under increased pressure when he deals with patients with multiple disease entities, and since about half of the aged population have more than one illness, this is very much an issue.

Not only must the clinician be concerned with the metabolism of drugs in the case of his patient with impaired respiratory or renal function, but he is also faced with the frequent complication of paradoxical drug effects on an already impaired autonomic or central nervous system. The biology of aging is not entirely known, and the psychopharmacology of aging has yet to be precisely defined.

For the future new approaches may be possible. At this time the value of drugs in the treatment of a variety of recognizable behavioral and affective difficulties is universally accepted. The possibility exists that intellectual and cognitive difficulties now a problem for many older persons can be modified by agents acting upon the cardiovascular, autonomic, or central nervous system. We need far greater understanding of such obvious variables as maintenance of adequate cerebral circulation and the control of hypertension as well as new approaches such as hyperbaria, anticoagulants, the regulation or modification of autonomic function, better autonomic-central nervous system interaction, and direct cortical acting drugs, just to name a few areas currently being explored.

We face new opportunities and will see new dilemmas. The possibility exists of new drugs to control the symptoms and, indeed, the process of aging. The problems of abuse and overuse, of a "drug dependent culture," of side effects — physiologic, psychologic, or social — and of costs and distribution all accompany such advances.

The conference and this report thus represent a beginning effort to identify crucial variables in treating aged patients. Ultimately the value of any component of good patient care lies in its effectiveness in promoting better long term personal adaptation of the individual in order that he or she may be able to maximize their ability to function in whatever their social matrix. This is no less the case with aging.

References

1. Osfelt, A., Frequency and Nature of Health Problems of Retired Persons in F.M. Carp (ed.) Retirement Process. Wash. D.C. U.S. Public Health Service Publication No. 1778, 1968.

2. Eptsein, L.J. and Simon, A., Alternatives to State Hospitalization for the Geriatric Mentally Ill. *Amer. J. Psychia.* 124: 955-961, 1968.

3. Lennard, H.C. et al.: *Mystification and Drug Misuse.* New York, Harper and Row, Publishers, Inc. 1971, p. vii.

Section 1

Bases of a
Psychopharmacology for the Aging

Norepinephrine, Dopamine and Serotonin:
CNS Distribution, Biosynthesis and Metabolism

Robert O. Friedel, M.D.

At the present time the bulk of experimental data relating biochemical factors to certain disorders of human behavior is converging in support of hypotheses implicating the biogenic amines norepinephrine (NE), dopamine (DA), and serotonin (5-HT). The theoretical importance of these substances depends on their putative role as CNS neurotransmitters involved in the central control of a variety of functions ranging from postural tone and appetite to sleep and feeling states. It is felt currently that an understanding of the biochemical etiology and the pharmacological treatment of mental disorders depends on the clarification of the related alterations in the distribution, synthesis, and metabolism of these monoamines. Our basic knowledge of CNS monoamines has increased greatly over the past twenty years, but is still incomplete. This chapter is a selective presentation of the major concepts currently advanced in this area.

I. Norepinephrine and Dopamine

Most of the information available regarding the distribution of the catecholamines and 5-HT in the CNS has resulted primarily from studies using the very sensitive and specific histochemical fluorescence method developed by the Scandinavian investigators (1). Using this technique it has been found that both ascending and descending NE neuron systems exist [Figure 1]. NE cell bodies located in the pons (locus coeruleus) and medulla oblongata (formatio reticularis), ascend primarily in the medial forebrain bundle and terminate in the telecephalon, diencephalon and cerebellum. Other NE containing neurons orginate in the medulla oblongata (nucleus reticularis lateralis), descend in the anterior and lateral funiculi of the spinal cord and probably connect there with motor neurons of both flexor and extensor groups and preganglionic sympathetic nerve cells.

11

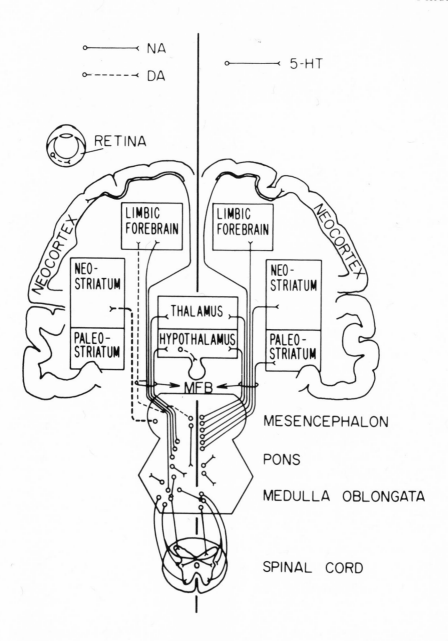

Figure 1.

Schematic drawing showing, in highly simplified form, the main monoamine neuron systems in the central nervous system. (From Andén et al., Ascending monoamine neurons to the telencephalon and diencephalon. Acta. Physiol. Scand. 67:313-326, 1966).

Three DA neuron systems have been identified [Figure 1]. One system originates in the substantia nigra and ascends through the crus cerebri and the internal capsule to terminate in the caudate nucleus and the putamen. Another major DA system arises in the middle mesencephalon, ascends in the lateral portion of the medial forebrain bundle and terminates in the limbic forebrain (nucleus accumbens and tuberculum olfactorium). DA neurons also originate in the arcuate and periventricular nuclei of the hypothalamus and converge onto the capillary plexus of the hypophyseal portal systems.

The biosynthesis and metabolism of NE and DA have received a considerable amount of study and are fairly well understood (2). The synthesis of NE and DA from tyrosine [Figure 2] takes places initially in the cytoplasm and is completed in the storage granules. It is believed that there are three pools of NE and DA within nerve terminals. The first is an *intragranular reserve pool* in equilibrium *with an intragranular mobile pool* which is released from the nerve ending by the action potential. Released NE and DA react with receptor sites on the postsynaptic membrane and then are removed by active transport back into the nerve terminal or inactivated by the enzyme catechol-O-methyl transferase (COMT) present on the postsynaptic membrane [Figure 3]. NE and DA taken back up into nerve ending into the *cytoplasmic mobile pool* and then are actively transported into the intragranular mobile pool. The mitochondrial enzyme monoamine (MAO) also controls the size of the cytoplasmic mobile pool.

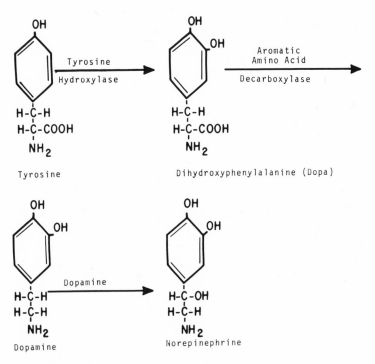

Figure 2. Biosynthesis of norepinephrine and dopamine.

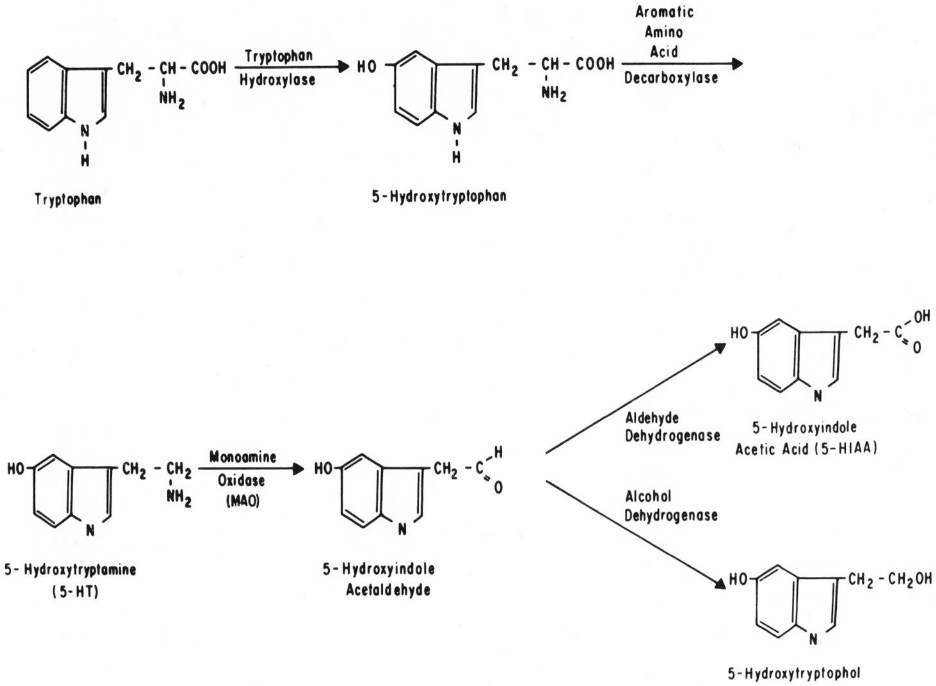

Figure 3. Metabolism of norepinephrine and dopamine.

II. Serotonin

Both ascending and descending pathways have been described for 5-HT neuron systems [Figure 1]. 5-HT containing neurons originate in the raphe nuclei of the lower brain stem and ascend through the medial forebrain bundle to terminate in the telencephalon, diencephalon and limbic forebrain. Other 5-HT neurons originating in the lower raphe nuclei descend in the anterior and lateral funiculi of the spinal cord to innervate the sympathetic lateral column and cell bodies of motor neurons of both flexor and extensor groups.

Serotonin is synthesized from the amino acid tryptophan [Figure 4]. The main degradative pathway for 5-HT probably involves its deamination by the enzyme MAO to the corresponding aldehyde which is then oxidized to 5-hydroxyindole acetic acid (5-HIAA) or reduced to 5-hydroxytryptophol (2).

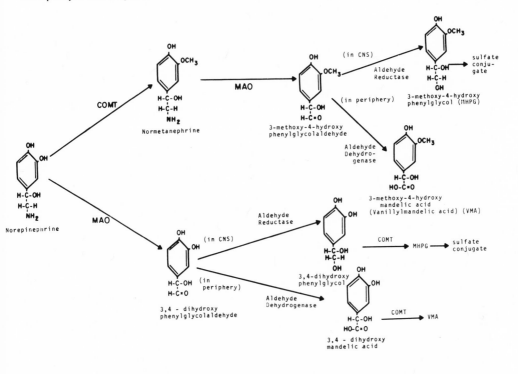

Figure 4. Biosynthesis and metabolism of serotonin.

References

1. Dahlström, A., and Fuxe, K.: Evidence for the existence of monoamine-containing neurons in the central nervous system. *Acta. Physiol. Scand.* 62:Suppl. 232:1-55, 1964.

2. Axelrod, J.: Brain monoamines: biosynthesis and fate. *Neuro-sciences Res. Prog. Bull.* 9:188-196, March, 1971.

Interaction of Learning and Memory with Age in the Rat

Oakley S. Ray, Ph.D.
Robert J. Barrett, Ph.D.

Introduction

This paper focuses on three issues which are important when rodents—rats or mice—are used in studying learning and memory and their interaction with the process of aging. A first question is: what data are now available in the literature? A second issue is primarily methodological and speaks to the question of the validity and generality of existing and future data in this area. The last consideration is the implication animal studies of learning, memory, and aging have for work at the human level.

The review of existing literature which will be presented is brief and only illustrative. The primary thrust of this paper is on the methodological issues involved in work in this area and we will support our concerns with data from our laboratory. The concluding section will also be brief since there are individuals here who are far better qualified to deal with the jump from animal behavior research to human behavior in the clinic.

The Available Literature

When long-term memory in animals is mentioned to a behavioral scientist two classic studies are immediately remembered. They are classic, however, only because they stand alone, not because they are monumental. The 1934 study by Liddell (1) which demonstrated two year retention of a classically conditioned motor response in sheep, and the 1950 report by Skinner (2) that pigeons retain a discriminated pecking response for four years do not give the present day researcher much to build upon. There are other long-term retention studies (3) but the data are sparse. A 1971 paper (4) commented "There is a paucity of animal studies concerned with long term memory" (p. 1348) and

17

"No data are available in the literature regarding long-term retention of learned avoidance behavior in rodents." (p. 1343).

This 1971 article contained shuttle box avoidance data for C57BL/6J female mice trained to avoid foot shock at the ages of 3, 6, 9, 12, and 15 months and then tested for retention at age 15 months. The authors reported that "shuttle box learning in mice declined with advancing age..."(p.1343) Another series of mice were all trained at the age of 3 months with retention testing at 3, 6, 9 or 12 months after acquisition. They found that retention "...decreased progressively with increasing acquisition-retention time intervals..."(p. 1343)

These data are congruent with other data in the literature. (5,6) Studies which train animals at ages considerably beyond sexual maturity usually report a decrease in the rate (amount) of learning with increasing age. Reviewing the literature is most discouraging though. Regularly, papers are published whose titles sound relevant: "Effects of Age on Learning and Retention..."(7) The abstract makes clear that the age variable is very restricted. The younger animals are appropriately and accurately described—i.e., they are usually one to two weeks past weaning—30 to 40 days of age—and well before sexual maturity. The upper age limit is quite truncated however. In most behavioral, developmental papers the "older" animals are 100 days old. In an animal whose life span is 20 to 24 months or more and sexual maturity occurs at 50-70 days, a 100 day old rat is little more than an awkward adolescent. Better titles for these papers would be "Learning and Retention at Several Ages in the Young Rat."

A similar problem exists when the literature on long-term memory retention is studied. Rarely, at any age level, has anyone looked at learning-retest intervals longer than 30 days. (See 8) We have also sinned—one of our early papers on the effects of electroconvulsive shock on memory included a long-term retention interval: 42 days! (9) We were quite proud of that since previous work from other labs had talked similarly about the intervals of, at most, 30 days (10,11). A 40% increase in retention interval over previous work in the field was quite good we felt. As will be clear, our views have changed somewhat—although we still sin occasionally.

Some of our earlier research with mice are representative of the kinds of data which have been published in this area. At the time of these studies our primary concern was on the effect of electroconvulsive shock on the retention of a passive avoidance response. To make possible the identification of the time at which the learning experience occurred we tested the animals in a one-trial passive avoidance unit—the Jarvik Box—which is shown in Figure 1.

There are two compartments, one brightly illuminated and the other dark, with a small opening between them. The animal is placed in the well-lighted side, facing away from the opening, and the time recorded before the subject moves into the dark side. When the animal enters the dark compartment foot shock is delivered and the subject is then removed to his home cage. The next day the animal is returned to the well-lighted

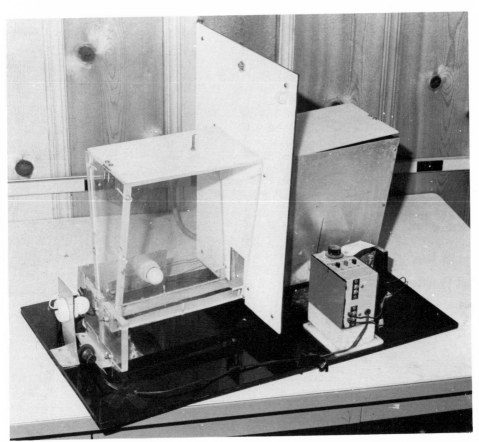

Figure 1.
Two compartment passive-avoidance unit. Animal is placed in the illuminated plexiglass compartment. When the animal enters the dark, metal compartment shock is delivered.

compartment. The response measure is the time interval between being placed in the start compartment on this second day and the entrance into the dark compartment where foot shock was delivered 24 hours before. This procedure is repeated on several consecutive days. The subject's latency of response, i.e., time to enter the dark compartment, was used as the measure of learning—learning to avoid foot shock by remaining in the start compartment. When an animal stayed in the start compartment for 600 seconds in one day he was removed and returned, without foot shock, to his home cage.

Figure 2 presents data from one study (12) and shows the average number of seconds each group remained in the start compartment on the second and third day of acquisition. Day one is the first training trial and response latencies are typically 10 to 20 seconds for all animals. Both sexes of three strains of mice were used with either no, 0.3, or 2.8 mA of foot shock being delivered when the dark compartment was entered. There are significant strain and sex factors but only the age and foot shock level results will be mentioned. Ss were either 60, 240, or 300 days old at time of testing as indicated in the figure.

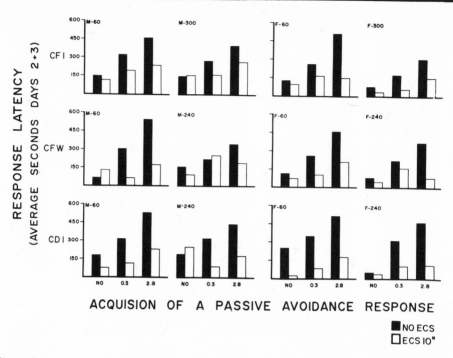

Figure 2.
Average latency for animals to enter the dark compartment of the passive-avoidance unit on the second and third day of testing (i.e., after foot shock had been delivered on days one and two).

As a brief summary of what is apparent in Figure 2—with increasing foot shock levels the response latency of all animals increased. For all six groups—three strains and two sexes—the increase in response latency was less for the older animals, i.e., they have not "learned" to avoid foot shock as well as the 60 day old animals. It should be noted that these data—where the correct response is to remain passive, as well as the shuttle box data (in the 1971 paper (4) already mentioned) where the correct response requires activity—suggest that rate of learning is slower in the older animal. As a point of caution, however, remember that what is being monitored is a change in behavior, not learning per se. To build the case that a change in behavior is due to learning it is necessary to show that other, nonassociative factors are not the basis for the performance change. This issue becomes central in the body of this paper.

As a final comment in this literature section we have presented data elsewhere (13) which shows that in 70 day old rats tested in the same passive-avoidance task (but a larger testing unit), retention 24 hours after a single foot shock is equally good, and essentially the same, whether a 1.4 or 2.8 mA foot shock is used. When animals given a single trial were tested 48 days later, retention was the same as at 24 hours if a 2.8 mA shock had been delivered, i.e., retention of the task persisted. If only 1.4 mA foot shock was used in the training trial there was a very large and significant decrease in response latency, i.e., retention of the passive avoidance behavior was good 48 days later if a high foot shock level was used in training but poor with a moderate shock level.

The Analysis of Animal Behavior

Our research emphasis for several years has attempted an analysis of the determinants of animal behavior—organismic and environmental. The study of animal factors which influence behavior has focused on strain, sex, and age. The environmental factors have included a broad spectrum of experimental manipulations some of which will be

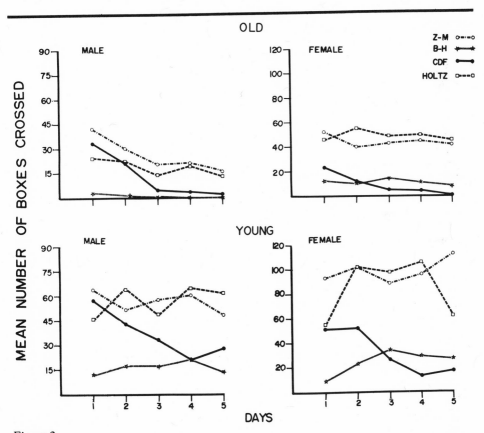

Figure 3.
Mean number of boxes crossed in the open field during five days of testing. (Note different male and female ordinates.)

mentioned in the following sections. In the process of presenting our data which are most relevant to the concerns of this conference, we will repeatedly point out some of the methodological problems which permeate animal research in the area of learning, memory, and aging.

Genetic Factors — One of the little used variables in behavioral research is that of strain differences. One of our first studies (14) looked specifically at the behavioral differences among four strains of commercially available rats. Animals used were albinos from Zivic-Miller Laboratories in Pittsburgh, black hooded from Simonsen Laboratories, albinos from Holtzman Laboratories, and the inbred Fischer Strain, CDF, from Charles River Laboratories. Both sexes, as well as young (60 day) and old (300-350 day) animals, were studied in a variety of behavioral procedures.

Activity level and habituation to a novel situation were studied in a standard four foot square open field marked off into one foot squares. Each animal was placed, one at a time, in the center of the open field and the number of squares it entered in a 5 minute period recorded. This procedure was repeated for 5 consecutive days and Figure 3 contains the results. Age, sex and strain differences in activity and in the decrease in

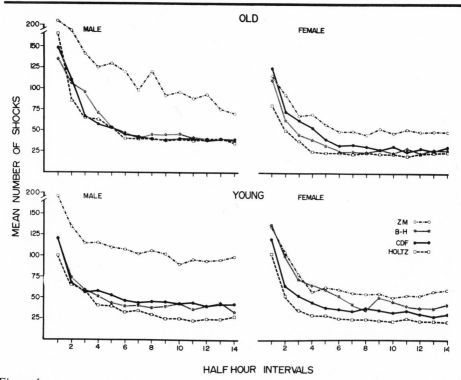

Figure 4.
Mean number of shocks received across 30-minute intervals during the 7-hour nondiscriminated-avoidance session.

activity over days (habituation) were clearly significant. Note especially that the Y-axis for females is different than for males. The young animals are clearly more active than the old animals. The two strains which will be of continuing interest here are the Zivic-Miller animals and the CDF's.

Figure 4 reports data from naive animals tested in a nondiscriminated avoidance situation. Here the animals are given a 0.5 mA, 0.5 second foot shock every 20 seconds unless they press a lever in the side of the experimental chamber—a Skinner Box. A lever press delays delivery of the foot shock for 20 seconds and by pressing at least once every 19 seconds the animal *could* avoid all foot shocks. The figure presents the number of foot shocks received in each 1/2 hour block for 7 hours of continuous testing.

Although the strain differences and sex differences are significant, the age of the *S*'s did not seem to have an impact on performance in this situation. Not quite the same result is evident in Figure 5 which presents data from a discriminated shuttle box

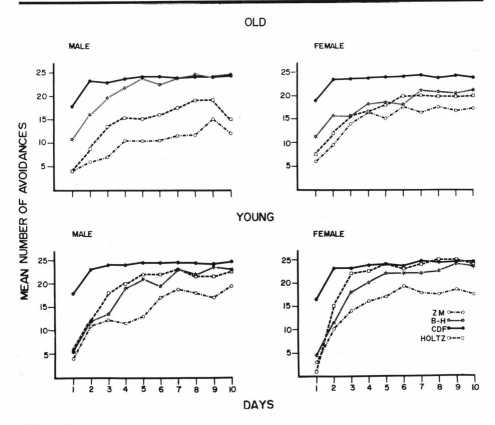

Figure 5.
Mean number of avoidances across 10 days of testing in the shuttle box.

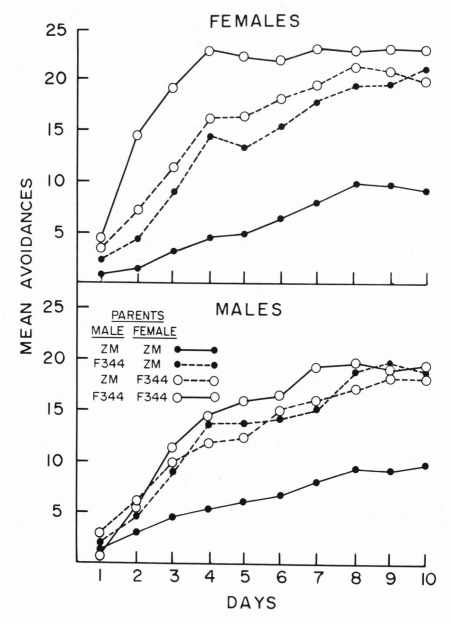

Figure 6.
    Mean number of avoidances across 10 days of testing in the shuttle box for the offspring of the indicated parents.

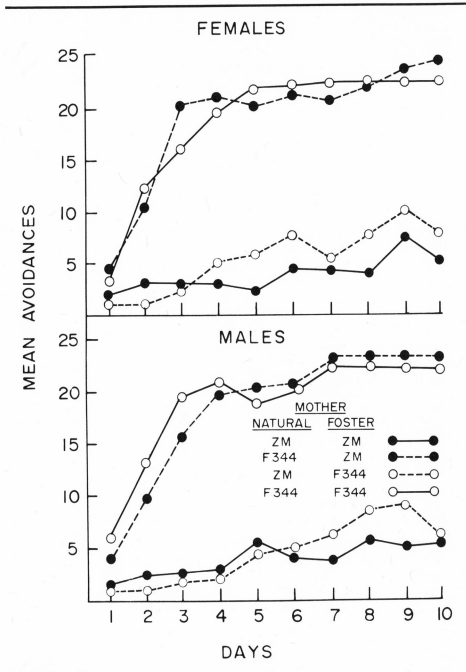

Figure 7.
    Mean number of avoidances across 10 days of testing in shuttle box for the foster
    care groups.

avoidance paradigm. In this procedure the animal is placed in the lighted side of a two compartment box and when the light switches to the other compartment the animal has 10 seconds in which to follow the light to the other compartment to avoid foot shock. If the animal does not move to the lighted compartment foot shock is delivered until it does move. A thirty second interval between trials was used and each animal was given 25 trials a day for 10 days. The figure plots the number of shock avoidance responses each day—i.e., the number of times the animals moved to the newly lighted compartment before foot shock was delivered.

In this task there are age related differences in performance which are strain and sex dependent. All CDF animals do well and all Zivic-Miller S's do poorly. The older male Zivic-Miller S's avoid shock only about 65% as often as the young S's but there are no aged related avoidance differences in the females of this strain.

Interestingly, the most active S's in the open field situation—the Zivic-Miller—do the poorest in this active avoidance situation. Conversely, the strain (CDF) that does best here (i.e., avoids foot shock most often) was the least active strain in the open field.

The strain of the animal was so clearly the most potent variable in the study just reported that we designed an experiment to explore the basis for the strain differences. (15) Animals from both the Zivic-Miller and Fischer strains were bred and crossbred in

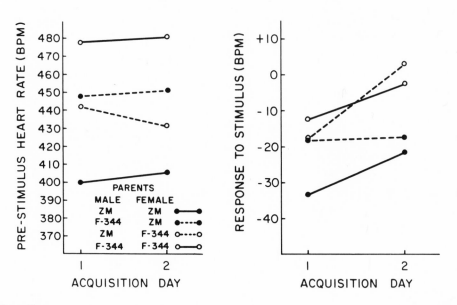

Figure 8.
Baseline heart rate (left) and heart rate changes during a shock-paired tone (right) for female offspring of the indicated parents.

our laboratory and the offspring reared to 80 days before testing. The Fischer animals are labeled F344 by Microbiological Associates, the supplier of these animals. Figure 6 presents shuttle box avoidance data from all four breeding conditions. The females show the effect better than the males, for both sexes the crossbreds have avoidance levels between the extremes of the basic strains.

Whether these differences are primarily genetic or preweaning (i.e., maternal care) factors is clearly shown in Figure 7. Offspring from Zivic-Miller/Zivic-Miller and Fischer/Fischer matings were all cross-fostered—some to same-strain mothers and some to other-strain mothers. Regardless of the preweaning care, behavior in this active avoidance task is related to the strain of the genetic mother, not the strain of the foster mother.

The same type result is shown in Figure 8. In this study female offspring of the four types of matings were tested in a situation in which a tone is paired with foot shock and heart rate measures recorded prior to and during the shock-paired tone. The four groups again separate on the basis of the strain of their parents. Note that the S's with the highest basal heart rate are the Zivic-Millers. They were the most active in the open field

Figure 9.
Symmetrical aversive Y-maze in which rat avoidance and discrimination performance can be studied.

and also did poorly in both shuttle box and nondiscriminated avoidance. That may or may not be important, but what certainly is important is the finding that these Zivic-Miller animals, as seen in the graph on the right, were the animals whose heart rate changed most to the tone which has been paired with foot shock. That is, the strain with the greatest response to the tone-paired shock is also the strain that performed poorly in the two shock-motivated tasks.

These studies have been cited for several reasons. One is to make the very strong point that the question of the strain which is selected for study is one of the most important which an investigator can ask. Failure to obtain an effect, or obtaining an effect, with an experimental manipulation may be more due to the strain used than to the manipulation imposed. A second point is that there seems to be a clear relationship, at least in these two strains, between activity level (as measured in the open field), reactivity to stimuli paired with shock (as in the heart rate change data), and performance in active shock-motivated behavioral tasks such as nondiscriminated and shuttle box avoidance.

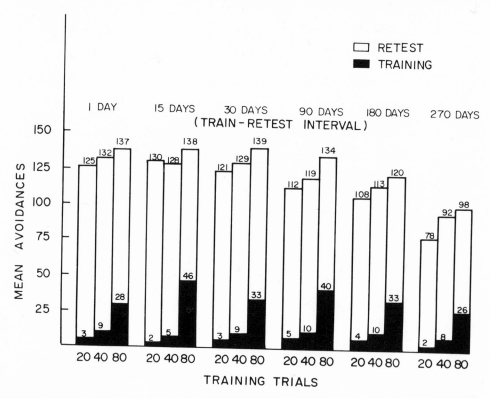

Figure 10.
Original learning (black rectangles) and retest performance (open rectangles) for separate groups of animals trained at 70 days of age and retested after the indicated intervals.

Performance, Learning and Memory—For the next experiment (16) a different task was used and only male, Fischer strain (F344) animals were studied. In this study our concern was threefold. Is there an age-related change in the acquisition of an avoidance response? Is there a decrement in retention of the avoidance response as the train-retest interval increases? Lastly, is there a relationship between the amount of original learning and performance of the behavior after varying intervals?

Completely automated symmetrical Y-mazes designed and constructed in our lab were used in this study. The apparatus is pictured in Figure 9. In these units the animal is placed in one arm, with a light present, and after 30 seconds the light switches randomly to a new arm. The animal has 10 seconds in which to move to the newly lighted arm to avoid foot shock. If this is not done in 10 seconds foot shock is delivered until the animal escapes to the correct, lighted arm. This arm now becomes the home arm and 30 seconds later the light again switches and so on.

In this study three training levels were used with the subjects given either 20, 40, or 80 trials on the original training day. The animals were returned to their home cages and separate groups were retested for retention of the avoidance response after either 1, 15, 30, 90, 180, or 270 days. Figure 10 contains the data from these groups.

Look first at the data on the left—the one day train-retest interval. The black rectangles at the bottom indicate the number of avoidances made on the original training day for those *S*'s who received 20, 40, or 80 trials. There is a clear superiority for those *S*'s receiving 80 trials. The open rectangles indicate the number of avoidances made by each of these groups when they were given 150 trials on retest the next day. Although there is a relationship between number of training trials and avoidance response on retest the major effect is the great improvement in performance shown by all three groups. This overnight improvement will be discussed later.

The black rectangles at each of the train-retest intervals plot the number of avoidance responses made by those *S*s when given 20, 40, or 80 trials at the age of 70 days. There are no significant differences among the retest groups on avoidances on the training day. The open rectangles at each train-retest interval again plot the mean number of avoidance responses made on retest after the indicated retention interval. Performance stays stable until about three months when retest avoidances begin to diminish. The decline in performance continues and is significant through the 270 day retention interval. It appears that there is a significant decrement in memory over this period.

To really test this, however, some control groups are needed. Not only have the 270 day retest animals been sitting in their cages for this period but they are now 340 day old animals. It seemed inappropriate to compare the performance of these 340 day old *S*'s with that of the 71 day old *S*'s.

Accordingly, along with the animals whose data have just been presented another set of animals was studied. These animals were all retested one day after training. Training

was done at the age when the animals in the experimental groups were retested, i.e., the
S's in the experimental group were trained at 70 days and retested at 85, 100, 160, 250,
and 340 days of age. The Ss in this control group were trained at those ages and tested
one day later. Their data are presented in Figure 11.

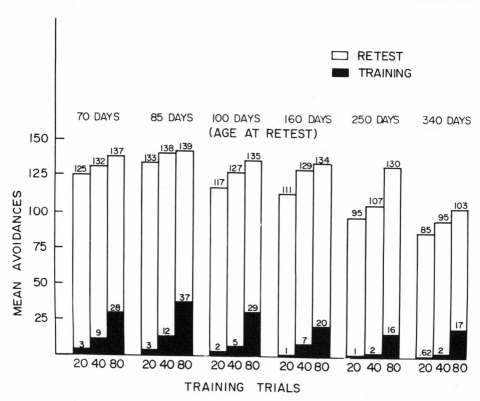

Figure 11.
Original learning (black rectangles) and retest performance (open rectangles) for separate
groups of animals trained at the indicated age and retested 24 hours later.

There are three major features. Note first the number of avoidances made on original
training (the solid black rectangles) when it occurred at the indicated ages. There is a
decline in acquisition avoidance responses after 85-100 days of age. The second point is
that there is still, even at age 340 days, a very large overnight increase in avoidance
behavior. The most important result, however, is that retest performance is clearly age
related. With increasing age, retest performance declines. The same held true for those S's
trained at age 70 days but the present data suggested that the decline in avoidance
responses is not related to a memory loss but to impaired performance.

The similarity between retest performance at particular ages, whether following a one-day or a many-day retention interval, is not just visual. Statistically there were no differences and the retest performance for both groups were combined in Figure 12. There is a difference in performance which is related to the number of original training trials but the three curves are parallel and thus the rate of performance decline is the same for all three training conditions.

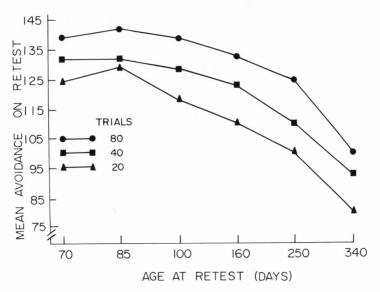

Figure 12.
Retest performance for *S*'s tested at the indicated ages. Combines retest data from Figures 10 and 11.

The performance decline is age related but not test-retest interval related so the question becomes what is the basis for the decline? Before addressing that, it is best to tie up some loose ends. One has to do with the great overnight increase in avoidance behavior.

Over 15 years ago a psychologist described a behavioral phenomenon which has since been named for him, the Kamin Effect. (17) He reported that performance in a shock motivated situation declined for one to four hours after partial acquisition of the task and then improved over the next 20 to 24 hours. If active avoidance responses are plotted, retest performance decreases from zero hours after acquisition to a low level one to four hours after acquisition and then improves to a high point 24 hours after original acquisition. Some have suggested that this decline in performance represents a decrease in the availability of the memory trace as it is transferred from short to long-term memory.(18)

We became interested in this performance decline—and its interpretation as a memory retrieval difficulty—because we were increasingly dissatisfied with shuttle box avoidance behavior as a measure of learning. The shuttle box situation is one in which the animal is given the task of learning when to move to the other compartment. If the animal follows the conditioned stimulus, the light-on stimulus in our studies, and avoids foot shock then it seems reasonable to conclude that the animal has learned that dark is associated with foot shock.

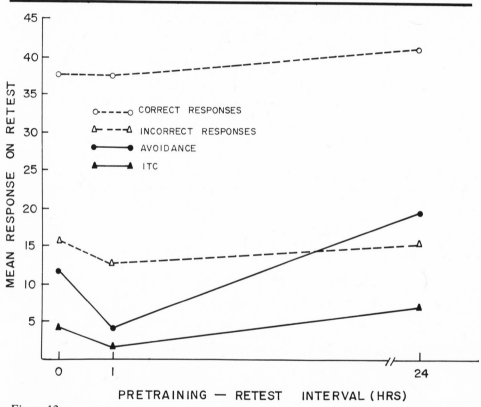

Figure 13.
Mean number of correct avoidances, correct responses (correct avoidances plus correct escapes), incorrect responses and intertrial crossings (ITC) as a function of pretraining-retest interval.

What if the animal does not follow the conditioned stimulus? Does it mean that he has not learned that darkness—light out—is paired with foot shock? Are there other factors which could be involved which would prevent the performance even though the animal has learned something about the task? Perhaps most importantly—in what way could it be shown that an animal has learned something about a task even though certain aspects of his performance would indicate otherwise?

We have attempted to solve this problem by testing animals in the symmetrical Y-maze rather than in a shuttle box. In the shuttle box the animal has only learned when to run. The response of running to avoid foot shock is the only performance measure in the shuttle box and it has been used as the index of learning. In a Y-Maze the animal has two tasks: he must learn *when* to run, but also must learn *where* to run. Not only must the response be made before foot shock is delivered, but the correct arm of the two possible arms must be selected. If performance of the avoidance response is interrupted in someway so that shock is delivered to the animal, it is still possible to monitor whether the animal escapes from the shock into the correct arm of the maze; i.e., in the Y-maze there are two obvious response measures: does the animal run in time to avoid shock? Does the animal run to the correct arm—no matter when he runs?

Study of the Kamin effect in the Y-maze could answer the question of whether the performance decline was due to difficulty of memory retrieval or a performance factor. Figure 13 shows the results of the study (19) designed to answer the question. Male F334 *S*'s were given 30 training trials in the Y-maze and then given 50 retest trials either 0, 1,

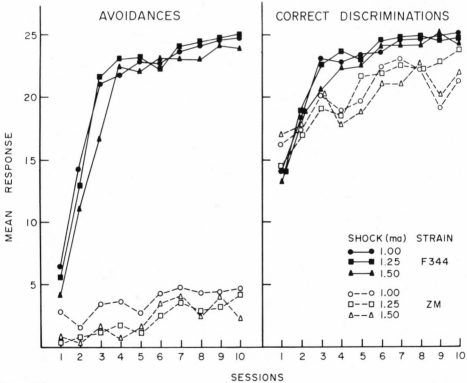

Figure 14.

Mean number of avoidances and correct discriminations over 25 trial sessions as a function of strain and shock intensity.

or 24 hours after original learning. Mean avoidances at each interval show the performance decline and recovery which is the Kamin effect. Plotting correct discriminations—i.e., did the animal go initially to the correct arm whether before or after shock was delivered—shows that there is no memory retrieval problem or loss of learning. There is only a decline in the performance of the avoidance response.

The importance of this additional response measure—correct discriminations, not just performance of the avoidance response—is clearly shown in Figure 14. In this study (20) groups of naive male Ss from the Fischer and Zivic-Miller strains were given 25 trials in the Y-maze each day with either 1.0, 1.25, or 1.5 mA foot shock as the unconditioned stimulus. There were no clear differences in avoidance behavior among the three foot shock levels used. If only avoidances are reported (as on the left of the figure) it appears that the Fischers are much faster learners than the Zivic-Miller rats. Consideration of the correct discriminations made by the two strains(as on the right side of the figure) suggests that the differences in behavior are primarily due to some other factor— one which is more closely tied to performance than to learning. Remember that these two strains are the strains which showed very different performance in shuttle box avoidance behavior. In the shuttle box, of course, there is a single response measure—avoidance—and from those data alone it would have seemed that the Fischer animals were much faster learners than the Zivic-Miller animals. The Y-maze data in Figure 14 clearly show that not to be true.

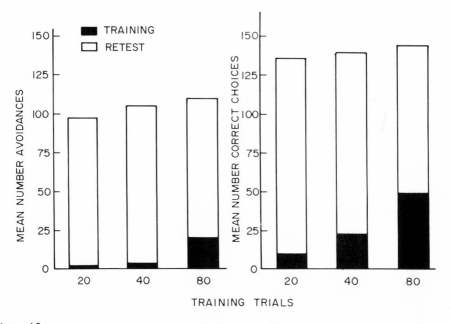

Figure 15.
Mean number of avoidances and correct choices on training and one-day retest in 270 day old F344 males.

We have not yet completed our analysis of the performance decrement which is related to the age of the animal but some data are available. One obvious question is whether the performance decrement in old *S*'s is the result of a learning deficiency or not. Unfortunately, in the long-term retention studies the equipment was not programmed to record discriminations. As a beginning answer to the question of the basis for the performance decrement in old animals the following study was conducted.

Figure 15 contains one-day retention data for 270 day old F344 males that were trained and tested in the Y-maze. The animals were given 20, 40, or 80 trials on the

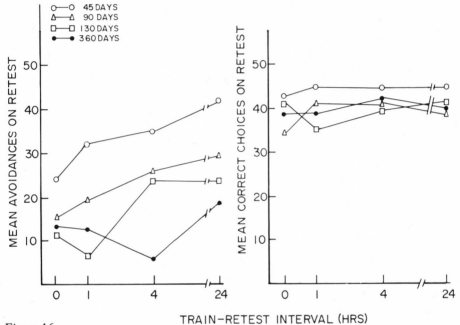

Figure 16.
Mean number of avoidances and correct choices as a function of age and train-retest interval.

training day and 150 retest trials one day later. The chart on the left plots avoidance responses. The black rectangles indicate the average number of avoidance responses made by each of the three groups on the training trials. The open rectangles in the left chart show the average avoidance responses when the *S*'s were retested one day later. Two points are obvious—increasing the number of training trials increases the percentage of avoidance responses on both the training and retest days; second, there is a large and significant increase in avoidance behavior when tested one day after training. Both of these results replicate the earlier study.

The data on the right plot total correct discriminations—the combination of avoidance responses and escape-from-shock responses to the correct arm. The data are virtually self-explanatory. In these 270 day old animals, as in the earlier study with 70 day old animals from both the Zivic-Miller and Fischer strains, avoidance behavior is a poor measure of learning. The discrimination data show clearly that the animals had learned a considerable amount in the task. The avoidance data suggest that there were nonassociative (i.e., nonlearning) factors blocking the performance of this response making avoidance a questionable index of learning, per se.

Although we have not yet collected data on intervening groups, this figure indicates that there is no evidence for an age-related decrement in learning ability at least up to an age of 270 days. There are, however, age-related changes in performance and we have started to study them. A project just completed tested Fischer strain animals either 45, 90, 130, or 360 days old in the Y-maze.

The Kamin paradigm was used and all animals were given 20 training trials and then given 50 additional trials either 0, 1, 4, or 24 hours after completion of the first 20 trials. Both avoidances and total correct discriminations—avoidances plus correct escapes—are plotted in Figure 16. Look first at the left chart where only avoidances are plotted. The two youngest groups do not show a Kamin effect and the number of correct responses increases as the interval becomes greater between training and retest. This is particularly clear in the 45 day old rats.

The 130 day old group shows the usual Kamin effect with the greatest performance decrement at the one hour interval. The performance decrement in the 360 day old animals is greatest four hours after training. When the total shapes of these four curves are considered it seems that the maximal effect of the performance decrement moves from the zero hour interval in the 45 day old group to longer intervals with each older group. That this effect is a reflection of performance rather than of learning is clear from the right chart which graphs total correct responses.

A comparison of the 24 hour avoidance responses and the 24 hour correct responses for the four age levels shows clearly that an avoidance measure by itself does not speak adequately to the question of age-related changes in learning. Yet this avoidance measure—usually in a shuttle box—is the response used almost exclusively in animal active-avoidance studies designed to investigate learning and memory. I will not belabor the point any more except to say that these data suggest that most of the research in the literature that is aimed at the problem of changes in learning as a function of age of the experimental animal has, in fact, been studying age-related performance factors.

The basis for this time dependent shock-related performance decrement is not completely clear. We have shown that the pituitary-adrenal axis is not the basis for the decrement (21). We have also shown that it is related to the interval between shock stress and retest, rather than between training and retest(19). We have reported (22) that the performance decrement is reversed by amphetamine and that the reversal is due to the attenuation of shock-induced behavioral suppression.

Our present feeling is that the performance decrement following shock results from a parasympathetic rebound to the sympathetic output in response to the stress produced by foot shock. This increase in parasympathetic activity is felt to induce the behavioral changes by blocking or overcompensating for the normal sympathetic response to the shock. We have not yet extended our drug studies to older animals.

The performance decline with age in both acquisition and retest performance which was stated earlier when several test-retest intervals were studied is probably best understood in the framework of parasympathetic rebound. The data suggest that one effect which occurs with age is an increase in the response to stress and a prolongation of the response to stress. Together the factors would impair the acquisition of the behavior on the training day, and this would lead to a decrease in performance on retention from that which would result if the task were better learned.

Several comments will conclude this section. One obvious conclusion is that when shock motivated behavior is used in animal studies, avoidance behavior alone is not an adequate measure of learning. This fact, by itself, means that most of the studies in the literature that say they deal with learning do not. This point becomes most important in designing future studies directed toward the basis of the performance decrement.

It is appreciated that the studies we have presented—even using 340 day old rats—may not approach the problem of the relationship of aging to learning and memory. Although we have found no decrement in learning in 270 day old animals, the use of older subjects in our automated Y-mazes may yield not just a decrease in performance but impaired learning.

Lastly, the identification of a non-learning decrement in performance with age poses more questions than it answers. Many of these are obvious. Perhaps the most important question now to be asked is whether an age-related change in learning, i.e., change in associative ability, can be clearly identified?

The Step to Mankind

We have written and rewritten this section more times then either of the first two. Each time this section gets shorter. One more rewrite and this section would vanish—perhaps wisely.

Our data suggest that the most important thing animal behavioral work in the area of aging can do for human work is to clearly emphasize the importance of a behavioral analysis approach. With poorly understood tasks being used to monitor unanalyzed behavior it is no surprise that the study of aging is in its infancy.

References

1. Liddell, H.S., James, W.T., and Anderson, O.D. (1934) The comparative physiology of the conditioned motor reflex: based on experiments with the pig, dog, sheep, goat, and rabbit. *Comp. Psychol. Monogr., 11,* No. 51.

2. Skinner, B.F. (1950) Are theories of learning necessary? *Psychol. Rev. 57,* 193-216.

3. Hoffman, H.S., Flesher, M., and Jensen, P.J. *Exp. Anal. Behav. 6,* 575, (1963).

4. Freund, Gerhard and Walker, Don W. The effect of aging on acquisition and retention of shuttle box avoidance in mice. *Life Sciences* Vol *10,* Part I, pp. 1343-1349, 1971.

5. Denenberg, V.W. and Kline, N.H. *J. Comp. Physiol. Psycho. 51,* 488, (1958).

6. Oliverio, A. and Bovet, D. *Life Sci. 5,* 1317 (1966).

7. Thompson, Richard W., Koenigsberg, Lewis A., and Tennison, James C. Effects of age on learning and retention of an avoidance response in rats. *J. Comp. Physiol. Psychol. 60,* No. 3, 457-459 (1965).

8. Kirby, R.H. *J. Comp. Physiol. Psychol. 56,* 158 (1963).

9. Ray, O.S. and Barrett, R.J. Step-through latencies in mice as a function of ECS-test interval. *Physiology and Behavior,* Vol. *4,* pp. 583-586 (1969).

10. Chevalier, J.S. Permanence of amnesia after a single posttrial electroconvulsive procedure. *J. Comp. Physiol. Psychol. 59:* 125-127 (1965).

11. Luttges, M.W. and McGaugh, J.L. Permanence of retrograde amnesia produced by electroconvulsive shock. *Science 156:* 408-140, (1967).

12. Ray, Oakley S. Passive avoidance acquisition and habituation as a function of strain, sex, age and electroconvulsive shock. Paper presented at Eastern Psychological Association Meeting, Phil. Pa. (1969).

13. Ray, Oakley S. Retention of passive avoidance response in mice. Paper presented at Eastern Psychological Association Meeting, Atlantic City, N.J. (1970).

14. Barrett, R.J. and Ray, O.S. Behavior in the open field, Lashley III maze, shuttle-box, and Sidman avoidance as a function of strain, sex, and age. *Developmental Psychology,* Vol. *3,* No. 1, 1970.

15. Barrett, R.J., Caul, W.T., and Ray, O.S. Genetic and environmental influences on classical and instrumental conditioning. In preparation.

16. Ray, Oakley S. and Barrett, Robert J. Long term retention in the rat. In preparation.

17. Kamin, L.J. The retention of an incompletely learned avoidance response. *Journal of Comparative and Physiological Psychology,* 1957, *50,* 457-460.

18. Grossman, S.P. *A textbook of physiological psychology.* New York: Wiley, 1967.

19. Barrett, Robert J., Leith, Nancy J., and Ray, Oakley S. Kamin Effect in rats: Index of memory of shock-induced inhibitions. *Journal of Comparative and Physiological Psychology,* 1971, Vol 77, No. 2, 234-239.

20. Barrett, Robert J., Leith, Nancy J., and Ray, Oakley S. A behavioral and pharmacological analysis of the variables mediating active-avoidance behavior in rats. *Journal of Comparative and Physiological Psychology* (In Press).

21. Barrett, Robert J., Leith, Nancy J., and Ray, Oakley S. The effects of pituitary-adrenal manipulations on time-dependent processes in avoidance learning. *Physiology and Behavior,* Vol. 7, pp 663-665. Pergamon Press, 1971.

22. Barrett, Robert J. and Ray, Oakley S. The effect of cholinergic-adrenergic manipulations on time dependent processes in avoidance learning. Paper presented at meeting of Psychonomic Society, St. Louis, Missouri, November, 1972.

Changes in Monoamine Oxidase with Aging

Alexander Nies, M.D.
Donald S. Robinson, M.D.
John M. Davis, M.D.
C. Lewis Ravaris, Ph.D., M.D.

Introduction

There has been a continuing and increasing interest in biogenic amine metabolism, particularly in the central nervous system, since these amines (norepinephrine, serotonin, dopamine) may play a role in the etiology of depression, mania, and parkinsonism. There are several lines of evidence from which the biogenic amine hypotheses of these disorders are drawn. For example, agents which are known to deplete neurons of amines, such as reserprine and alpha-methyl-dopa, can precipitate depressive illness in a significant percentage of patients, particularly if there is a past personal or family history of depression. In addition, pharmacologic agents useful in treating depression, such as the tricyclic antidepressants and monoamine oxidase inhibiting group of drugs are known to affect biogenic amine metabolism and function in the CNS. Finally, there are studies of blood and urinary excretion of amines and their metabolites which suggest that depressed and manic patients may exhibit differences from normals in amine metabolism. Such studies have been periodically reviewed over the past several years (1, 2, 3, 4). In regard to parkinsonism, the earlier reports implicating a defect in biogenic amine metabolism, specifically dopamine (5, 6) culminated in the successful treatment of this condition with the amino acid precursor to dopamine, dihydroxyphenylalanine (DOPA) (7).

The affective disorders as a group show a definite relationship to age, with an increased incidence and prevalence with age (8). Furthermore, individual affective disorders, such as manic-depressive or bipolar depressive illnesses, are well-known to have a natural history characterized by increasing frequency, severity and duration of attacks, with increasing resistance to treatment with advancing years (9, 10). The recurrent depressions of the later years also are known to have a relatively poor prognosis for full recovery (11).

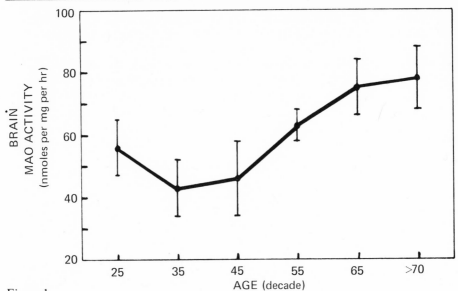

Figure 1.

    Mean MAO activity of human hindbrain (with standard error of the mean, S.E.M.) for each decade (n moles per milligram protein per hour).

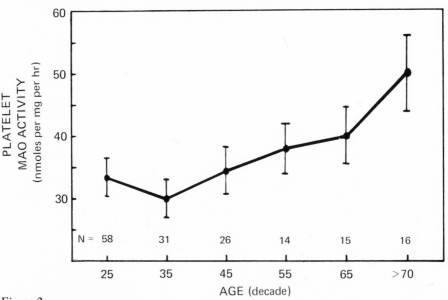

Figure 2.

    Mean MAO activity (±S.E.M.) of platelets from control subjects (N=162 for each age decade (n moles per milligram protein per hour).

Idiopathic parkinsonism also is age related in that onset is in the later years with progressive degeneration with age (12). Of further interest is the fact that post-encephalitic parkinsonism may develop many years after the initial illness, suggesting that an age-related factor may contribute to this later onset (13,14).

In this study, the effect of age on monoamine oxidase (MAO) activity in three human tissues was studied because oxidative deamination by this group of enzymes is one of the major degradative pathways for biogenic amines. Cellular MAO activity in human hindbrain and platelets and a soluble plasma MAO were compared across age decades, and the levels of two amines and one metabolite were compared to MAO levels in hindbrain. Like other tissue MAOs, platelet MAO is particulate bound, and although human brain MAO occurs as four isoenzymes (15), and platelet MAO as only one isoenzyme (16), there are similarities in relative substrate affinity and inhibitor potency, suggesting some overlap in the characteristics of the MAOs of brain and platelets (17). This raises the possibility that platelet MAO activity may, to some extent, and in some circumstances, be an indicator of brain MAO activity. On the other hand, since plasma MAO is a non-particulate, soluble enzyme, with cofactor requirements which differ from tissue MAO, it is probably of less significance as a possible index of nervous tissue MAO activity (17).

Methods

Autopsy brain specimens were obtained from 55 patients who had died from a variety of medical illnesses. Since liver disease may alter MAO levels (18), three cases with significant liver disease were excluded. The hindbrains were removed and stored as described previously; neither lapse of time between death and autopsy nor lengths of storage were related to amine or MAO levels (19). Hindbrains were assayed for serotonin (5-HT), 5 hydroxyindoleacetic acid (5HIAA) and norepinephrine (NE) by the methods of Bogdanski *et al* (20), Udenfriend *et al* (21), and a modification of the method of Anton and Sayre (22), respectively. MAO levels were also determined in 24 of the hindbrains by the ^{14}C-benzylamine method (17).

MAO levels were determined in platelets and plasma of 71 normal males and 91 normal females, 21 to 84 years of age. These subjects were chosen for the absence of a personal or family history of psychiatric illness, were currently taking no medications, and had never received a major psychotropic drug. In addition, platelet and plasma MAO were determined in 61 males and 161 females with a clinical diagnosis of a primary depressive illness from the inpatient and outpatient services of a university hospital and the private practices of two psychiatrists. Patients with schizophrenia, alcoholism, drug dependence, and organic mental syndromes were excluded.

Results

MAO activity increased with age in human hindbrain (Fig. 1), and in platelets (Fig. 2), and plasma (Fig. 3) of normal subjects. The correlations of MAO with age were 0.57

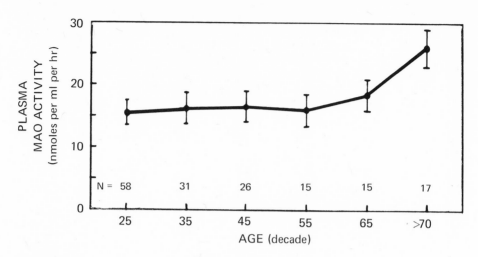

Figure 3.
　　Mean MAO activity (±S.E.M.) of plasma from control subjects (N=162) for each age decade (n moles per ml. per hour).

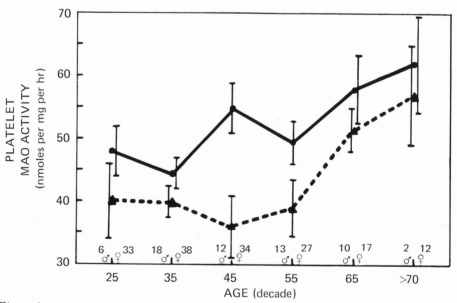

Figure 4.
　　Mean MAO activity (± S.E.M.) of platelets from 61 depressed males (▲————▲) and 161 depressed females (●————●) for each age decade (n moles per milligram protein per hour).

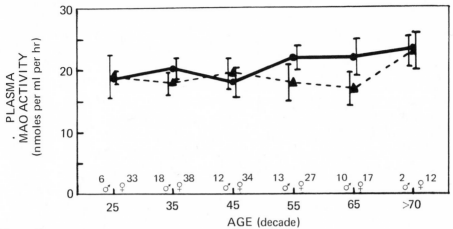

Figure 5.

Mean MAO activity (±S.E.M.) of plasma from 61 depressed males (▲————▲) and 161 depressed females (●————●) for each age decade (n moles per ml. per hour).

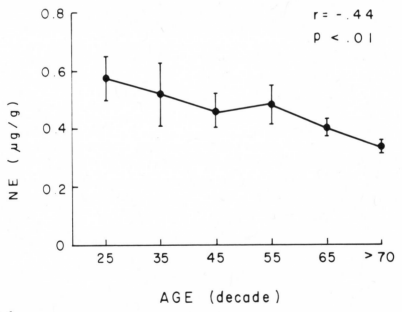

Figure 6.

Mean concentration (±S.E.M.) of human hindbrain norepinephrine (NE) for each age decade (μg/gm).

(p<0.005) in hindbrain, 0.39 (p<0.001) in platelets, and 0.47 (p<0.001) in plasma. Platelet MAO also increases with age in two other groups, depressed male and females, and in addition is higher in females than in males for each decade (Fig. 4). This sex effect on platelet MAO also occurs in the control subjects (not shown). There is less of a sex effect on plasma MAO (Fig. 5); however, the effect in the decades over 50 is statistically significant.

NE levels in hindbrain decreased with age as shown in Fig. 6 (r=−0.49, p<0.001). Neither 5-HT (r=0.12) nor 5-HIAA (r=−0.18) correlated with age (Fig. 7) and although there is a trend for the 5-HIAA/5-HT ratio to increase with age (r=−0.22), this also is not significantly non-zero. In addition, 5-HT levels did not correlate with 5-HIAA levels (r=−0.09).

When NE and 5-HIAA content are compared to MAO activity rather than age, (Fig. 8), the NE levels show a negative correlation with MAO (r=−0.54, p<0.005) and the 5-HIAA levels a positive correlation with MAO (r=0.55, p<0.005). When the multiple correlation coefficients were computed to partial out the effects of age and MAO on NE and 5-HIAA, accounting for age did not significantly influence the correlations, suggesting that the predominant effect on NE and 5-HIAA is due to MAO.

In view of the higher mean platelet MAO in females in each age decade and the suggestion of a similar effect on plasma MAO in the older decades, it is of interest that the MAO activity of hindbrains from females had a mean of 66±7 n moles per milligram per hour compared to a mean of 61±4 n moles per milligram per hour for the hindbrains obtained from males. This, although not statistically significant, is consistent with the results in platelets.

Discussion

The literature on the biological concomitants of aging contains numerous references to the effects of age on enzyme activity in various tissues in many species. Bjorksten (23) and Zorzoli (24) provide useful reviews of this subject. One of the confounding features of many of these studies is the difficulty in distinguishing between maturation and aging, especially when immature animals are studied. In general, the tendency is for enzyme activity to decrease with age, although there are numerous exceptions (23).

The effect of age on enzyme systems involved in biogenic amine synthesis and degradation, especially in the central nervous system, has been less well studied. Studies have found brain monoamine oxidase levels to increase with maturation in certain species (25, 26, 27). MAO activity of heart increases with aging and cardiac hypertrophy in a number of species (28, 29, 30). In 1940 Birkhauser, using a manometric technique with tyramine as substrate, reported that subjects over age 60 had higher brain MAO activity than subjects under 60, who in turn had higher levels than children (31). Our studies of three sources of MAO are consistent in showing a positive correlation of the activity of this group of enzymes with age in human hindbrain, platelet, and plasma. This evidence

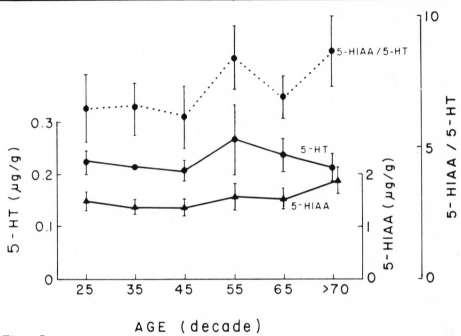

Figure 7.
Mean concentration (±S.E.M.) of human hindbrain serotonin (5-HT), 5-hydroxyindoleacetic acid (5-HIAA), and 5-HIAA/5-HT ratio for each age decade (mg/gm).

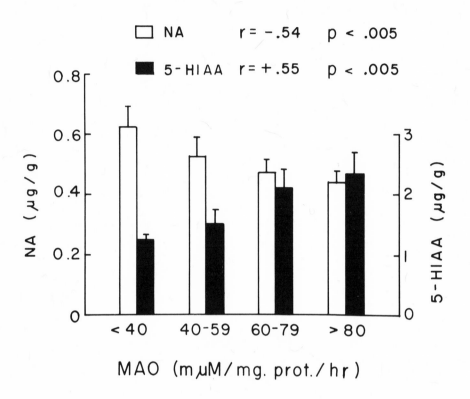

Figure 8.
Relationship of mean hindbrain concentration (±S.E.M.) of norepinephrine (NA –
□) and 5-hydroxyindoleacetic acid (5-HIAA – ■) to hindbrain MAO activity
grouped by levels of MAO activity. There is a significant negative correlation of NA
(r = –0.54, p<0.005) and a significant positive correlation of 5-HIAA (r=0.55,
p<0.005) with MAO activity.

suggests that an age-related increase in MAO activity is general biological phenomenon. The fact that NE concentrations correlated negatively and 5-HIAA concentrations positively with brainstem MAO suggest that this enzyme may play a major role in regulating intracellular concentrations of biogenic amines. It is possible that the increased levels in lumbar cerebrospinal fluid of 5-HIAA observed in elderly patients by Bowers and Gerbode (32) and of 5-HIAA and homovanillic acid by Gottfries *et al* (33) may be a consequence of age-related increases in brain MAO activity.

It has recently been shown that tyrosine hydroxylase, the rate-limiting enzyme in catecholamine synthesis, decreases with age in the striatum of accident victims. In contrast, two other enzymes, choline acetylase and glutamic acid decarboxylase, did not change with age (34). This study, together with our findings, makes it imperative that age be controlled in studies of clinical material involving brain tissue and cerebrospinal fluid, particularly in investigations of the biogenic amine hypotheses of depression and parkinsonism.

The relationship of the enzymes involved in biogenic amine metabolism to human disease is beginning to be explored. Liver disease has been shown to increase MAO levels (18), but the relationship of this to the alterations in CNS function associated with liver disease is unexplored. McGeer has shown that striatal tyrosine hydroxylase is lower in parkinsonian patients than in accident victim controls (34). We have reported that platelet MAO in a large series of depressed patients is higher than in age-matched controls (35), but there is considerable variation from individual to individual and it is necessary to group the data by age decades to bring out the effect (compare Fig. 2 and Fig. 4). Our findings do not agree with those of Murphy and Weiss who found that platelet MAO in patients with a history of bipolar depression (whose illness has had manic and depressed episodes) is significantly lower than in patients with nonbipolar depression and normal controls. Their groups had similar mean ages so that an age effect probably does not account for the decreased MAO in the bipolar group, although the effect of age on MAO as determined by their technique was not reported (36). Since benzylamine was the substrate in our studies and Murphy and Weiss used tryptamine, this may at least partly account for the disagreement, particularly since indoleamines are not particularly good substrates for platelet MAO (16,17). However, there are limitations to our data. Our series of depressed patients was accumulated over a two and one half year period of time; although the controls were obtained in groups at various times during this period, the depressed and normal series cannot be considered to be entirely concurrent. Since the platelet assay may be susceptible to vagaries with time, this makes it imperative that future studies of platelet MAO in depression use concurrent age and sex matched controls and perhaps preferably both an indoleamine and phenylethylamine substrate.

Of related interest are the reports that catechol-O-methyl transferase (COMT), another enzyme in a major amine degradative pathway, shows reduced activity in red blood cells from depressed women patients (37), with women with nonbipolar depressive illnesses showing the most marked reductions in COMT activity (38). However, from these two reports it is not clear that an age effect can be entirely ruled out.

The negative correlation of NE and the positive correlation of 5-HIAA with MAO reported in the present study are consistent with other evidence that mitochondrial MAO, by influencing intracellular levels of free amines, can secondarily influence the synthesis of these amines by an end-product feedback mechanism (39, 40). On the other hand, it is unclear whether the MAO increase with age is secondary to other changes in amine metabolism (such as decreased synthesis resulting from decreased tyrosine hydroxylase activity) or represents a primary difference. Since there is evidence that it is newly synthesized amines which are released by nervous stimuli and therefore can be considered most functionally active (41), it is likely that the absolute levels of intracellular amines are not a critical index of normal transmitter function. Therefore, it is conceivable that the increase in MAO with age is part of a compensatory mechanism to increase amine turn-over, thereby making available newly synthesized amine for synaptic transmission.

Although there are suggestions of neurally mediated short-range changes in MAO activity (42), and more prolonged changes induced by endocrine (43,44), behavioral (45), and social (46) stimuli, the results of this study suggest that these take place against a background of gradually increasing MAO activity in the CNS and other tissues with age. Unpublished data comparing twins and controls indicate that genetic factors also play a role in the regulation of MAO activity (47).

Epidemiologic studies have established that the incidence and prevalence of the affective disorders increase with age (8). The fact that MAO levels also increase with age makes it tempting to speculate that this relation of age to enzyme activity might be a predisposing factor to depression which accentuates changes in brain amines precipitated by other events. Similarly, age-related changes in MAO may play a role in the pathogenesis of parkinsonism, which has been suggested to be a late consequence of subclinical or undiagnosed encephalitis, presenting clinically as paralysis agitans after a wide range of latent intervals (13,14).

Bibliography

1. Bunney WE, Davis JM: Norepinephrine in depressive reactions. Arch. Gen. Psychiat. *13*: 483-494, 1965.

2. Schildkraut JJ, Kety SS: Biogenic amines and emotion. Science *156*:21-30, 1967.

3. Glassman A: Indoleamines and affective disorders. Psychosom. Med. *31:* 107-114, 1969.

4. Davis, JM: Theories of biological etiology of of affective disorders. Int. Rev. Neurobiol. *12*: 145-175, 1970.

5. Carlsson A: The occurrence, distribution and physiological role of catecholamines in the nervous system. Pharmcol. Rev. *11*:490-493, 1959.

6. Ehringer H, Hornykiewicz O: Verteilung von noradrenalin und dopamin (3-hydroxytyramin) im gehirn des menschen und ihr verhalten bei erkrankungen des extrapyramidalen systems. Klin. Wsch. *38*: 1236-1239, 1960.

7. Cotzias CG, Von Woert MH, Schiffer LM: Aromatic amino acids and the modification of parkinsonism. N. Eng. J. Med. *276*: 374-379, 1967.

8. Rawnsley K: Epidemiology of affective disorders. Recent Developments in Affective Disorders. Brit. J. Psychiat., Special Publication No. 2, pp. 27-36, 1968.

9. Perris C: A study of bipolar (manic depressive) and unipolar recurrent depressive psychoses. Acta Psychiat. Scand. *42* (Suppl 194): 7-189, 1966.

10. Van der Velde CD: Effectiveness of lithium carbonate in the treatment of manic-depressive illness. Am J. Psychiat.*127*: 345-351, 1970.

11. Shternberg EY, Rokhlina ML: Some general characteristics of depression in old age. Zhurnal neuropatalogii i psikhiatrii imeni ss korsakova *70*: 1356-1364, 1970.

12. Brain WR, Walton JN: Brain's Diseases of the Nervous System. pp 522-534, Oxford University Press, London, 1969.

13. Poskanzer DC, Schwab RS: Cohort analysis of parkinson's syndrome: evidence for a single etiology related to subclinical infection about 1920. J. Chron. Dis. *16*: 961-973, 1963.

14. Brown EL, Knox EG: Epidemiologic approach to parkinson's disease. Lancet *I*: 974-976, 1972.

15. Collins GGS, Sandler M, Williams ED, Youdim MBD: Multiple forms of human brain mitochondrial monoamine oxidase. Nature *225*: 817-820, 1970.

16. Collins GGS, Sandler M: Human blood platelet monoamine oxidase. Biochem. Pharmacol. *20*: 289-296, 1971.

17. Robinson DS, Lovenberg W, Keiser H, Sjoerdsma A: The effects of drugs on human blood platelet and plasma amine oxidase activity *in vitro* and *in vivo*. Biochem. Pharmacol *17*: 109-119, 1968.

18. McEwen CM, Castell DO: Abnormalities of serum monoamine oxidase in chronic liver disease. J. Lab. Clin. Med. *70*: 36-47, 1967.

19. Bourne HR, Bunney WE, Colburn RW, Davis JM, Davis JN, Shaw DM, Coppen AJ: Noradrenaline 5-hydroxytryptamine and 5-hydroxyindoleacetic acid in hindbrains of suicidal patients. Lancet *II*: 805-808, 1968.

20. Bogdanski DF, Pletscher A, Brodie BB, Udenfriend S: Identification and assay of serotonin in brain. J. Pharmacol. Exp. Therapeut. *117*: 82-88, 1956.

21. Udenfriend S, Weissbach H, Brodie BB: Methods of Biochemical Analysis, Ed. by D. Glick, Bol VI, pp 95-130, Interscience, New Yor, 1958.

22. Anton AH, Sayre DF: A study of the factors affecting the aluminum oxidetrihydroxyindole procedure for the analysis of catecholamines. J. Pharmacol Exp. Therapeut. *138*: 360-375, 1962.

23. Bjorksten J: Enzymes and cellular metabolism, *in* Enzymes in Mental Health, Ed. by GJ Martin, B Fisch, JB Lippincott Co., Philadelphia, 1966.

24. Zorzoli A: Enzymes and cellular metabolism, *in* Men, Molecules and Aging, Ed. by S Bakerman, Thomas, Springfield (Ill.), 1967.

25. Nachmias VT: Amine oxidase and 5-hydroxytryptamine in developing rat brain. J. Neurochem. *6*: 99-104, 1960.

26. Kuzuya H, Nagastusa T: Flavin and monoamine oxidase activity in the brain, liver, and kidney of the developing rat. J. Neurochem. *16*: 123-125, 1969.

27. Karki N, Kuntzman R, Brodie BB: Storage, synthesis and metabolism of monoamines in the developing brain. J. Neurochem. *9*: 53-58, 1962.

28. Novick WJ: The effect of age and thyroid hormones on the monoamine oxidase of rat heart, Endocrinology *69:* 55-59, 1961.

29. Horita A: Cardiac monoamine oxidase in rat. Nature *215*: 411-412, 1967.

30. DeChamplain J, Krakoff LR, Axelrod J: Increased monoamine oxidase activity during the development of cardiac hypertrophy in the rat. Circ. Res. *23*: 361-369, 1968.

31. Birkhauser H: Fermente im gehirn geistig normaler menschen. Helvet. Chim. Acta. *23*: 1071-1086, 1940.

32. Bowers MB, Gerbode F: The relationship of monoamine metabolites in human cerebrospinal fluid to age. Nature *219*: 1256-1257, 1968.

33. Gottfries DG, Gottfries I, Johansson B, Olsson R, Person T, Roos BE, Sjostrom R: Acid monoamine metabolites in human cerebrospinal fluid and their relations to age and sex. Neuropharmacol. *10*: 665-672, 1971.

34. McGreer PL: The chemistry of the mind. Am Scientst *59:* 221-229, 1972.

35. Nies A, Robinson DS, Ravaris CL: Amines and monoamine oxidase in relation to aging and depression in man. Psychosom. Med. *33*: 470, 1971.

36. Murphy DL, Weiss R: Reduced monoamine oxidase activity in blood platelets from bipolar depressed patients. Am J. Psychiat. *128*: 1351-1357, 1972.

37. Cohn DK, Dunner KL, Axelrod J: Reduced catechol-O-methyltransferase activity in red blood cells of women with primary affective disorder. Science *170*: 1323-1324, 1970.

38. Dunner DL, Cohn DK, Gershon ES, Goodwin FK: Differential catechol-O-methyltransferase activity in unipolar and bipolar affective illness. Arch. Gen. Psychiat. *25*: 348-353, 1971.

39. Kopin IJ: Storage and metabolism of catecholamines: the role of monoamine oxidase. Pharmacol. Rev. *16:* 179-191, 1964.

40. Spector S, Gordon R, Sjoerdsma A, Udenfriend S: End product inhibition of tyrosine hydroxylase as a possible mechanism for regulation of norepinephrine synthesis. Molec. Pharmacol. 3: 549-555, 1967.

41. Glowinski J, Axelrod J, Iversen L: Regional studies of catecholamines in the rat brain. IV Effect of drugs on the disposition and metabolism of H^3-norepinephrine and H^3-dopamine. J. Pharmacol. Exp. Therapeut. *153*: 30-31, 1966.

42. Welch BL, Welch AS: Control of brain catecholamines and serotonin during acute stress and after d-amphetamine by natural inhibition of monoamine oxidase: an hypothesis, *in* International Symposium on Amphetamines and Related Compounds, pp 415-466, Ed. by E. Costa, S. Gerrattini, Raven Press, New York, 1970.

43. Levin RF, Oates JA, Vendsalu A, Sjoerdsma A: Studies on the metabolism of aromatic amines in relation to altered thyroid function in man. J. Clin. Endocrinol. *22*: 1242-1250, 1962.

44. Klaiber EL, Kobaiyashi Y, Broverman DM, Hall F: Plasma monoamine oxidase activity in regularly menstruation women and in amenorrheic women receiving cyclic treatment with estrogens and a progestin. J. Clin. Endocrinol. Met. *33*: 630-638, 1971.

45. Eleftheriou BE, Boehlke KW: Brain monoamine oxidase in mice after exposure to aggression and defeat. Science *155*: 1693-1694, 1967.

46. Henry JP, Stephens PM, Axelrod J, Meuller RA: Effect of psychosocial stimulation on the enzymes involved in the biosynthesis and metabolism of noradrenaline and adrenaline. Psychosom. Med. *33*: 227-237, 1971.

47. Nies A, Robinson DS, Lampert R, Lamborn KR: Platelet and plasma monoamine oxidase in identical and fraternal twins compared to randomly paired age and sex matched controls. Unpublished manuscript.

Age-related Changes in Tissue Levels of Cyclic AMP

G.A. Robison, Ph.D.
M.J. Schmidt, Ph.D.
G.C. Palmer, Ph.D.

Introduction

The role of cyclic AMP as a second messenger mediating many of the peripheral actions of a number of hormones is by now well recognized (Sutherland *et al.*, 1968; Robison *et al.*, 1971b). By extrapolation, it has seemed reasonable to suppose that cyclic AMP may also mediate some of the actions of neurohumoral agents within the central nervous system (Greengard and Costa, 1970). The catecholamines have been of special interest from this point of view. There is evidence that in peripheral tissues most if not all of the effects of these agents which are known to result from an interaction with adrenergic *beta* receptors may in fact be mediated by increased levels of cyclic AMP, secondary to increased activity of adenyl cyclase (Robison and Sutherland, 1970; Robison *et al.*, 1972a). The catecholamines are also capable of producing large increases in the level of cyclic AMP in brain slices and cultured brain cells *in vitro* (eg., Kakiuchi and Rall, 1968a,b; Schmidt *et al.*, 1970; Gilman and Nirenberg, 1971 a,b; Clark and Perkins, 1971), and an intriguing recent finding has been that urinary excretion of cyclic AMP rises during the period just preceding the onset of the manic phase in patients with manic-depressive illness (Paul *et al.*, 1971). The potential importance of brain catecholamines in regulating brain function and behavior has been recognized for many years (eg., Kety, 1966; Schildkraut and Kety, 1967).

More recently it has become apparent that cyclic AMP may have an important role to play during the growth and development of mammalian and other cells, and the main purpose of the first part of this article will be to summarize the evidence for this. Because the role of cyclic AMP in the brain is still obscure, it is not clear that this evidence can be applied in any meaningful way to the psychopharmacology of the aging patient. It seems possible or even likely, however, that changes in cyclic AMP will ultimately be seen to have great relevance within this context.

Microbiological Studies

The ability of glucose to suppress cyclic AMP formation in *E. coli,* or of a lack of glucose to stimulate cyclic AMP formation in these organisms (Makman and Sutherland, 1965), was for many years an observation of uncertain significance, approximately as uncertain as the ability of histamine to raise brain cyclic AMP levels seems today. As reviewed elsewhere (Pastan and Perlman, 1970; Robison *et al.,* 1971b), it is now known that cyclic AMP is required for the synthesis of a number of inducible enzymes in *E. coli* and other organisms, and that glucose suppresses the synthesis of these enzymes by reducing the level of cyclic AMP. Glucose also prevents flagella formation and hence motility in these organisms, and this also appears to result from reduced levels of cyclic AMP (Yokota and Gots, 1970).

More recently, and of possibly greater relevance from the standpoint of human biology, it has been discovered that the level of cyclic AMP in the bacterial host is an important factor determining the viral decision between lysogeny and lysis (Hong *et al.,* 1971). It was known previously (Lwoff, 1953) that when a temperate bacteriophage infects a bacterial cell, a decision is made during the first few minutes that results in either lysogeny or lysis. In lysogeny, the phage chromosome is incorporated into the bacterial chromosome and may remain dormant there for many generations. Alternatively, the phage may replicate, leading to a burst of progeny and ultimately to lysis of the bacterial cell. It is now known from the work of Hong and her colleagues that when the level of bacterial cyclic AMP is low, as in the presence of glucose (or in mutants lacking adenyl cyclase under any conditions), then lysogeny occurs at a drastically reduced frequency and lysis is favored. By contrast, when the level of cyclic AMP is high, then lysogeny is favored over lysis. Normal rates of lysogenization could be restored if exogenous cyclic AMP was added to mutants lacking adenyl cyclase. Hong *et al* also studied mutants deficient in a cyclic AMP-binding protein which had previously been shown to be required for inducible enzyme synthesis (Zubay *et al.,* 1970), but cyclic AMP did not promote lysogeny in these organisms. It would thus appear that both cyclic AMP and the cyclic AMP-binding protein are required in order for viral DNA to be incorporated into the bacterial chromosome.

Studies with Tumor Cells

Had the foregoing observations on lysogeny been made earlier, they might well have suggested a role for cyclic AMP in cancer. It had been known for many years (see Lwoff, 1962) that a variety of chemicals and other stimuli, such as ultraviolet irradiation, were capable of inducing the previously dormant virus (the prophage) in lysogenic bacteria to replicate, thus leading to lysis, and all of these stimuli were known to be carcinogenic when applied to mammalian cells. Huebner and his colleagues (see Todaro and Huebner, 1962, for a recent review) have postulated that cancer results from the unsuppressed activity of a virus-like particle which they have referred to as the oncogene. The oncogene is thought to be present in most if not all cells, and may play an important functional role, possibly as part of what Bullough (1967) referred to as the "mitosis operon," during early embryogenesis. Later, as differentiation proceeds, the oncogene becomes repressed, presumably by a mechanism similar or analogous to the mechanism by which viral activity is repressed in lysogenic bacteria. If the oncogene ever gets derepressed, according to this theory, then the previously differentiated cells are transformed to malignant cells which are no longer responsive to the normal controls of cell multiplication. In support of the oncogene theory, the expected expression of viral activity has in fact been detected in embryos of experimental animals, and, in further line with theory, such expressions are greatly diminished after birth and during early life.

As it turned out, an important role for cyclic AMP in cancer had already been suggested by more direct evidence. For example, Johnson *et al* (1971) showed that the addition of cyclic AMP to viral-transformed cells in tissue culture would restore to these cells many of the morphological and other characteristics of normal fibroblasts. An important functional characteristic that was restored by cyclic AMP was contact inhibition of growth, according to which cells stop multiplying after a certain cell density has been reached. Sheppard (1971) showed that spontaneously - and viral - transformed 3T3 cells (a line of cells derived from mouse embryo fibroblasts) would stop multiplying at a density not far above the normal saturation density of the untransformed cells, if they were grown in the presence of exogenous cyclic AMP, but that unrestrained growth would resume if the cyclic AMP (added as the dibutyryl derivative) was removed.

These and other findings (eg., Heidrick and Ryan, 1971; Makman, 1971) suggested that there might be a correlation between the level of cyclic AMP in tumor cells and the rate of cell replication, with high levels of cyclic AMP being associated with slow growth, and low levels being associated with rapid growth. Such an association was demonstrated directly by Heidrick and Ryan (1971) and by Otten *et al* (1971), who studied a series of tumor cells with widely differing growth rates, and later by Sheppard (1972) in normal and transformed 3T3 cells.

The question of whether cell-to-cell contact leads to increased levels of cyclic AMP, or whether cyclic AMP causes the cells to become more sensitive to each other, is controversial at present. Otten and his colleagues observed that in normal 3T3 cells subject to contact inhibition, cyclic AMP levels rose approximately 4-fold at confluency, whereas the levels remained low in malignant cells not subject to contact inhibition. Heidrick and Ryan were unable to even detect cyclic AMP in strain L cells until the cells had become confluent. These results might suggest that normal (i.e., density-dependent) cells possess a mechanism through which cell-to-cell contact leads to an increase in the level of cyclic AMP. It could then be suggested that when this mechanism fails, for whatever reason, the resulting fall in the level of cyclic AMP leads to derepression of the oncogene, which would in turn lead to the unrestrained growth we know as cancer. In Sheppard's experiments, on the other hand, cyclic AMP levels were high in untransformed cells even during the growth phase, and did not increase further either before or after the stationary phase had been reached. This important discrepancy between laboratories remains to be solved. The major point of agreement is that contact-inhibited cells contain steady-state levels of cyclic AMP which are at least twice as high as in transformed cells not subject to contact-inhibition.

It will perhaps go without saying that cancer could also occur even without a fall in the level of cyclic AMP, if one or more other mechanisms controlling cell replication were to fail. Conversely, it should be clear that a fall in the level of cyclic AMP will not lead to cancer if the affected cells are otherwise incapable of mitosis. In other words, a fall in the level of cyclic AMP will be neither necessary nor sufficient to produce cancer in all cells. However, an increasing body of evidence is accumulating (see, for example, Otten *et al.,* 1972) to suggest that this may be the final common cause of many if not most cases of cancer, regardless of the mechanism through which the initial defect is brought about.

Cyclic AMP and Development

With the foregoing observations in mind, the possibility of an important role for cyclic AMP during development can be considered. A hypothetical scheme to illustrate what might happen during embryogenesis is presented in Fig. 1. According to this scheme, cyclic AMP levels in gametes are approximately the same as in mature diploid cells, but begin to fall more or less rapidly following fertilization. Experimental data to support this conjecture are unfortunately not available. Cyclic AMP levels have not been measured in mammalian zygotes, and experiments with sea urchin and chicken eggs, which are heavily laden with yolk, are difficult to interpret. Spermatozoa contain levels of cyclic AMP which are at least as high as in other cells (Butcher *et al.,* 1965; Garbers *et al.,* 1971; Gray, 1971), and the nucleotide also occurs in sea urchin and chicken eggs, but what happens during early embryogenesis is unclear. The overall cyclic AMP was not different in fertilized and infertile chicken eggs, but at least 95% of the cyclic AMP measured in these experiments was present in yolk (Gray, 1971). Attempts to measure cyclic AMP in blastodermic discs were unsatisfactory because of heavy contamination with yolk; it may or may not be significant, therefore, that the apparent blastoderm level fell after fertilization from a value about twice that of yolk to a level the same as in yolk. When the eggs were incubated at 38 degrees the yolk content of cyclic AMP fell to approximately 25% of its preincubation value within 48 hours, i.e., during early embryogenesis. These preliminary results would seem to be in line with the hypothetical curve plotted in Fig. 1. In sea urchin eggs, by contrast, the levels seemed low at the time of fertilization (approx. 0.1 n mole/g wet packed cells) and were not significantly lower after 100 minutes, roughly time for one mitotic division to have occurred (Gray, 1971). However, since cyclic AMP has not been measured in the cells of adult sea urchins, it is not clear how or if the egg levels can be related to development in higher forms. Regardless of whether the level of cyclic AMP is low to begin with or falls from an initially higher level, the same purpose should be served, which is to permit the rapid cell division characteristic of early embryogenesis. The supposition that reduced levels of cyclic AMP are necessary at this stage is based largely on the aforementioned studies with tumor cells, and is strengthened by recent studies of the proliferative skin disease psoriasis. Voorhees and his colleagues

(1972) have shown that psoriatic epidermal cells contain approximately half as much cyclic AMP as in normal cells. The antimitotic action of epinephrine in these cells is presumably mediated by cyclic AMP (Voorhees and Duell, 1971; Bronstad *et al.*, 1971); the possible relation of cyclic AMP to the action of the epidermal chalone (Bullough, 1967) remains to be established.

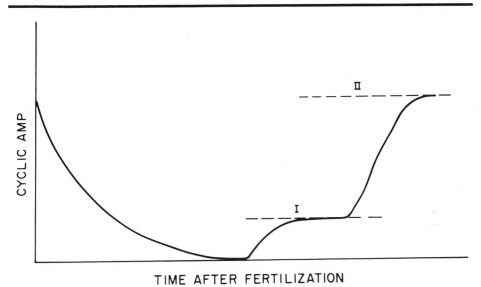

TIME AFTER FERTILIZATION

Figure 1.
Hypothetical changes in cyclic AMP during development. Level at zero time refers to the zygote, whereas level II refers to any mature differentiated cell. See text for further discussion.

Returning to the hypothetical sequence illustrated in Fig. 1, and based largely on the work of Heidrick and Ryan (1971) and Otten, Johnson, and Pastan (1971), it can be suggested that at some point in the course of development some and perhaps most cells develop a mechanism through which adenyl cyclase can be stimulated or deinhibited as a result of cell-to-cell contact. This leads to an increase in the intracellular level of cyclic AMP, up to what we might refer to as baseline level I. This might be taken by the cell as a signal to stop replicating, or at least to reduce its rate of mitosis from what it was, and to devote more of its time and energy to differentiation. In biological terms, the cell will now be forced to spend more of its time in the G_1 phase of the cell cycle, during which time DNA is available for transcription. Some cells, of which neurons are a good example, may eventually fall into a G_1 rut, apparently becoming incapable of further mitosis. In certain other cells, however, a fall in cyclic AMP below base-line I would be expected to lead to neoplastic growth, as discussed previously.

Later, as differentiation proceeds, most cells will develop hormone receptors and other mechanisms for regulating their content of cyclic AMP. In general, this will lead to a further increase, up to what we refer to in Fig. 1 as baseline level II. At this stage cyclic AMP begins to play its well established and best studied role as a regulator of highly differentiated cell function. Increases above this baseline will lead to one effect, the stimulation or inhibition of a process possibly secondary to the phosphorylation of a protein (Kuo and Greengard, 1969; Walsh *et al.*, 1971), whereas a fall below it will lead to the opposite effect.

The most familiar role of cyclic AMP in later life is as a second messenger mediating the effects of a variety of hormones, as illustrated schematically in Fig. 2. It should be

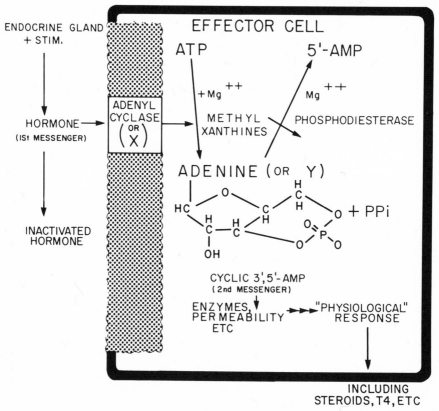

Figure 2.
The second messenger system involving adenyl cyclase.

emphasized, however, that other roles for this nucleotide may yet be discovered. There is now evidence, for example, that some of the effects of light on the retina may be mediated by cyclic AMP (Bitensky *et al.*, 1971), raising the possibility that cyclic AMP may be involved in many sensory phenomena.

The danger of excessively low levels of cyclic AMP has already been emphasized, but the danger of prolonged high levels should also be noted. This is particularly well illustrated by recent studies of cholera (eg., Evans *et al.,* 1972; Guerrant *et al.,* 1972). Apparently cholera enterotoxin is capable of producing (by an unknown mechanism) an irreversible increase in functional adenyl cyclase activity in intestinal mucosal cells, leading to prolonged high levels of cyclic AMP. This in turn leads to increased permeability of these cells, which appears to account for the excessive loss of fluid and electrolytes characteristic of this disease.

Finally, in this section, we should emphasize that the hypothetical scheme presented in Fig. 1 is undoubtedly oversimplified, and may even be incorrect in broad outline. It is conceivable, for example, that the level of cyclic AMP may change during the cell cycle, and such changes could be more important than the overall steady state level measured in large populations of unsynchronized cells. Furthermore, we have ignored an important group of cells which are actually *stimulated* to replicate by cyclic AMP, and which therefore do not fit in with the scheme outlined in Fig. 1 at all. These would include, for example, thymic lymphocytes (MacManus *et al.,* 1971) and hematopoietic stem cells (Byron, 1972). This phenomenon may seem less puzzling when it is realized that the ability to replicate rapidly is an essential part of the differentiated function of these cells. It seems possible that they possess a special cyclic AMP-sensitive mechanism not shared by most cells, and that just as some cells are stimulated to release hormones, for example, so also are the cells stimulated to replicate.

But no matter how oversimplified the scheme suggested in Fig. 1 may ultimately prove to be, it is almost certainly less simplistic than earlier views which ignored the possible role of cyclic AMP in development altogether. Continued research in this area should lead to results of great biological interest, and possibly of therapeutic value as well.

Cyclic AMP in the Brain

Although the role of cyclic AMP in the brain is obscure, it nevertheless seems appropriate at this conference to summarize the results of some of our research in this area. Figure 3 shows how the steady state level of cyclic AMP in the rat brain changes as a function of age. As an incidental point, and in support of the scheme suggested in Fig. 1, this figure also shows that cyclic AMP may fall to very low levels in embryonic tissue. The level in rat brain increases a few days before birth, then remains stable for approximately a week, and then begins to increase again, reaching adult levels after about 30 days (Schmidt *et al.,* 1970).

The increasing levels beginning a few days after birth can be correlated up to a point with the effect of norepinephrine on rat brain slices *in vitro* (Fig. 4). In these experiments, chopped slices were incubated in the absence of norepinephrine for 44 minutes, during which time the level of cyclic AMP gradually falls to a low steady state level. Norepinephrine ($5 \times 10^{-6}M$) was then added to half the samples, and 6 minutes later the tissue was fixed for the assay of cyclic AMP. It can be seen that a response to this concentration of norepinephrine could not be detected for at least the first three

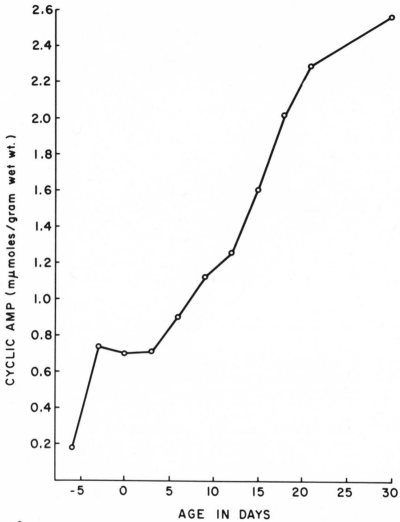

Figure 3.
Whole brain cyclic AMP levels in rats of different ages. Brains were removed from the heads of rats which had been quick-frozen in liquid nitrogen. After pulverization and homogenization, cyclic AMP was measured in purified extracts. From Schmidt *et al.* (1970).

days after birth; the response develops rapidly thereafter, reaching a peak after about 10 days of age. A higher and maximally effective concentration (5×10^{-5}M) produced a measurable effect in slices from 3 day old rats, but not at earlier times (Schmidt *et al.*, 1970). Since adenyl cyclase is present in rat brain even before birth, these data were initially interpreted as reflecting the development of adrenergic receptors. It seems equally possible, however, that receptors were present even before an effect on cyclic

AMP could be detected, and that what develops during early postnatal life is a mechanism which enables the hormone-receptor interaction to influence adenyl cyclase. An apparently similar development of sensitivity to catecholamines has been studied in mouse brain cultures by Seeds and Gilman (1971).

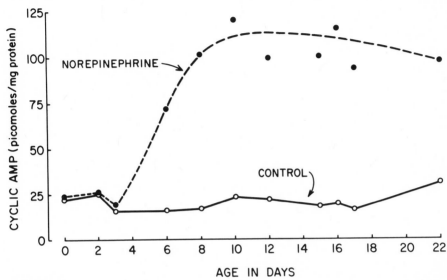

Figure 4.
> Response of developing rat brain to norepinephrine. Brains were cut in half and then chopped in the cold with the aid of a McIlwain tissue chopper. Suspensions were then incubated for 50 minutes, with or without 5×10^{-6}M norepinephrine during the final 6 minutes. After tissue fixation, cyclic AMP was measured in purified extracts. From Schmidt *et al.,* 1970.

We can note that the reduced response seen in brain slices from older animals (Fig. 4) seems to be characteristic of many tissues, and presumably reflects decreasing sensitivity of adenyl cyclase to hormonal stimulation. This is difficult to study in broken cell preparations of brain, because such preparations respond poorly to hormones under all conditions tested, but it has been studied in other tissues. In liver preparations, for example, Bitensky *et al* (1970; see also Bar and Hahn, 1971) found that the magnitude of the response to both epinephrine and glucagon decreased with increasing age, with the response to epinephrine being decreased more than the response to glucagon. Deteriorating receptor activity with age is probably not confined to receptors related to adenyl cyclase. For example, Elsas *et al* (1971) have studied the loss of responsivity of the rat diaphragm muscle to insulin. To what degree these changes are the cause and to what degree an effect of other age-related changes remains to be seen.

The most striking example that we have encountered of this type of change occurs in the developing rabbit brain (Fig. 5). Unlike the rat, rabbit brain slices respond to norepinephrine with a measurable increase in cyclic AMP even on the day of birth. The magnitude of this response thereafter increases in most brain areas, reaching a peak at about 9 to 14 days of age. It then begins to decrease until, as noted previously by Kakiuchi and Rall (1968b), a response in adult brain slices can hardly be detected. The cerebellum is seen to be something of an exception, since its response to norepinephrine does not markedly change with age, and is at least as great in the adult as it is in newborn tissue (Schmidt and Robison, 1971).

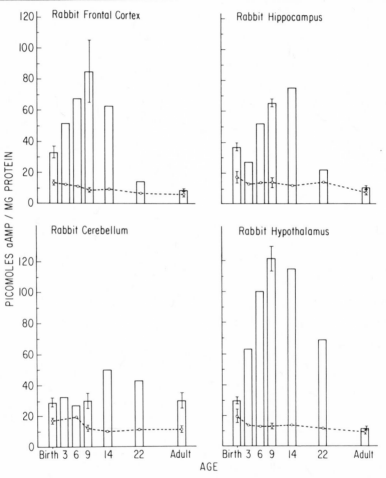

Figure 5.

The cyclic AMP response to norepinephrine in 4 areas of the developing rabbit brain. After dissection in the cold, suspensions of chopped tissue were incubated for 50 minutes, with or without 5×10^{-5}M norepinephrine during the final 6 minutes. Dashed lines represent control levels of cyclic AMP, while bars represent the effect of norepinephrine. From Schmidt and Robison (1971).

We have more recently studied the response of the developing rabbit cerebral cortex to histamine (Palmer *et al.,* 1972b). Histamine has only a slight effect on rat brain cyclic AMP, at least under most conditions (Krishna *et al.,* 1970), but it was known to have a pronounced effect on rabbit brain slices (Kakiuchi and Rall, 1968b). We found that sensitivity to histamine developed initially along a time-course similar to that seen with norepinephrine (Fig. 6), but that it declined much more gradually, so that even in slices from adult animals a very substantial 5-fold increase could be seen. Another difference between the effects of histamine and norepinephrine in rabbit brain is that the increased levels of cyclic AMP seen in response to histamine tend to be well-maintained, whereas

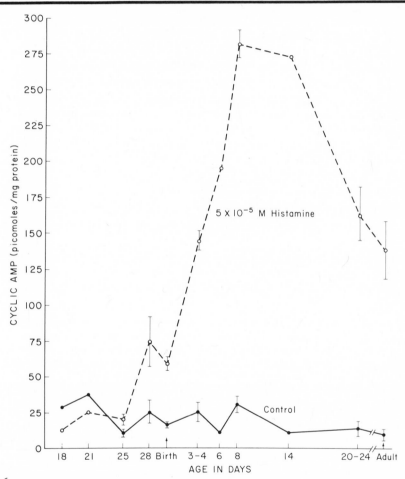

Figure 6.

The cyclic AMP response to histamine in the cerebral cortex of the developing rabbit brain. Suspensions of chopped tissue were incubated for 50 minutes, with or without the indicated concentration of histamine during the final 6 minutes, following which cyclic AMP was measured. From Palmer *et al.* (1972b).

with norepinephrine they begin to fall after a few minutes even in the continued presence of the antagonist. The functional significance of these species differences in the cyclic AMP response of brain to different biogenic amines is unknown at present. Perhaps the knowledge that they exist will eventually be helpful in future attempts to understand how brain function is regulated.

Interpretation of these studies with brain slices is complicated by several factors, one being that we do not know which cells are responsible for the observed changes in cyclic AMP. Although cyclic AMP appears to occur in neurons (e.g., Breckenridge and Bray, 1970; McAfee *et al.*, 1971), it also occurs in glia (Gilman and Nirenberg, 1971b; Clark and Perkins, 1971). The changes in cyclic AMP which have been observed in cultured glial tumor cells in response to biogenic amines are very striking, and, if these cells are at all indicative of the capacity of normal glial cells, they could account for most if not all of the cyclic AMP produced in response to these agents in brain slices. Clark and Perkins found that the magnitude of the cyclic AMP response to norepinephrine in cultured glial cells (a human astrocytoma cell line) was much greater during the period of rapid proliferation than at later times when the cell density was high, whereas the smaller response to histamine remained more-or-less constant. A rapid proliferation of glial cells might well contribute to the unusual pattern of responsivity seen in the developing rabbit brain, although the differences between the rabbit and rat do not seem explicable on this basis. Of possible significance is the fact that cyclic AMP levels in the developing rat brain (Fig. 3) correlate closely with the relative proportion of oligodendrocytes in nervous tissue of this species (Vaughn, 1969; see also Jacobson, 1970).

Thus there are several indications that most of the cyclic AMP present in brain may be located in glia rather than neurons. Unfortunately, the function of glial cells in the brain seems almost as obscure as the function of cyclic AMP; perhaps a better understanding of one of these will lead to a better understanding of the other, and vice versa.

Another factor complicating the interpretation of changes in cyclic AMP in brain slices is that we have been unable to reproduce these results *in vivo*. Using microwave irradiation as the means of tissue fixation (Schmidt *et al.*, 1971), we were able to show an increased level of cyclic AMP in all areas of the rat brain following decapitation. We were further able to show large increases in hepatic cyclic AMP in response to glucagon and in adrenal cyclic AMP in response to ACTH (Blumberg *et al.*, 1972). However, when either large or small amounts of norepinephrine were injected intraventricularly, there was no change in brain cyclic AMP (Schmidt *et al.*, 1972), despite the large changes that we and many others had noted *in vitro* (e.g., Fig. 4). Amphetamine, which is thought to act centrally by stimulating the release of newly-synthesized norepinephrine, also had no detectable effect on the level of cyclic AMP in brain. There is, therefore, a puzzling discrepancy between our *in vitro* and *in vivo* results which we have so far not resolved.

Lack of Effect of Thyroidectomy

Our studies of the developing rat brain were initiated with the hypothesis in mind that a defect in the formation of action of cyclic AMP might be responsible for some forms of mental retardation in humans. An interesting experimental model is provided by the thyroidectomized rat, since there is a critical period in this species, roughly during the first ten days of life, during which deprivation of thyroid hormone results in faulty brain development and permanent impairment of learning ability. Administration of thyroid hormone to thyroidectomized rats during this critical period permits normal development, but thyroxine is not effective if given after the tenth day of age (Hamburgh, 1968; Jacobson, 1970). The thought that cyclic AMP might be involved in this was based on the report by Krishna *et al* (1968) that thyroxine appeared to stimulate the synthesis of adenyl cyclase in rat adipose tissue.

Upon investigation, however, we found that thyroidectomy at birth had no detectable effect on the development of brain adenyl cyclase, phosphodiesterase, cyclic AMP levels *in vivo,* responsivity to norepinephrine *in vitro,* or on protein kinase activity either in the presence or absence of cyclic AMP, despite the fact that the typical signs of hypothyroidism were produced (Schmidt and Robison, 1972). At about 15 days of age we noted that endogenous cyclic AMP levels in the brains of the thyroidectomized rats were significantly lower than in normal animals, and by 40 days of age were down to 60% of normal. The pathological significance of this is unclear at present. It would appear, in any event, that the early steps in the action of thyroid hormone in brain are not closely related to cyclic AMP.

Pharmacological Studies

In view of our inability to see similar changes *in vivo*, drug-induced changes in brain cyclic AMP *in vitro* obviously have to be viewed with caution. Some interesting results have nevertheless been obtained, and can be summarized briefly here.

Most catecholamine-induced increases in cyclic AMP in peripheral tissues seem to be mediated by adrenergic *beta* receptors (Robison and Sutherland, 1970; Robison *et al.,* 1972a), and this also appears to be true in some brain areas, such as the cerebellum of rabbits (Kakiuchi and Rall, 1968a) and humans (Shimizu *et al.,* 1971). By contrast, adrenergic *alpha* receptors had been found to suppress the level of cyclic AMP in some cells (eg., Robison *et al.,* 1971a, 1972b) but had never been found to mediate an increase. We reasoned that if inhibitory *alpha* receptors existed in brains, we should see a larger increase in cyclic AMP in response to norepinephrine if the norepinephrine was added in the presence of an *alpha* adrenergic blocking agent such as phentolamine. This was tested using slices of rat hypothalamus, and, far from the predicted result, we found that phentolamine was actually a more potent antagonist of norepinephrine, on a mole per mole basis, than was the *beta* adrenergic blocking agent propranolol (Palmer *et al.,* 1972c). Essentially similar findings were made by Chasin *et al* (1971) using slices of guinea pig brain. These findings suggest that adrenergic *alpha* receptors in some brain areas may mediate an increase in the level of cyclic AMP. Whether the *alpha* receptors are located in the cells responsible for the change in cyclic AMP, or whether the effect is indirect, is unknown at present.

We were unable to see an effect of dopamine of cyclic AMP in rat brain slices, but increased levels in response to dopamine in bovine ganglia have since been reported (Kebabian and Greengard, 1971). Stimulation of retinal adenyl cyclase by dopamine has also been reported (Brown and Makman, 1972). The receptors involved in these effects seem clearly to be dopaminergic in nature, rather than adrenergic, and the possibility has thus to be considered that some of the central effects of dopamine may be mediated by cyclic AMP. Brain tissue is so heterogeneous that our negative findings with rat brain slices do not argue strongly against this possibility.

Chlorpromazine had been found to prevent the accumulation of cyclic AMP in brain slices in response to several stimuli (Kakiuchi and Rall, 1968b; Kakiuchi et al., 1969). We later tested chlorpromazine and a series of analogs and metabolites for their ability to inhibit the effect of norepinephrine in slices of rat hypothalamus and brain stem (Palmer et al., 1971; 1972a), and an interesting correlation was observed between their effects in vitro and their psychopharmacological activity in vivo. When added at a concentration of 10^{-5}M, none of the phenothiazine derivatives affected the basal level of cyclic AMP, but chlorpromazine and prochlorperazine markedly inhibited the increase produced by 5 x 10^{-5}M norepinephrine. The 7-hydroxy metabolite of chlorpromazine, which is almost as active as the parent compound pharmacologically (Manian et al., 1965), was also active in vitro. The 8-hydroxy metabolite was less active, in line with its lower pharmacological activity, and all of the other metabolites tested, which are essentially devoid of pharmacological activity, were likewise without effect in vitro. We also found that haloperidol, a butyrophenone derivative with pharmacological properties resembling those of chlorpromazine, also antagonized the effect of norepinephrine in brain stem slices. Among tricyclic antidepressants, imipramine had a slight inhibitory effect in hypothalamic slices, while protriptyline had no effect in either brain area; these findings fit the correlation in that imipramine does have weak chlorpromazine-like sedative properties while protriptyline does not. These various correlations (see also Uzunov and Weiss, 1971) suggest that at least part of the pharmacological activity of the phenothiazine tranquilizers could be related to their ability to suppress cyclic AMP accumulation in the brain. It is of interest in this regard that Himwich (1967) found that 10-fold higher doses of chlorpromazine were required to block the alerting response in 9 to 14 day old rabbits than were required to block this response in adults. This period of relative insensitivity to chlorpromazine coincides closely with the period of greatest sensitivity to norepinephrine (and histamine), as shown in Fig. 5.

Since we were unable to detect increased brain levels of cyclic AMP in response to adrenergic stimuli in vivo, we did not study the effects of phenothiazine derivatives under these conditions. However, in the course of studies with amphetamine, a very striking fall in the level of cyclic AMP was noted in both hypothalamus and brain stem in response to p-chloroamphetamine (Palmer et al., 1972a). In these experiments, p-chloroamphetamine was injected 4 hours before the rats were killed, and the slices incubated for 50 minutes as usual, but the same effect can be demonstrated without incubation (J. Blumberg, unpublished observations). The significance of this effect of p-chloroamphetamine is unknown at present, but may conceivably be related to the long-lasting inhibition of tryptophan hydroxylase produced by this drug (Bush *et al.,* 1972).

Another drug that causes a fall in brain levels of cyclic AMP *in vivo* is RO-4-1284, a benzoquinolizine derivative which stimulates the rapid release of presynaptic stores of brain amines (serotonin as well as norepinephrine), leading ultimately to depletion of these stores (Sulser and Bush, 1971). A significant reduction in the level of cyclic AMP (to less than half of normal in most brain areas) was seen within 30 minutes of the intraperitoneal injection of RO-4-1284, while the tricyclic antidepressant DMI, which prevents reuptake of norepinephrine, partially inhibited the effect (Blumberg *et al.,* 1972). The overall significance of these observations is far from clear at present. The lack of effect of DMI by itself in these experiments represents another instance of non-correlation between *in vitro* and *in vivo* results, since Kodama *et al* (1971) did demonstrate increased cyclic AMP formation in response to DMI in brain slices.

Possible Role in Affective Disorders

The increased urinary excretion of cyclic AMP during the switch phase from depression to mania in manic-depressive patients (Paul *et al.,* 1971) represents an intriguing observation pointing to a possible role for cyclic AMP in mental illness. Cyclic AMP levels in cerebrospinal fluid from manic and depressed patients had previously been found to be the same as in normal patients (Robison *et al.,* 1970), but, as pointed out by Paul and his colleagues, a different result might have been obtained had the samples been collected during the switchphase. It remains entirely conceivable that changes in cyclic AMP in certain brain cells may have a very important influence on mood and behavior. On the other hand, whether these changes would be reflected by changes in urinary excretion or even cerebrospinal fluid levels seems more doubtful, since so many cells and tissues throughout the body may contribute to these values (Broadus *et al.,* 1971). The interesting observation by Paul and his colleagues nevertheless suggests that continued research in this direction may be rewarding.

Concluding Remarks

An important role for cyclic AMP in regulating the function of highly differentiated cells in peripheral tissues has been established. Cyclic AMP may also play an important role during early development, and some of the evidence for this was reviewed in the first part of this paper. However, despite the many advances which have been made in understanding the role of cyclic AMP in other structures, its role in the brain remains obscure.

Some of the reasons for believing that cyclic AMP probably does play a role in the brain can be briefly summarized. The enzymes for synthesizing and metabolizing cyclic AMP are very active in brain, and cyclic AMP occurs there in high concentrations. Norepinephrine and other biogenic amines found in the brain are capable of producing large increases in the level of cyclic AMP when added to brain slices *in vitro*, and at least one of central effects of norepinephrine, the inhibition of cerebellar Purkinje cell firing, can be fairly accurately mimicked by exogenous cyclic AMP (Hoffer *et al.*, 1971). The behavioral effects of cyclic AMP, when injected directly into the brain (as the dibutyryl derivative), are very striking. These effects, which have been summarized by Gessa *et al.* (1970) and observed also by us (Strada *et al.*, 1968), include pronounced motor stimulation, recurring convulsions, and catatonia, the precise syndrome varying with the site of injection and species. Tagliamonte *et al.* (1971) have also observed stimulation of serotonin synthesis in the brain in response to exogenous cyclic AMP, in line with the postulated effect on tryptophan hydroxylase.

Taken together, the observations mentioned in this and preceding sections are compatible with a number of possible roles for cyclic AMP in the modulation of brain function. Complicating factors which tend to preclude a more definitive conclusion are a) our lack of understanding of the physiological role of agents known to alter cyclic AMP in brain slices *in vitro*, b) our lack of knowledge of which cells are specifically responsible for these changes, and c) our inability to detect similar or analogous changes *in vivo* in response to stimuli which might be expected to produce them.

With these considerations in mind, we turn reluctantly to the possible relation of cyclic AMP to aging. Based on the limited number of studies which have been carried out to date with experimental animals, it would appear that the ability of most cells and tissues to produce cyclic AMP in response to environmental stimuli increases up to a point, with increasing age, and thereafter begins to decline. Could this decreasing ability to produce cyclic AMP be responsible for any of the disorders commonly seen in the aging patient? In the case of peripheral systems, some plausible guesses could be made. It could be predicted, for example, on the basis of our present understanding of the role of cyclic AMP, that elderly patients would have a greater incidence of cancer (for reasons outlined in this paper), hypertension (because reduced levels of cyclic AMP lead to increased tone of smooth muscle), and thrombosis (because platelets aggregate more readily when cyclic AMP levels are low). But to what extent reduced levels of cyclic AMP are in fact responsible for these disorders remains to be established.

Turning finally to the psychiatric disorders so commonly seen in aging patients, such as loss of memory, depression, confusional states, and so on, it is clear that the possible role of cyclic AMP in these disorders will remain for some time to come entirely within the realm of conjecture. But while answers are scarce, the basic question seems very much worth asking. Although we cannot prevent old age, we might be able, if we knew more about it, to make it a more enjoyable period of life than it presently seems to be. We hope that continued research on the possible role of cyclic AMP in aging will eventually contribute to this goal.

References

Bär, H-P. and P. Hahn (1971). *Canad. J. Biochem.*, 49: 85.

Bitensky, M.W., V. Russell and M. Blanco (1970). *Endocrinology,* 86: 154.

Bitensky, M.W., R.E. Gorman and W.H. Miller (1971). *Proc. Nat. Acad. Sci.,* 68: 561.

Blumberg, J.B., J.T. Hopkins, M.J. Schmidt and G.A. Robison (1972) In preparation.

Bleckenridge, B. McL. and Bray, J.J. (1970). *Adv. Biochem. Psychopharmacol.,* 3: 325.

Broadus, A.E., J.G. Harman, N.I. Kaminsky, J.H. Ball, E.W. Sutherland and G.W. Liddle (1971). *Ann. N.Y. Acad. Sci.,* 185: 50.

Bronstad, G.O., K. Elgjo and I. Oye (1971). *Nature New Biol.,* 233: 78.

Brown, J.H. and M. Makman (1972). *Proc. Nat. Acad. Sci.,* 69: 539.

Bullough, W.S. (1967). "The Evolution of Differentiation." Academic Press, New York.

Bush, E.S., J.A. Bushing and F. Sulser (1972). *Biochem. Pharmacol.,* in press.

Butcher, R.W., Ho, R.J., Meng, N.C. and Sutherland, E.W. (1965). *J. Biol. Chem.,* 240: 4515.

Byron, J.W. (1972). *Exptl. Cell Res.,* 71: 228.

Chasin, M., Rivkin, I., Mamrak, F., Samaniego, S.G. and Hess, S.M. (1971). *J. Biol. Chem.,* 246: 3037.

Clark, R.B. and Perkins, J.P. (1971). *Proc. Nat. Acad. Sci.,* U.S.A., 68: 2757.

Elsas, L.J., R.C. MacDonell and L.E. Rosenberg, (1971). *J. Biol. Chem.,* 246: 6452.

Evans, D.J., L.C. Chen, G.T. Curlin and D.G. Evans (1972). *Nature New Biol.,* 236: 137.

Garbers, D.L., W.D. Lust, N.L. First and H.A. Lardy (1971). *Biochemistry,* 10: 1825.

Gessa, G.L., G. Krishna, J. Forn, A. Tagliamonte and B.B. Brodie (1970). *Adv. Biochem. Psychopharmacol.,* 3: 371.

Gilman, A.G. and Nirenberg, M. (1971a). *Nature,* 234: 357.

Gilman, A.G. and Nirenberg, M. (1971b). *Proc. Nat. Acad. Sci.,* U.S.A., 68: 2165.

Gray, J.P. (1971). "Cyclic AMP and cyclic GMP in gametes." Ph.D. Dissertation, Vanderbilt University.

Greengard, P. and Costa, E. (1970). "Role of Cyclic AMP in Cell Function," Raven Press, New York.

Guerrant, R.L., L. C. Chen and G.W.G. Sharp (1972). *J. Infect. Dis.,* 125: 377.

Hamburgh, M. (1968). *Gen. Comp. Endocrinol.,* 10: 198.

Heidrick, M.L. and W.L. Ryan (1971). *Cancer Res.,* 31: 1313.

Himwich, H. (1967). *In* "Regional Development of the Brain in Early Live," ed by A. Minkowski (Davis, Philadelphia), p. 293.

Hoffer, B.J., Siggins, G.R., Oliver, A.P. and Bloom, F.E. (1971). *Ann N.Y. Acad. Sci.,* 185: 531.

Hong, J-S., G.R. Smith and B.N. Ames (1971). *Proc. Nat. Acad. Sci.,* 68: 2258.

Jacobson, M. (1970). "Developmental Neurobiology." Holt, Rinehart and Winston, Inc., New York.

Johnson, G.S., R.M. Friedman, and I. Pastan (1971). *Proc. Nat. Acad. Sci.,* 68: 425.

Kakiuchi, S. and Rall, T.W. (1968a). *Molec. Pharmacol.,* 4: 367.

Kakiuchi, S. and Rall, T.W. (1968b). *Molec. Pharmacol.,* 4:479.

Kakiuchi, S., T.W. Rall and H. McIlwain (1969). *J. Neurochem.,* 16: 485.

Kety, S.S. (1966). *Pharmacol. Rev.,* 18: 787.

Kodama T., Y. Matsuka, T. Suzuki, S. Tanaka, and H. Shimizu (1971). *Biochim. Biophys. Acta,* 252: 165.

Krishna, G., S. Hynie and B.B. Brodie (1968). *Proc. Nat. Acad. Sci.,* 59:884.

Krishna, G., Forn, J., Voight, K., Paul, M and Gessa, F.L. (1970). *Adv. Biochem. Psychopharmacol.,* 3:155.

Kuo, J.F. and P. Greengard (1969). *Proc. Nat. Acad. Sci.,* 64: 1349.

Lwoff, A. (1953). *Bacteriol. Rev.,* 17: 269.

Lwoff, A. (1962). "Biological Order." MIT Press, Cambridge, pp. 62-86.

McAfee, D.A., Schorderet, M. and Greengard, P. (1971). *Science,* 171: 1156.

MacManus, J.P., J.F. Whitfield and T. Youdale (1971). *J. Cell. Physiol.*, 77: 103.

Makman, M.H. (1971). *Proc. Nat. Acad. Sci.*, 68: 2127.

Makman, R.S. and E.W. Sutherland (1965). *J. Biol. Chem.*, 240: 1309.

Manian, A.A., D.H. Efron and M.E. Goldberg, (1965). *Life Sci.*, 4: 2425.

Otten, J., G.S. Johnson and I. Pastan (1971). *Biochem. Biophys. Res. Commun.*, 44: 1192.

Otten, J., J. Bader, G.S. Johnson and I. Pastan (1972). *J. Biol. Chem.*, 247: 1632.

Palmer, G.C., Robison, G.A. and Sulser, R. (1971). *Biochem. Pharmacol.*, 20: 236.

Palmer, G.C., Robison, G.A., Manian, A.A. and Sulser, F. (1972a). *Psychopharmacologia*, 23: 201.

Palmer, G.C., M.J. Schmidt and G.A. Robison (1972b) *Submitted for publication.*

Palmer, G.C., F. Sulser and G.A. Robison (1972c). *Submitted for publication.*

Pastan, I. and R. Perlman (1970). *Science*, 1969: 339.

Paul, M.I., H. Cramer and W.E. Bunney (1971). *Science*, 171: 300.

Robison, G.A. and E.W. Sutherland (1970). *Circulation Res.*, 26: I-147.

Robison, G.A., A.J. Coppen, P.C. Whybrow and A.J. Prange (1970). *Lancet*, II: 1028.

Robison, G.A., B. Cole, A. Arnold and R.C. Hartmann (1971a). *Ann. N.Y. Acad. Sci.*, 180: 324.

Robison, G.A., R.W. Butcher and E.W. Sutherland (1971b). "Cyclic AMP." Academic Press, New York.

Robison, G.A., R.W. Butcher and E.W. Sutherland (1972a). *In* "Biochemical Actions of Hormones," Vol. II, ed. by G. Litwack (Academic Press, New York), pp. 81-111.

Robison, G.A., P.E. Langley and T.W. Burns (1972b). *Biochem. Pharmacol.*, 21: 589.

Schildkraut, J.J. and S.S. Kety (1967). *Science*, 156: 21.

Schimmer, B.P. (1971). *Biochim. Biophys. Acta*, 252: 567.

Schmidt, J.H. and Robison, G.A. (1971). *Life Sci., Pt. I,* 10:459.

Schmidt, M.J. and G.A. Robison (1972). *J. Neurochem.,* 19: 937.

Schmidt, M.J., Palmer, G.C., Dettbarn, W-D. and Robison, G.A. (1970). *Develop. Psychobiol.,* 3:53.

Schmidt., M.J., Schmidt, D.E. and Robison, G.A. (1971). *Science,* 173: 1142.

Schmidt, M.J., J.T. Hopkins, D.E. Schmidt. and G.A. Robison (1972). *Brain Research,* in press.

Seeds, N.W. and Gilman, A.G. (1971). *Science,* 174: 292.

Sheppard, J.R. (1971). *Proc. Nat. Acad. Sci.,* 68: 1316.

Sheppard, J.R. (1972). *Nature New Biol.,* 236: 14.

Shimizu, H., S. Tanaka, T. Suzuki and Y. Matsukado (1971). *J. Neurochem.,* 18: 1157.

Strada, S.J., D.M. Buxbaum and G.A. Robison (1968). *Unpublished observations.*

Sulser, F. and E.S. Bush (1971). *Ann. Rev. Pharmacol.,* 11: 209.

Sutherland, E.W., G.A. Robison and R.W. Butcher (1968). *Circulation,* 27: 279.

Tagliamonte, A., P. Tagliamonte, J. Forn, J. Perez-Cruet, G. Krishna and G.L. Gessa (1971). *J. Neurochem.,* 18: 1191.

Todaro, G. and R.J. Huebner (1972). *Proc. Nat. Acad. Sci.,* 29: 1009.

Uzunov, P. and Weiss, B. (1971). *Neuropharmacol.* 10: 697.

Vaugh, J.E. (1969). *Z. Zellforsch. Mikroskop.,* 94: 293.

Voorhees, J.J. and E.A. Duell (1971). *Arch. Dermatol.,* 104: 352.

Voorhees, J.J., E.A. Duell, L.J. Bass, J.A. Powell and E.R. Harrell (1972). *Arch. Dermatol.,* in press.

Walsh, D.A., J.P. Perkins, C.O. Brostrom, E.S. Ho and E.G. Krebs (1971). *J. Biol. Chem.,* 246: 1968.

Weiss, G., Shein, H.M., and Snyder, R. (1971). *Life Sci., Pt. I,* 10: 1253.

Yokota, T. and J.S. Gots (1970). *J. Bacteriol.,* 103: 513.

Zubay, G., D. Schwartz and J. Beckwith (1970). *Proc. Nat. Acad. Sci.,* 66: 104.

A Pituitary Factor Inhibiting the Effects of the Thyroid:

Its Possible Role in Aging

W.D. Denckla, M.D.

Hypothyroidism produces many of the symptoms of premature aging, including greying hair, when it occurs in young persons. The successful "rejuvenation" of young hypothyroid patients with thyroid hormone treatment encouraged early investigators in the 19th century to believe that this endocrine deficiency might contribute to the pathogenesis of aging. Early in this century Benedict and others showed that the O_2 consumption rate, as measured by basal metabolic rate (BMR) methods, declined with age. Since a low BMR was supposed to be a relatively specific diagnostic test for hypothyroidism, early investigators were encouraged to treat the aged with thyroid. The treatment was a failure. Medicine was faced with a paradox. Thyroid replacement cured the symptoms of hypothyroidism in young persons. However, when these same symptoms occurred in old, normal persons, replacement was ineffective. With the advent of protein bound iodine measurements as a test for the level of thyroid hormones in the blood, an additional complexity was added. The protein bound iodine levels were found to be constant throughout life (5). Faced with the accumulated evidence, investigators have long ago abandoned any hope of relating hypothyroidism to aging.

Recent experiments with rats in my laboratory suggest that this hope may have been prematurely abandoned. The pituitary may secrete a factor after puberty which might progressively block the effects of thyroid hormones on peripheral tissues.

The methods for measuring O_2 consumption have been somewhat improved compared to the various BMR methods (2,3). O_2 consumption measured by the new method will be called minimal O_2 consumption rates (MOC). Because of the far greater convenience of anesthesia, all the rats reported in this paper were measured under anesthesia. A simple closed circuit instrument was developed compared to the original instrument. O_2

77

consumption was measured by the rate of movement of a bolus of water in a horizontal glass tube. The tube was connected to a small plastic chamber containing the rat. The chamber contained soda lime for CO_2 absorption and was immersed in a water bath. Rectal temperatures were continuously monitored and the bath temperatures were adjusted to make certain all test rats had the same normal rectal temperatures. MOC was expressed in cc's of O_2 at STP/100 gms fat free body weight/min (3). All rats were fed a low iodine diet (3).

The MOC, in agreement with others (1), was found to decline 4 fold with age (Table I). The total MOC of intact rats can be considered to consist of two parts. The athyroidal MOC was considered to be the MOC of hypophysectomized or thyroidectomized rats. The thyroidal MOC was calculated as shown in Table I by subtracting the athyroidal MOC from the total MOC. These studies indicated that the athyroidal MOC declined approximately 2 fold with age while the thyroidal MOC decreased 6—8 fold.

All known endocrine glands were ablated in 40 week old rats (Table II). Only primary (thyroidectomy) or secondary (hypophysectomy) thyroid ablation lowered the MOC. With the exception of pancreatectomy, these same ablations were repeated in 3 week old rats with the same results. These experiments indicated that whatever the cause of the MOC decline with age, it most probably involved only the thyroid or the pituitary.

The MOC after either thyroidectomy of hypophysectomy in 3 week old rats was followed for 24 weeks post-operatively. After an initial 8 weeks wait for the decay of the effects of endogenous thyroid hormones, the MOC remained constant during the period of observation at 1.68±.12 cc's of O_2. Intact rats at 27 weeks had a total MOC of 1.31±0.07. A comparison of these two rats produced the puzzling finding of a rat without thyroid function with an MOC which was higher than an intact rat of the same age (p value 0.01). This finding suggested that either pituitary or thyroid ablation might have arrested the production of a factor which was normally responsible for the MOC decline with age.

Rats were thyroidectomized at 3 weeks of age and given a physiological replacement dose of thyroxine (75 ugm/kg/d). The MOC was followed during the 8 weeks of injection. The response to this amount of thyroxine declined significantly during the course of the injections from 2.73±0.19 to 1.69±0.10 cc's of O_2 (p value 0.01). The injections were stopped. After waiting 8 weeks for the decay of the effects of the exogenous thyroxine, the antithyroidal MOC was found to have declined from a preinjection value of 1.56±0.12 to a final value of 0.85±0.05 (p value 0.001). Thyroxine treatment of thyroidectomized rats apparently could lower the thyroidal and the athyroidal MOC in a normal fashion.

Rats were hypophysectomized at 3 weeks of age. They were given the same treatment as the thyroidectomized rats above. Unlike the thyroidectomized rats, hypophysectomized rats showed no decrease in the response to thyroxine during the course of the injections and no decrease in the athyroidal MOC measured after the injections were stopped.

Various pituitary extracts were made from adult bovine anterior pituitaries in order to find a fraction which inhibited the effects of exogenously administered thyroxine in rats hypophysectomized at 3 weeks. Ellis' C fraction (4),kindly prepared by Dr. Kenneth Gibson, was found to be active when injected at a rate of 30 mg/kg/day for 4 weeks. The MOC's of the pituitary extract injected and control rats were respectively 2.58±0.18 and 3.65±0.21, n=18 (p value 0.001).

The question remained whether the sensitivity to thyroxine normally changed with age. Dose response curves were performed in which the MOC of rats hypophysectomized at 3 weeks of age were compared to the MOC of rats hypophysectomized or thyroidectomized at 40 weeks of age. A 3 fold decrease in sensitivity to thyroxine was observed in the older rats. From 3 to 40 weeks of age in the rat there appeared to be at least a 2 fold decrease in the degradation rate of thyroxine (6). Consequently, if the degradation rates were taken into consideration the actual decrease in tissue sensitivity would be 6 fold with age. This decrease could account for the 6 fold decrease in the thyroidal MOC which occurred between 3 and 40 weeks despite constant plasma levels of thyroid hormones.

For the dose response curves the 40 week old rats were used within 2 months after operation. It was somewhat disappointing that hypophysectomized rats had the same sensitivity to thyroxine as the thyroidectomized 40 week old rats. Pituitary ablation should have removed the purported peripheral inhibitor of thyroxine and the hypophysectomized rats should have been more sensitive than thyroidectomized rats to the administered thyroxine. In preliminary experiments it was observed that hypophysectomized rats eventually regained sensitivity to thyroxine found in 3 week old rats. However, the rats had to be kept for approximately 7 months post-operatively. Thyroidectomized rats kept a similar amount of time did not regain sensitivity to thyroxine.

It is not suggested that the presence of the inhibitor is completely equivalent to thyroidectomy. The MOC is the only effect of thyroid hormones which these experiments indicate may be inhibited by the new factor. However, these experiments at least raise the possibility that some of the other beneficial effects of thyroid hormones may also be inhibited and this inhibition may contribute to the pathogenesis of aging.

References

1. Davis, J.E. Effect of Advancing Age on Oxygen Consumption of Rats, Am. J. Physiol. *112*, 28-33, 1937.

2. Denckla, W.D., Minimal Oxygen Consumption in the Female Rat Some New Definitions and Measurements, J. Appl. Physiol. *29*, 263-274, 1970.

3. Denckla, W.D., A New Interpretation of the VO2 Max, J. Appl. Physiol. *31*, 168-173, 1971.

4. Ellis, S., Studies on the Serial Extraction of Pituitary Proteins, Endocrinology *69*, 554-570, 1961.

5. Gregerman, R.I. and Crowder, S.E., Estimation of Thyroxine Secretion in the Rat by Radioactive Turnover Technique, Endocrinology *72*, 382-392, 1963.

6. Kumerasan, P., and Turner, C.W., Effect of Advancing Age on Thyroid Hormone Secretion Rate of Male and Female Rats, Pro. Soc. Exp. Biol. Med. *124*, 752-754, 1967.

Section 2

Complications of Drug Use

Dyskinesia in the Aging

George W. Paulson, M.D.

This article discusses dyskinetic phenomena in the aged, involuntary movements which are manifested as inappropriate or excessive movements of the limbs, face, or even of the entire trunk. There is, of course, no way that all disorders of movements can be discussed, or even completely listed today. For clinicians, especially we who are aging, new movements and new theories of movements constantly appear and they appear with bewildering rapidity. Some of these are dyskinesias which are rediscovered, some represent movements perceived for the first time because new concepts have arisen, and some unfortunately are produced by our medications and by our surgical colleagues. All movement is a continuous combination of afferent and efferent phenomena in the nervous system and the nervous system lacks water-tight compartments. Even sensory disorders can be reflected in the motor system. Some movement patterns are under central control with feedback or servomechanisms linking one region of the nervous system to another. It is apparent, therefore, that an anatomical, physiologic, clinical, or theoretical framework could be used for classification of the dyskinesias. The list that follows utilizes all of these features in a manner which I prefer to call non-obsessive rather than simply disorganized.

"Normal" or non-organic movements may appear or become more prominent in aged individuals. There is no evidence that normal associated gestures and non-verbal communication and gesticulation diminish with age, except insofar as the universal, inexorable slowing suppresses these cultural stigmata. An enthusiastic Italian doesn't fail to enliven his speech by waving his hands just because he is receiving Medicare.

It has long been noted that mentally or developmentally retarded individuals may have associated movements in one limb when the other is used. For example, contralateral imitative movements, pinching, finger spreading, etc., may be retained in retarded children in contrast to the gradual inhibition of such overflow in the normal child. In the most extreme degree of reflected movements or overflow, "mirror" movements are seen. Associated movements of the hemiplegic limb when the sound limb is used is more common following hemiplegia in children than in the aged. Nevertheless, it seems likely that repetitive hand movements, drumming movements, or finger spreading could reappear in the contralateral limb as the patient ages. Studies of these association patterns and their correlation with dementia have not been performed so far as I know. (Already you can sense that much of the emphasis during this presentation concerns release of lower structures when higher ones are damaged.)

Facial synkinesias, perhaps resulting from injury to the peripheral or central nervous system, are occasionally seen in the aged. There is no evidence that I know of that synkinesias following Bell's palsy are more common in older patients; in fact, I believe the reverse is true. Some of the other facial movements that are seen are conveniently explained as release of lower nuclear connections when higher cortical inhibition has been eroded or suppressed. One example is the corneomandibular response, which consists of a contralateral movement of the chin when the eye is forcefully closed. This reflex may present as a fragmentary phenomenon in the aged, and can occur without the noxious corneal stimulation usually required to elicit it. In extreme examples, the patient's chin protrudes whenever the lids blink forcefully. Another movement which I believe can be seen in normal individuals and which I have noted not only in aged individuals but also in four patients with multiple sclerosis, is a movement of the chin in a direction opposite to eye movements.

It is probable that some irritative phenomena, such as hiccups, are more intractable when they occur in the aged than in the young. We cannot be too surprised at this when we remember the problems of sensory overflow such as postherpetic neuralgia or tic douloureux that are more characteristic of older patients.

Other "supracortical" disorders(1) are less normal, for example, blepharospasm. Blepharospasm can be quite troublesome in parkinsonian patients though it may diminish with therapy. Blepharospasm can also result from hysteria, though hysteria is a hazardous diagnosis in aged individuals. We have recently reported three cases of Meige's syndrome in older women.(2) In Meige's syndrome,(3) blepharospasm gradually increases through the years and eventually produces rhythmical contractions of the entire face. The contractions are partially relieved by anxiety or intense concentration, but eventually become socially and physically incapacitating. "Supracortical" factors, if you will temporarily forgive that expression, may play a role in occupational cramps and the psychogenic contractures noted in the aged. Habits and rhythmical or stereotyped phenomena such as rocking, which are so common in the young or blind, may also be observed in a group of elderly patients who are listening to music or attending to religious exercises. Most of us would hesitate to call such rocking abnormal. Why, we do it ourselves! Tics and stuttering in fact tend to diminish with the passage of years, with the exception of an apparent increase in all types of mouthing phenomena.

Cortical imbalance and cortical discharges can occur, and, since irritability of the cortex can reflect partial denervation or isolation of regions, it should not be a great surprise to us that some patients with focal atrophic processes develop seizures. Over fifteen years ago, members of the Duke neurology staff suggested an association between cortical atrophy and seizures in the aged, and clinical experience supports their observations. Epilepsy can continue for a lifetime, or can occur de novo in the aged. Just as in the very young seizures may reflect metabolic disease, the same is true in the aged. Metabolic imbalance such as the hyperosmolar state seen in uncontrolled diabetics, can lead to focal or generalized seizure disorders secondary to complex cortical and subcortical irritability. The peculiar, and at times rhythmical, contractions of the limbs that are observed acutely after a cerebrovascular accident, particularly in individuals with metabolic disorders or alcoholism, is an intriguing process rarely seen in the very young.

Tremors, like cataracts, seem to await us all if we live long enough. Ecclesiastes XII comments that "the keepers of the house shall tremble" and this has been interpreted to represent the trembling of the hands frequently present with senility. The normal changes of aging include features of extrapyramidal disease. In addition, the familial benign, or essential, tremor tends to worsen with the passage of years and can appear for the first time in old age. Its linkage with advancing years has led to the opinion that benign tremor is associated with longevity, which is a nice but probably untrue statement used to reassure patients. A few clinicians have attempted to separate benign tremor from senile tremor. Both senile and benign tremor are increased by action. In senile tremor, relatively specific actions such as handwriting are more likely to exaggerate the movement. Since pathological differentiation is not yet possible and clinical differentiation is a matter of opinion, to attempt the distinction between senile and benign tremor is fruitless. I am sure there are patients who have a combination of both benign and parkinsonian-type tremor. Naturally the tremor associated with parkinsonism occurs increasingly in older people, since it is primarily a disease of those over fifty-five.

Chorea, even Huntington's Chorea, can appear in late life. Occasionally, unfortunately rarely, however, Huntington's disease at this age may be seen without the association of dementia. Acute senile chorea has been reported. In the instances in which I have seen it, it has followed an acute and apparently viral illness in which recovery was succeeded by a severe generalized choreo-athetotic movement. Hemichorea can be noted as a portion or fragmentary manifestation of hemiballismus following a vascular accident.

Torticollis or torsion spasms can be confused with chorea and is not rare in the practice of neurology. The spasmodic torticollis seen in middle-aged individuals, often female, is the type of disorder that both psychiatry and neurology have attempted to assign to its sister discipline. Even dystonia musculorum deformans, though classically reported as an autosomal recessive trait of Jewish children, can appear as an autosomal dominant disorder. In the dominant form of the disorder, more common in Ohio than the recessive form, the disease presents in later life as torticollis or as a mild dystonic posturing.

Partial destruction or irritation of subcerebellar and vestibular structures can lead to a series of abnormal movements. The phenomenon of oculogyric crisis, perhaps hiccups, and some of the other synkinesias, even some cases of Bell's palsy, may represent damage to structures in this region. Myoclonus as a clinical phenomenon can also originate from neurons in this area, and one way to think of myoclonus is to attribute it to instability of neurons between cortex and spinal cord. Myoclonic phenomena are disturbing prognostically whether they are seen in childhood or in adult life. It is now known that some infectious diseases such as Jakob's disease are noted in the middle-aged or aged patients and myoclonus can be a conspicuous feature in some of these individuals. Benign nocturnal myoclonus that is an almost universal normal phenomenon tends to diminish with the passage of years.

Peripheral structures can probably lead to abnormal movements, as for example the myokymia or twitching beside the eye colloquially known as "live flesh" and seen in all ages in a setting of fatigue. Myokymia in the malar region is more ominous, suggestive of demyelination or a pontine tumor. Facial spasm and facial hemispasm is more common in older individuals than in the young.

Even lesions in the spinal cord can lead to abnormal movements. Destruction of the posterior columns, with loss of position sense, can lead to "piano-playing" movements of the fingers when the eyes are closed. Though these may appear as gentle "searching" movements, some have a more dramatic appearance, and look like asterixis.

A series of abnormal movements have been reported in patients who have been receiving drugs, and the most classic example is tardive dyskinesia. It is now well accepted that this movement disorder, which consists of tongue movements, finger movements and toe movements, as well as postural change, can be related to prolonged ingestion of phenothiazines.(4) The tardive dyskinesias do not invariably disappear when phenothiazines are discontinued, and in some individuals tardive dyskinesia is seen for the first time after the drug is stopped. We will have more discussion today about tardive dyskinesia and I will not belabor it here. We do need an explanation for the clinical distinction between (a) the acute dystonic response to phenothizaines seen largely in children, (b) the pseudoparkinsonism of longer dosage, and (c) the tardive dyskinesia secondary to chronic ingestion of the drug. Are receptor sites transformed; or are central metabolic stores flooded, or depleted?

Similar dyskinesias have been reported in children receiving dexedrine,(5) but this has not been reported in adults, so far as I know. On the other hand, I have seen several aging patients with extreme trembling, agitation and confusion who were on medications such as imipramine. Similar doses would have been readily tolerated by a younger individual. This phenomenon of a paradoxical reaction to any type of sedative is familiar to all of us. It has been suggested that excessive restlessness and agitation can be observed in monkeys in which both basal ganglia and frontal structures are damaged. I do not know of any good studies correlating level of activity, or the response to drugs, to pathologic changes in the brains of senile individuals. Surely there is a difference between those with incessant restlessness, and those with bradykinesia; but since we can't exactly correlate the lesions in parkinsonism to the level of activity, we may have to wait a few years to find a pathologic explanation for some of our questions. It is possible that differences in the metabolic pathways are crucial in advanced years and that such changes produce atypical responses to drugs.

Degenerative disorders are frequently associated with either hypokinesia or hyperkinesia, although many of these have been poorly described and infrequently diagnosed. The Shy-Drager syndrome, the various disorders in which supernuclear palsy may appear, and striatonigral degenerations(6) are examples of this. Many of these appear somewhat like a variety of parkinsonism with the hypokinesia more striking than tremors or adventitious movements. Even the highly skilled may have trouble distinguishing sub-groups of the degenerative disorders that affect the basal ganglia and I would not expect your skill to increase because of a few brief words here. It seems likely that this area of medicine, along with all of the dementias, will be increasingly harvested for research. Certainly there is no shortage of problems.

In listing the movements above, it is apparent that dyskinesia can originate from lesions in many portions of the brain, and that the exact pathophysiologic basis is usually obscure. Dyskinesias are common in the aged, at least partly because lesions involving the central nervous system are cumulative with years. Abnormal movements involve not only cortical but many sub-cortical structures as well.

Several fundamental questions remain. Is the fact that the aged often respond differently to drugs, particularly sedative drugs, any clue as to metabolic differences? In some instances, surely yes, but these metabolic differences may be in organs other than the brain. Lesions do not have to be cerebral ones to lead to cerebral manifestations. It seems true, particularly if one attempts to generalize from the experience with phenothiazines, that the aged can be more vulnerable to drugs, and are vulnerable in a different way than youngsters. Today we will continue to discuss the fact that one of the more common manifestations of drugs in the aged is an abnormal movement, or an abnormal pattern of a normal movement.

Thank you for the chance to join you today.

References

1. Liversedge, L.A.: Involuntary Movements in *Handbook of Clinical Neurology* Vol. I, edit. Vinken, P.J. and Bruyn, G.W., 1969, 277-292.

2. Paulson, G.: Meige's Syndrome, *Geriatrics,* Vol. 27, No. 8, 69-73, 1972.

3. Meige, H.: Les convulsions de la face, une forme clinique de convulsion faciale,

bilaterale et mediane. *Rev. neurol.* (Paris) 2 (1910), 437–443.

4. *Psychotropic Drugs and Dysfunctions of the Basal Ganglia,* edited by George E. Crane and Russell Gardner, Jr., U.S. Government Printing Office, Washington, D.C.

5. Mattson, R.H., and Calverley, J.R.: Dextroamphetamine Sulfate Induced Dyskinesias. *JAMA,* Vol. 224, 1968, 400-402.

6. Adams, R.D.: The Striatonigral Degenerations in *Handbook of Clinical Neurology,* Vol. VI, edit. Vinken, P.G. and Bruyn, G.W., 1968, 694-702.

Attempts at Pharmacological Management of Tardive Dyskinesia

William E. Fann, M.D.
John M. Davis, M.D.
Ian C. Wilson, M.D.
C. Ray Lake, M.D., Ph. D.

One of the more perplexing side-effects of drug therapy, first described by Sigwald and coworkers (34) in 1959, and now generally known as tardive dyskinesia (TD), a hyperkinetic state secondary to prolonged exposure to neuroleptics (2, 7, 8, 9), has proven difficult to treat pharmacologically. A variety of agents has been used in attempts at reversing it. Patients most likely to evince TD are those withdrawn, after long exposure, from neuroleptics; continued therapy tends to mask or reduce the symptoms (10,11). On this evidence, some investigators have tried high doses of phenothiazines, especially the piperazine derivatives (5, 35, 4), as well as haloperidol (33, 24), in treating these conditions. The rationale for using these agents is that they block activity of dopamine (DA) in the CNS and, since TD may be due to DA over-activity at certain striatal neurons, reducing the effect of DA should cause a diminution of the abnormal movements. The short-term efficacy of these agents suggests that this reasoning is correct. However, methyldopa, a compound known to compete with DA in vitro and a commonly used antihypertensive, did not show any clear effect in relieving symptoms of TD (23). Others have tried the potent biogenic amine depleting agent, reserpine (30,32) and its congener, tetrabenzine (19), with some success. Amantadine, an anti-viral agent with mild CNS stimulant properties, has also been suggested (36), but the findings from these investigations, and even the criteria used in them for TD, have been challenged (12). The vitamin pyridoxine has been tried, also without success (13), and levodopa, a precursor of dopamine used successfully in treating Parkinsonism has provided no help in TD (24).

Since the condition seems to be brought about by prolonged exposure to neuroleptics and since some of the predominant activity of these compounds is to block central adrenergic mechanisms, a rational pharmacology might therefore be to use a drug that has central adrenergic stimulant properties. For this reason we tried caffeine, amphetamine,

89

and methylphenidate. Methylphenidate has been used successfully to reverse acute neurotoxic side-effects of phenothiazines (17). Pilot studies in TD yielded no response to caffeine or amphetamine but some modest profit with methylphenidate, a tertiary amine with central stimulant properties similar to amphetamine (18,24). Because methylphenidate reverses some acute neuroleptic neurotoxic effects and because our open pilot study suggested that it may be effective in TD, we undertook a double-blind, placebo controlled study using regular daily oral doses of this agent, as part of an ongoing project to study the pharmacology of this distressing condition and attempt to meliorate it.

Methods

A group of 30 hospitalized patients diagnosed by independent clinicians as having TD were taken into the study. EKG, physical examination, hematology, and urinalysis were done prior to and after the study. Daily blood pressure and pulse were taken on each of the patients and recorded. The patients were housed on their regular treatment wards and escorted once weekly to the office of the rater where they were examined 10 minutes each and rated, using Crane's neurological scale. This method has, in our hands, provided highly reliable results. NOSIE forms were completed weekly by the ward aides. Global ratings were made from verbal reports collected from the ward staff and other ancillary personnel with parameters being overall function and ability to carry out activities of daily living. Video tapes were made of each subject before, during, and after treatment, rerun in random sequence, and rated blind. Half the subjects were placed randomly on placebo for methylphenidate and half on active drug. All subjects were started on 20 mg. per day of methylphenidate (or its placebo equivalent) and increased for each by weekly increments pari passu to a maximum of 80 mg. per day. At the end of 6 weeks the two groups were crossed over. All subjects remained on prescribed neuroleptics, 200-800 mg/day chlorpromazine (or equivalent (20)). None of the neuroleptics were other than phenothiazines.

Another group of 10 subjects showing movements diagnosed as being TD was given careful physical and laboratory evaluations, and where no contraindication was found, was given physostigmine 40 µg/Kg I.V. Methylscopolamine, a compound which antagonizes the peripheral but not the central nervous system effects of physostigmine was given simultaneously mixed in the same syringe. Each subject was rated clinically on an open basis at the time immediately before, during, 45 minutes and one day after physostigmine injection. In addition, each subject was videotaped immediately before, 45 minutes and 24 hours after injection and ratings of changes were made by neurologists from these tapes on a blind basis.

Results

Seventeen of thirty subjects completed the full 12 weeks of the study. In the remaining thirteen patients, an increase in psychiatric symptoms, becoming unruly or unmanageable, in five militated for discontinuing methylphenidate; eight others were removed from the study for administrative reasons. The seventeen who completed the study were compared on several ratings between methylphenidate and placebo.

The weekly blind ratings showed no definite or consistent changes in the neurological symptomatology for either group at any time. The NOSIE scales for those patients remaining on the study showed no significant changes. No differences were found from serial assessment of the video tapes. On the global weekly neurological ratings by the nurses and ward staff, six showed some increase in hyperkinesia, eight showed no change and three were judged to be improved while on methylphenidate. Benefit in these three was adjudged by their becoming able to feed themselves, tie shoe-strings, carry cafeteria trays, dress themselves. This improvement was lost when methylphenidate was withdrawn. Side effects included a transient (5 day) 20 mmHg rise in systolic BP in one patient, a transient moderate (trace − 2+) proteinuria in five female patients, and, in three, EKG changes which were without clinical corollary.

Discussion

Methylphenidate, a CNS stimulant, has been tried in treatment of TD in 17 subjects and has yielded no definitive results. Six of the subjects became symptomatically worse, eight showed no change and a small number (three subjects) showed some benefit. Such results, scattered across a full range of possibilities, and lack of agreement between measuring instruments can be interpreted several ways. First, the lack of agreement is probably due to the subject's voluntary control of the movements during the novel brief interview and taping sessions whereas the global ratings were taken from observations made with the patient unaware or distracted by routine. Since voluntary modification of their symptoms for 5-10 minutes is possible even in severely afflicted subjects, this appears to be a likely factor, especially in light of high reliability of the weekly interview results. This, of course, cannot completely rule out errors of technique which may have contributed but suggests that these were not strong determinants.

Secondly, the increase in hyperkinesia of TD in some of the patients is in keeping with present knowledge of central nervous system pharmacology. That methylphenidate relieves dystonia due to acute neuroleptic toxicity but aggravates symptoms of the tardive type suggests differences in the pathophysiology of acute vs chronic drug-induced conditions that also fit present theories. Enhancement of striatal dopaminergic mechanisms by methylphenidate should increase choreo-athetoid movements in a manner similar to these side-effects in levo-dopa therapy of Parkinson's Disease (3,25) and corroborates the report that another central stimulant, amphetamine, provokes or aggravates dyskinesias (23). Moreover, an increase in psychiatric symptoms in some of the subjects is not surprising since methylphenidate, a CNS stimulant, increases psychomotor activity, and thereby evokes bizarre behavior in already disturbed persons. (16).

Thirdly, the most plausible explanation for improvement of function in the three subjects is their having had a Parkinson-like component (viz., rigidity, bradykinesia) to their neurological disease which was meliorated by methylphenidate (20). Serial ratings of these components were not included in this study but by examination before and during treatment these 3 subjects showed a decrease in these elements suggesting such a response to methylphenidate. In some patients Parkinsonism and TD coexists (14) and can be quite difficult to differentiate. This, of course, does not rule out melioration of TD by methylphenidate, but we consider it unlikely. In any case, since more subjects became symptomatically worse on methylphenidate (N = 6) or showed no change (N = 8) than showed improvement (N = 3) we conclude that methylphenidate is not effective in improving symptoms of TD.

Since centrally acting adrenergic and dopaminergic agents meliorate Parkinsonism and augment or provoke hyperkinesia, whereas cholinergic agents relieve some of the choreo-athetosis of Huntington's Disease (a condition symptomatically similar to TD) and intensify Parkinsonism (1,15,32,22), it may follow that TD is due to weakening of central cholinergic mechanisms and not a reduction of adrenergic or dopaminergic mechanisms. This suggests that prolonged exposure to anticholinergic effects of the neuroleptics is perhaps responsible for the manifestations of TD. On the other hand, dopaminergic systems may become hypersensitive under prolonged antagonism by the neuroleptics, either through an effect on receptor sites or an increase in transmitter synthesis. In any case, our rationale for the use of methylphenidate in TD, based on our data in acute neurological side-effects, would appear to be incorrect though we were encouraged by data from the pilot study. The acute neurotoxic side-effects, presumptively due to antagonism of central dopaminergic mechanisms would, therefore, respond to central dopaminergic agonist or cholinergic antagonist (e.g., an anticholinergic agent). Widespread experience shows agents of these types to indeed be genuinely effective in reversing acute drug-induced neurotoxicity.

Physostigmine, a centrally active anticholinesterase, has been reported to reduce the involuntary movements of Huntington's Disease (1), a hereditary neurological condition similar in its manifestation to TD, and does this presumably by stimulating an increased activity in cholinergic mechanisms. These authors (1) suggest that a deficient cholinergic function exists in HD. On the other hand, physostigmine provokes or augments the rigidity and tremor of parkinsonism (26) presumably by increasing a relative or absolute cholinergic dominance over opposing dopaminergic activity. In addition, parkinsonian symptoms are antagonized by anticholinergic agents (5), whereas HD and TD are aggravated by such treatment (25,26).

Such findings indicate that HD (and TD) and Parkinson's Disease are opposite, as regards the reaction to cholinergic and anticholinergic agents, in their major clinical manifestations. In Parkinson's Disease there exists presumably a relative dopaminergic deficit and concomitant cholinergic dominance (37). Physostigmine would, therefore, amplify this imbalance and intensify the symptoms. On the other hand it has been proposed that, in HD, there is a relative weakening of striatal cholinergic systems with subsequent dopaminergic dominance. In this condition physostigmine may help restore a balance of neurochemical activity and thereby diminish the hyperkinesis (26). Because TD is similar to a neurological disease (i.e. HD) that shows improvement with physostigmine, it is of interest to examine the reaction of patients with TD to physostigmine. We have undertaken such an investigation but the results are incomplete at this time.

Ten chronically hospitalized subjects showing evidence of TD were taken into the study. Careful physical examination and laboratory results showed no contraindication to giving physostigmine. To block peripheral effects of physostigmine without interferring with its central activity, each patient was premedicated with the quarternary anticholinergic, methylscopolamine, 0.25 mg. subcutaneously — the compound used by other investigators for this same purpose in similar studies (1,15,26) — followed by physostigmine, 40 µg/Kg, intravenously. Neurological examinations were performed by two raters immediately before, 45 minutes, and one day after the physostigmine injection, using global ratings, neurological rating scales of hands, limbs, feet, head and face movements. The subjects were videotaped at the same times of live rater examination and the tapes re-run in random sequence for rating, using the same scales, by neurologists on a blind basis.

Tentatively we find that no significant changes occurred in either the general neurological status or in the involuntary movements of arms, legs, neck, and trunk or face movements of these patients. There was nearly complete inter-rater agreement on all measurements. Side effects included vomiting, diarrhea, increased bowel activity, and some salivation.

The absence of clinical changes following physostigmine may be interpreted in several ways. First there is the possibility that the dose was not adequate for a central effect. However, the presence of definite peripheral cholinergic effects despite strong premedication with anticholinergics would weigh against this conclusion. Moreover, the i.v. dose (40 µg/Kg) used in this study is the same i.v. dose (40 µg/Kg) used to diminish the involuntary movement in HD (1,26). Secondly, it is conceivable that the condition in these patients may have been too far advanced to allow a discernible response. The range of impairment, however, was wide enough in these propositi that we feel they collectively represented a good test for the compound, though it may be that, despite the gross clinical evidence of moderate impairment, the loss of cholinergic neurons was so extensive that clinical effect could not occur. Thirdly, technical errors of examination might have contributed to these results though the nearly complete inter-rater agreements marshals some evidence against this conclusion, albeit without infinite degrees of confidence. Definitive deductions, however, must await further refinement of our data.

References

1. Aquilonius, J.M. and Sjostrom, R. Cholinergic and Dopaminergic Mechanisms in Huntington's Chorea. *Life Sciences* 10:405-414, 1971.

2. Ayd, F.J. Persistent Dyskinesia: A Neurologic Complication of Major Tranquilizers. *Int. Drug Ther. Newsletter,* 1:No. 6, 1966.

3. Barbeau, A. Importance of Pathogenesis of Abnormal Movements During L-Dopa Therapy of Parkinson's Disease. *Neurol.* (Minneapolis) 20: 366, 1970.

4. Bucci, L. The Dyskinesias: A New Therapeutic Approach. *Dis. Nerv. Sys.* 32:324-328, 1971.

5. Carruthers, S.G. Persistent Tardive Dyskinesia. *Brit. Med. J.* 3:572, 1971.

6. Christensen, E., Moller, J.E., Baurbye, A. Neuropathological Investigation of 28 Brains from Patients with Dyskinesia. *Acta Psychiat. Scand.* 46: 14-23, 1970.

7. Crane, G.E. Dyskinesia and Neuroleptics . *Arch. Gen. Psychiat.* 19:700-703, 1968.

8. Crane, G.E. Tardive Dyskinesia in Patients Treated with Major Neuroleptics. *Am. J. Psychiat.*, 124 (Supp.) 40-48, 1968.

9. Crane, G.E. Tardive Dyskinesia in Schizophrenic Patients Treated with Psychotropic Drugs. *Aggressologie,* 19:209-218, 1968.

10. Crane, G.E. and Paulson G. Involuntary Movements in a Sample of Chronic Mental Patients and Their Relation to the Treatment with Neuroleptics. *Int. J. Neuropsychiat.,* 3:286-91, 1967.

11. Crane, G.E., Ruiz, P., Kernohan, W.J., Wilson, W., and Royalty, N. Effects of Drug Withdrawal in Tardive Dyskinesia. *Activitas Nervosa Superior,* 11:30-35, 1969.

12. Crane, G.E. More on Amantadine in Tardive Dyskinesia. *N. Eng. J. Med.* 285:1150-1151, 1971.

13. Crane, G.E. Failure of Pyridoxine in Tardive Dyskinesia. *N. Neurol. Neurosurg. Psychiat.* 33:511-512, 1970.

14. Crane, G. Motor Disorders Induced by Neuroleptics: A Proposed New Classification. *Arch. Gen. Psychiat.* 24:179-184, 1971.

15. Duvoisin, R.C. Cholinergic-anticholinergic Antagonism in Parkinsonism. *Arch. Neurol.* 17:124-136, 1967.

16. El-Yousef, M.K., Davis, J.M., Janowsky, D.S., Serkeke, H.J. Methylphenidate as a Provocative Test in Schizophrenia. *The Pharmacologist* 63, July, 1972.

17. Fann, W.E. Use of Methylphenidate to Counteract the Acute Dystonic Reactions to Phenothiazines. *Amer. J. Psychiat.* 1:1293-1294, 1966.

18. Ferguson, J.T., and Funderbark, W.H. Further Evaluation of the New Drug Methyl

Phenidyl Acetate in Treating the Mentally Ill. *J. Pharmacol. and Exper. Therap.* 116:20, 1956.

19. Godwin-Austin, R.B. and Clark, T. Persistent Phenothiazine Dyskinesia Treated with Tetrabenazine. *Brit. Med. J.* 3:25-26, 1971.

20. Held, J.M., Cromwell, R.L., Frank, E.T., and Fann, W.E. Effect of Phenothiazines on Reaction Time in Schizophrenics. *J. Psychiat. Res.* 7:39-45, 1970.

21. Holiday, A.M., Nathan, P.W. Methyl Phenidate in Parkinsonism. *Brit. Med. J.* 1:1652-1655, 1961.

22. Kazamatsuri, H., Chien, C., and Cole, J.O. Treatment of Tardive Dyskinesia II. Short-Term Efficacy of Dopamine Blocking Agents Haloperidol and Thiopropazate. *Arch. Gen. Psychiat.* 27:100-103, 1972.

23. Kazamatsuri, H., Chien, C., Cole, J.O. Treatment of Tardive Dyskinesia III. Clinical Efficacy of a Dopamine Competing Agent, Methyldopa. *Arch. Gen. Psychiat.*27:824-827, 1972.

24. Klawans, H.L. Levodopa in Tardive Dyskinesia. *J. Neurol. Sci.* 14:189-192, 1971.

25. Klawans, H.L. The Pharmacology of Tardive Dyskinesias. *Amer. J. Psychiat.* 130:82-86, 1973.

26. Klawans, J.H. and Rubovitz, R. Central Cholinergic-anticholinergic Antagonism in Huntington's Chorea. *Neurol.* 22:107-116, 1972.

27. Mattson, R.H. and Calverly, J.R. Dextroamphetamine-SO_4 Induced Dyskinesias. *JAMA* 204:400-402, 1968.

28. Natenshon, A.L. Clinical Evaluation of Ritalin. *Dis Nerv. Syst.* 17:392-396, 1956.

29. Papavasiliou, P.S., Gellene, R., Cotzias, G.C. Modification of Parkinsonism: Dyskinesias Accompanying Treatment with Dopa in Psychotropic Drugs and Dysfunctions of the Basal Ganglia. Ed. Crange, G., Gardner, R., pp. 140-147. U.S. Pub. Health Serv. Public. Number 1938. Washington, D.C. U.S. Govt. Printing Off., 1969.

30. Peters, H.A., Daley, R.F., Sato, S. Reserpine for Tardive Dyskinesia. *N. Eng. J. Med.* 286:106, 1972.

31. Prange, A.J., Jr., Wilson, I.C., Morris, C.E., and Hall, C.O. Preliminary Experience with Tryptophan and Lithium in Treatment of Tardive Dyskinesia. Psychopharmacology Abstracts, 1972. In press.

32. Sato, S., Daley, R., Peters, H. Resperine Therapy of Phenothiazine Induced Dyskinesia. *Dis. Nerv. Syst.* 32:680-682, 1971.

33. Siegel, J.C., Mones, R.J. Modification of Choreoform Activity by Haloperidol. *JAMA* 216:675-676, 1971.

34. Sigwald, J., Bonttier, D., Raymondeaud, C., et al. Quatre cas de dyskinesie facio-bucco-linuo-masticatrice a l'evolution prolongee secondaire a un traitement par les neuroleptiques. *Re. Neurol.* 100: 751-755, 1959.

Affective Changes Associated with L-DOPA Therapy

H. Keith Brodie, M.D.

Introduction

The dramatic therapeutic effects of L-DOPA in the treatment of Parkinson's disease have focused attention on psychiatric changes accompanying the administration of this compound (1). While the neurologists were busy studying the effects of DOPA in patients with extrapyramidal disorders, the psychiatrists were assessing the efficacy of L-DOPA in the treatment of depression (2). Based on the hypothesis that depression may be associated with a deficiency in catecholamines proposed by Bunney, Davis, and Schildkraut in the mid-Sixties (3,4), several research groups attempted to administer L-DOPA to depressed patients in order to reverse the presumed deficit in dopamine or norepinephrine (2,5). This paper reviews several of these studies, emphasizing some of the human mood changes associated with the administration of L-DOPA, as well as some of the biochemical effects of this compound. This discussion is particularly relevant in a conference on aging, because most of the patients who will be receiving L-DOPA for the treatment of Parkinson's disease are patients who are sixty years old or older, some of whom will have a mood change caused by the administration of L-DOPA. Most of the data reviewed in this chapter has been published elsewhere (6).

Methods

Our patients were studied in a metabolic research unit specifically designed for the collection of behavioral and biochemical data on a longitudinal basis. All of our patients were severely depressed and required hospitalization. Their symptoms of depression included psychomotor retardation or agitation, weight loss, anorexia, sleep disturbances, and depressive thought content often of psychotic proportions dominated by feelings of worthlessness, hopelessness, preoccupation with guilt, and suicidal ideation. Those patients who were agitated tended to show anxiety, pacing, and hand-wringing, while the retarded patients evidenced slow speech, slowed movement and social withdrawal. For the purposes of the study, we divided our patients into two groups: those with a history of manic depressive illness we referred to as the Bipolar patients, while those patients who had never had an attack of manic depressive illness in the past were referred to as Unipolar patients. This nosologic system was first proposed by Leonhard (7).

The patient's clinical state was independently assessed by a trained nursing research

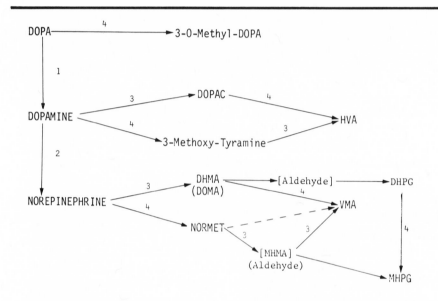

Enzymes:

1. DOPA decarboxylase
2. Dopamine-β-hydroxylase

3. Monoamine oxidase (MAO)
4. Catechol-o-methyl-transferase (COMT)

Metabolites:

DOPAC - 3,4 dihydroxyphenylacetic acid
HVA   - Homovanilic acid
DHMA (DOMA) - Dihydroxymandelic acid
VMA   - 3-methoxy-4-hydroxy-mandelic acid

NORMET - Normetanephrine
MHMA - 3-methoxy-4-hydroxy-mandelic aldehyde
MHPG - 3-methoxy-4-hydroxy-phenyl-glycol
DHPG - 3,4-dihydroxyphenylglycol

Figure 1.
Major Metabolites of DOPA, Dopamine and Norepinephrine

team, who rated the patients twice daily on a 15 point multi-item scale (8). L-DOPA and placebo were administered double blind in a non-random design so that periods of drug and placebo were available for comparison within each patient. Because of the side effects of L-DOPA administration, primarily on the gastrointestinal tract, L-DOPA was administered in conjunction with a peripheral decarboxylase inhibitor, MK 485, which in preventing peripheral decarboxylation necessitated the use of *less* L-DOPA to achieve an increase in brain dopamine levels (9). For those patients not receiving the peripheral decarboxylase inhibitor, L-DOPA dosage was started at 0.5 gm. and built up slowly until either clinical improvement was achieved, or unacceptable side effects were encountered. The maximum dose averaged 8 gm. For the patients on MK 485, the L-DOPA dose required was approximately 1/10 of that used without the inhibitor. Thus, the maximum dose was approximately 800 mg. 24 hour urine pools were collected daily and were frozen for determinations. Whenever possible, cerebral spinal fluid was obtained before and during DOPA administration and analyzed for homovanillic acid and 5-hyroxyindoleacetic acid (10,11).

Results

The metabolism of norepinephrine, dopamine, and DOPA is presented in Figure 1(12). Of 18 depressed patients studied, only 4 showed any anti-depressant response to L–DOPA treatment. For this reason we are not advocating the use of L-DOPA in the treatment of depression. The clinical course of one patient who improved on L-DOPA is presented in Figure 2. Note that the diminution in depression did not occur during

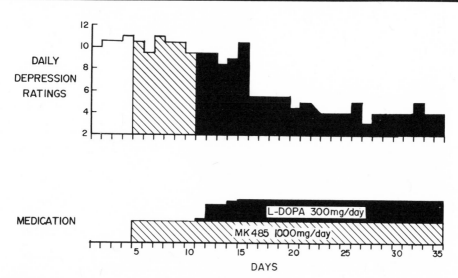

Figure 2.
Improvement in Depression Following L-DOPA Plus MK-485.

administration of the peripheral decarboxylase inhibitor but only when L-DOPA was administered in doses above 250 mg. daily. The development of mania during the course of L-DOPA administration to a depressed patient is presented in Figure 3. We noted that mania occurred primarily in patients who had prior histories of manic depressive illness. Of the 18 patients studied, 6 out of 7 Bipolar patients became hypomanic or manic during L-DOPA administration compared to only 1 out of 11 Unipolar patients. This is significant at the p<0.01 level using chi-square analysis (x^2 = 7.6) (13).

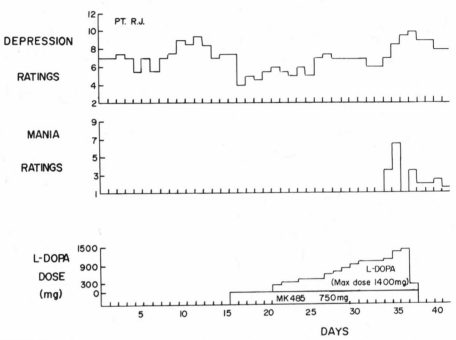

Figure 3.
Occurrence of Hypomania During the Administration of L-DOPA Plus MK-485.

An intensive study of the first seven patients we treated with DOPA, who were rated every four hours, showed that their anger levels increased during the course of L-DOPA treatment. Verbal expression of anger increased by 65% and angry facial expression increased by 25%. All 7 patients showed an increase in global ratings for anger when comparing the 5 days prior to DOPA treatment to the last 5 days on DOPA.

Our biochemical studies of cerebrospinal fluid indicated that the administration of L-DOPA was associated with a marked increase in homovanillic acid levels in spinal fluid and that the administration of L-DOPA with a peripheral decarboxylase inhibitor resulted in a modest increase in homovanillic acid levels. This data is presented in Table 1.

Table I

Cerebrospinal Fluid Metabolites and L-DOPA Administration

DOPA Dose	Number of Determinations	HVA* NG/ML	5–HIAA* NG/ML
Pretreatment	4	30±7	25±6
DOPA (8-9 gms)	2	425±92	20±3
MK485 + DOPA (Av. Dose 650 mg)	5	68±20	29±3

*Mean ± S.E.M.

In summary, our biochemical evidence is convincing that the administration of L-DOPA caused more dopamine to be formed in human brain, and that the administration of L-DOPA was associated with an increase in anger in those depressed patients studied. L-DOPA administration was not associated with a marked decrease in depression, but in those patients with a history of manic depressive illness, it did precipitate mania or hypomania.

Discussion

The finding that the administration of L-DOPA differentiated between Unipolar and Bipolar depressed patients is supported by other pharmacologic studies designed to differentiate these two groups (14). Coppen (15) has noted that the administration of lithium carbonate to Bipolar patients resulted in an improvement in their depression, as well as a prophylaxis against recurrent depressive episodes, whereas lithium carbonate administered to Unipolar depressed patients was of no therapeutic value. In addition, a statistical analysis of depressed patients treated with tri-cyclic antidepressants revealed that, whereas Unipolar patients responded well to the antidepressant effects of these compounds, Bipolar depressed patients showed very little improvement; in fact, some were noted to become hypomanic during administration of the drugs (14). Recently, Murphy (15) has shown that patients with Bipolar disease have a significant diminution of approximately 45% in levels of monoamine oxidase in blood platelets, when compared to normals, or to Unipolar patients. This may possibly explain the development of hypomania in those Bipolar depressed patients treated with DOPA, if mania is associated with an excess of dopamine or norepinephrine. The deficiency of monoamine oxidase present in these patients could possibly account for an increase in dopamine and/or brain norepinephrine predisposing these patients to the development of mania.

The finding that the administration of L-DOPA caused an increase in verbal expression of anger and also angry facial expression with a net increase of global anger ratings is of interest. This is supported by findings in the animal literature which reveal that L-DOPA increases aggressive behavior in both rats and mice when administered alone or in combination with a monoamine oxidase inhibitor (17, 18). Although it is important to note the difference between human anger and the expression of aggressive behavior in rats, the fact that DOPA elicited both is of interest and may indicate that dopaminergic pathways are responsible for the mediation of anger or aggressive behavior. Munkvad and Randrup (18) have proposed that dopamine formation is responsible for that part of aggressive behavior which can be labeled stereotypic, such as repetitive biting, and that norepinephrine synthesis is responsible for threat and attack patterns. If this is indeed the case, then L-DOPA administration to humans may be associated with one or both of these elements of animal aggression.

Summary

In an attempt to review mood changes associated with L-DOPA administration we have presented data based on observations of depressed patients treated with L-DOPA. We noted little antidepressant effect on this compound; however, we did observe the development of anger in most patients studied and also a high incidence of mania in those depressed patients with a history of Bipolar disease. This latter finding may be explained by enzymatic differences between the Unipolar and Bipolar patient groups.

It is of note that these same affective changes, i.e., anger and hypomania, have been observed in Parkinson's patients treated with L-DOPA (19), and consequently, it may be important to try other drugs in the treatment of Parkinson's disease in those patients with a history of Bipolar illness or with a history of violent and aggressive behavior.

References

1. Cotzias, G. C., Papavasiliou, P. S., and Gellene, R.: Modification of Parkinsonism-chronic treatment with L–DOPA, *New England Journal of Medicine,* 280:338, 1969.

2. Bunney, W. E., Jr., Janowsky, D. S., Goodwin, F. D., Davis, J. M., Brodie, H. K. H., Murphy, D.L., and Chase T.N.: Effect of L-DOPA on depression, *Lancet,* 1:885, 1969.

3. Bunney, W.E. and David J.M.: Norepinephrine in depressive reactions, *Archives of General Psychiatry,* 13:483, 1965.

4. Schildkraut, J. J.: The catecholamine hypothesis of affective disorders: A review of supporting evidence, *American Journal of Psychiatry,* 122: 509, 1965.

5. Klerman, G. L., *et al.*: Clinical experience with dihydroxyphenylalanine (DOPA) in depression, *Journal of Psychiatric Research,* 1:289, 1963.

6. Goodwin, F.K., Murphy, D.L., Brodie, H.K.H., and Bunney, W.E., Jr.: L-Dopa catecholamines, and behavior: a clinical biochemical study in depressed patients, *Biological Psychiatry,* 2:341, 1970.

7. Leonhard, K.: Aufteilung der Endogenen Psychosen, 2nd ed. Berlin, Akademie Verlag, 1959.

8. Bunney W.E., Jr., and Hamburg, D.A.: Methods for reliable longitudinal observation of behavior, *Archives of General Psychiatry,* 9:280, 1963.

9. Goodwin, F.K., Brodie, H, K. H., Murphy, D.K., and Bunney, W.E., Jr.: Administration of a peripheral decarboxylase inhibitor with L-DOPA to depressed patients, *Lancet,* 1:908, 1970.

10. Ashcroft, G. and Sharman, D.F.: Changes in the concentration of 5-OR indolyl compounds in cerebrospinal fluid and caudate nucleus, *British Journal of Pharmacology,* 19:153, 1962.

11. Gerbode, F., and Bowers, W.: Measurement of acid monoamine metabolites in human and animal cerebrospinal fluid, *Journal of Neurochemistry,* 15:1053, 1960.

12. Kopin, I. J.: Metabolism and Disposition of Catecholamines in the Central and Peripheral Nervous Systems, in Levine, R. (Ed.) *Endocrines and the Central Nervous System,* Res. Publ. Nerv. Ment. Dis., Vol 43, Baltimore, Williams and Wilkins Company, 1966, pp. 343-353.

13. Murphy, D. L., Brodie, H. K. H., Goodwin, F. D., and Bunney, W. E., Jr.: L—Dopa: induction of hypomania in bipolar manic-depressive patients, *Nature,* 229:135, 1971.

14. Bunney, W. E., Jr., Brodie, H. K. H., Murphy, D. K., and Goodwin, F. K.: Psychopharmacological differentiation between two subgroups of depressed patients, *Proceedings 78th Annual Convention of the American Psychological Association,* 829, 1970.

15. Coppen, A., Noguera, R., Bailey, J., Burns, B. H., Swani, M. S. Hare, E. H., Gardner, R., and Maggs, R.: Prophylactic lithium in affective disorders, *Lancet,* 2:275, 1971.

16. Murphy, D. L. and Weiss, R.: Reduced monoamine oxidase activity in blood platelets from Bipolar depressed patients, *American Journal of Psychiatry,* 128:1351, 1972.

17. Vanderwende, C.: Psychotic symptoms induced in mice by the intravenous administration of solutions of 3,4 dihydroxyphenylalanine (DOPA), *Archives of International Pharmacodynamics,* 137:145, 1962.

18. Randrup. A., and Munkvad, I.: *Aggressive Behavior,* Garattini, S. and Sigg, E. B. (Eds.), New York, Wiley and Sons, Inc., 1969, p. 228.

19. Goodwin, F. K.: Psychiatric side effects of LevoDOPA in man, *Journal of the American Medical Association, 218: 1915, 1971.*

Abuse Potential of Mild Analgesics

Donald R. Jasinski, M.D.

It is generally held that drugs such as heroin and morphine, as well as other narcotic analgesics, share certain pharmacological properties which are indicative of their ability to produce dependence of the morphine type (1–4). These properties of morphine and morphine-like drugs are (a) the production of a characteristic set of subjective effects and euphoria, and (b) the production of physical dependence. The exact relationship and relative importance of these pharmacological properties to the initiation and maintenance of "addiction" are not clear since the pathophysiology of addiction is a matter of great debate.

In this regard, certain compounds have been judged to have lower abuse potential or dependence liability than morphine. These compounds can be divided into two groups:

The first group are those which are judged to be unable to produce a high degree of euphoria or physical dependence because toxic, dose-limiting, side effects occur with the administration of large doses. The second group are narcotic antagonists that possess properties which resemble those of morphine, including analgesia, but which precipitate rather than suppress abstinence in morphine-dependent subjects.

An example of the first group is d-propoxyphene (Darvon). In single doses d-propoxyphene produces a high degree of opiate-like euphoria when administered intravenously (5–7). In addition, like morphine, d-propoxyphene will produce pupillary constriction, nausea, vomiting, and respiratory depression. With chronic administration of d-propoxyphene, physical dependence can be produced since mild, morphine-like withdrawal symptoms and signs were observed with nalorphine precipitation tests and upon abrupt withdrawal of d-propoxyphene (5). The dose levels which could be achieved with chronic administration were limited by the appearance of nervousness and a toxic psychosis. Further, when large doses of *d*-propoxyphene were substituted in subjects dependent upon 240 mg of morphine per day, *d*-propoxyphene in one subject resulted in the production of convulsions which precluded attempts to suppress abstinence with large doses of *d*-propoxyphene. The tissue-irritant properties of *d*-propoxyphene results in sclerosing of the veins with repeated intravenous administration. Thus, even though *d*-propoxyphene is essentially a morphine-like agent capable of producing morphine-like euphoria, morphine-like physical dependence as evidenced by both direct addiction and substitution studies in morphine-dependent subjects, the presence of convulsant properties, tissue-irritant properties and its ability to produce a toxic psychosis as well as the fact that *d*-propoxyphene is only available as an oral preparation, purposely made difficult for parenteral injection, has been felt to be responsible for the low incidence of abuse of oral preparations of *d*-propoxyphene.

These same principles have been applied to judgments of the abuse potential of the compound used as an antidiarrheal agent, diphenoxylate (Lomotil) (8). Single doses of diphenoxylate administered orally and parenterally produced pupillary constriction, respiratory depression, and a high degree of morphine-like physical dependence and will completely substitute for and suppress abstinence in morphine-dependent subjects. When administered in single doses there is a latency in the onset of pupillary constriction and morphine-like euphoria, which probably is a consequence of diphenoxylate being converted to an active metabolite. Further, diphenoxylate is for all practical purposes water insoluble which precludes parenteral injection. Even though diphenoxylate has been shown to have morphine-like properties, its insolubility in aqueous solution and latency to long onset of action have led to the judgment that diphenoxylate has a lower abuse potential than other opiate-like drugs. There is included in the commercial preparation of diphenoxylate a small dose of atropine to deter self-administration of large doses of diphenoxylate, since ingestion of large doses would be accompanied by atropine intoxication.

In the early 1950s it was observed by Lasagna and Beecher that the narcotic antagonist nalorphine was itself an analgesic, which in subsequent studies was found to be unsuitable for clinical use because of the production of side effects (9). Characterization of the properties of nalorphine (10,11) revealed the production of effects which resembled those of morphine, including analgesia, pupillary constriction and respiratory depression, as well as some morphine-like subjective effects, but with larger increases in dosage two additional types of subjective effects occurred, one type resembling those produced by sedative-hypnotics including production of such symptoms as lethargy, weakness, loss of energy and drunkenness, and the second type resembling those produced by psychotomimetic agents including irritability, sensory distortions, racing thoughts, and, in the extreme, derealization, depersonalization and production of a toxic psychosis. When administered to morphine-dependent subjects, the antagonist did not substitute for morphine, but rather precipitated abstinence. Chronic administration of nalorphine (11) was shown to produce physical dependence which was qualitatively and quantitatively different than morphine-like physical dependence. The most important differentiating characteristic was the observation that the nalorphine abstinence syndrome was not associated with drug-seeking behavior.

Thus it was felt that nonaddicting analgesics could be developed among the narcotic antagonists, since compounds such as nalorphine did not possess the ability to produce morphine-like euphoria, morphine-like physical dependence or to substitute for and suppress abstinence in morphine-dependent subjects, properties which were held to be of importance in predicting the dependence liability or abuse potential. The presence of psychotomimetic and sedative effects limited the clinical usefulness of nalorphine.

Subsequently, a large number of compounds having morphine antagonistic properties were synthesized in the hope that suitable agents could be found which would have low abuse potential. Of these compounds, pentazocine (Talwin) is the one having major clinical use. Pentazocine is a weak narcotic antagonist which was initially shown to produce only a mild degree of morphine-like effects and to produce physical dependence, since an abstinence syndrome was seen upon abrupt withdrawal. However, pentazocine would not substitute for and suppress abstinence in morphine dependent subjects, and as a consequence could not be classified as a narcotic since classification as a narcotic under the Narcotic Manufacturing Act of 1960 requires a compound to be both addiction forming and addiction sustaining (12). This phrase was interpreted to mean that a compound should be able to substitute for and suppress abstinence in morphine dependent individuals.

Other weak narcotic antagonists were developed and studies revealed that certain of these compounds were essentially morphine-like agents in man, with limited morphine-like activity such that they can act as antagonists (7). These compounds were judged to be capable of producing dependence of the morphine type in man. Subsequent studies were conducted to determine if pentazocine, too, was a partial agonist of morphine (13). The results of these studies indicated that single doses of pentazocine up to 40 mg produced morphine-like subjective effects whereas larger dosages of 60 mg of pentazocine produced typical nalorphine-like effects characterized by psychotomimetic and sedative effects. Chronic administration of large doses of pentazocine produced physical dependence, since an abstinence syndrome emerged when the compound was abruptly withdrawn. This abstinence syndrome, unlike the nalorphine abstinence syndrome, was characterized by drug-seeking behavior since the subjects were uncomfortable and demanded relief of their symptoms with administration of drug. This presence of drug-seeking behavior during abrupt withdrawal distinguishes pentazocine abstinence from abstinence from antagonists such as nalorphine and cyclazozine. During chronic administration of pentazocine, doses of nalorphine to 12 mg did not precipitate abstinence but the pure antagonist, naloxone, to doses of 4 to 6 mg precipitated an abstinence syndrome which resembled that precipitated in subjects dependent upon morphine. However, it was demonstrated that pentazocine is capable of acting as an antagonist and precipitating abstinence in subjects dependent upon 240 mg of morphine per day, and is 1/50th as potent as nalorphine in this regard. Pentazocine will not substitute for morphine and suppress abstinence in subjects dependent upon 60 mg of morphine per day. This inability to substitute for morphine in subjects dependent upon 60 mg per day distinguishes pentazocine from those antagonists which are partial agonists of morphine. Pentazocine still cannot be clearly identified as a morphine or nalorphine-like analgesic, but has properties which resemble both (13). Although pentazocine represents an advance in the search for a nonaddicting analgesic and is probably less capable of producing dependence than agents such as *d*-propoxyphene, pentazocine does produce euphoria and physical dependence characterized by drug-seeking behavior. These properties could lead to abuse, and pentazocine should be prescribed cautiously and judiciously.

Thus, on the basis of the pharmacology, a number of compounds judged to be non-narcotic or having low abuse potential possess properties which resemble those of morphine and are thought to be of importance in predicting or being indicative of their abuse potential. Consequently these agents should be prescribed with caution and judiciousness since it must be recognized that these properties may lead to problems of abuse, especially in circumstances where patients are allowed to self administrate.

Bibliography

1. Martin, W.R. and Fraser, H.F.: A comparative study of physiological and subjective effects of heroin and morphine administered intravenously in postaddicts. J. Pharmacol. Exp. Ther. *133:* 388-399, 1961.

2. Martin, W.R.: Assessment of the dependence producing potentiality of narcotic analgesics. In Radouco-Thomas, C. and Lasagna, L. (Eds.): *International Encyclopedia of Pharmacology and Therapeutics,* pp. 155-180, Ch. 9, Sec. 6, Vol. I, Pergamon Press, Glasgow, 1966.

3. World Health Organization: Evaluation of dependence-producing drugs. Report of a WHO Scientific Group. Wld. Hlth Org. Techn. Rep. Ser. 287, 1964.

4. Fraser, H.F., Van Horn, G.D., Martin, W.R., Wolbach, A.B., and Isbell, H.: Methods for evaluating addiction liability (A) "Attitude" of opiate addicts toward opiate-like drugs, (B) A short-term "direct" addiction test. J. Pharmacol. Exp. Ther. *133:* 371-387, 1961.

5. Fraser, H.F. and Isbell, H.: Pharmacology and addiction liability of *dl-* and *d*-propoxyphene. Bull. Narcotics *12:* 9-14, 1960.

6. Fraser, H.F., Martin, W.R., Wolbach, A.B. and Isbell, H.: Addiction liability of an isoquinoline analgesic, 1-(p-chloro-phenethyl-2-methyl-6,7-dimethoxy-1,2,3,4-tetrahydroisoquinoline.) Clin. Pharmacol. Ther. *2:* 287-299, 1961.

7. Jasinski, D.R., Martin, W.R. and Hoeldtke, R.: Studies of the dependence-producing properties of GPA-1657, profadol, and propiram in man. Clin. Pharmacol. Ther. *12:*

613-649, July-Aug. 1971.

8. Fraser, H.F. and Isbell, H.: Human pharamacology and addictiveness of ethyl-1-(3-cyano-3,3-phenylpropyl)-4-phenyl-4-piperidine carboxylate hydrochloride (R-1132, Diphenoxylate). Bull. Narcotics *13*: 29-43, Jan-Mar. 1961.

9. Lasagna, L. and Beecher, H.K.: The analgesic effectiveness of nalorphine and nalorphine-morphine combinations in man. J. Pharmacol. Exp. Ther. *112:* 356-363, 1964.

10. Martin, W.R., Fraser, H.F., Gorodetzky, C.W. and Rosenberg, D.E.: Studies of the dependence-producing potential of the narcotic antagonist 2-cyclo-propylmethyl-2'-hydroxy-5,9-dimethyl-6,7-benzomorphan (cyclazocine, Win 20,740,ARC II-C-3). J. Pharmacol. Exp. Ther. *150:* 426-436, 1965.

11. Martin, W.R. and Gorodetzky, C.W.: Demonstration of tolerance to and physical dependence on N-allylnormorphine (nalorphine). J. Pharmacol. Exp. Ther. *150:* 437-442, 1965.

12. Fraser, H.F. and Rosenberg, D.E.: Studies on the human addiction liability of 2'-hydroxy-5,9- dimethyl-2(3,3-dimethylallyl)-6,7-benzomorphan (Win 20,228); a weak narcotic antagonist. J. Pharmacol. Exp. Ther. *143:* 149-156, 1964.

13. Jasinski, D.R., Martin, W.R. and Hoeldtke, R.D.: Effects of short- and long-term administration of pentazocine in man. Clin. Pharmacol. Ther. *11*: 385-403, May-June 1970.

Clinical Problems in Treating the Aged With Psychotropic Drugs

John M. Davis, M.D.
William E. Fann, M.D.
M. Khaled El-Yousef, M.D.
David S. Janowsky, M.D.

The purpose of this paper is to review the use of psychotropic drugs in the aged. Psychotropic agents can be an effective tool in a physician's armamentarium in treating mental disorders in the aged. However, these drugs can also be inappropriately used. The aged may be more susceptible to certain drug side effects. In addition, since they are more apt to have medical problems, there is more likelihood of drug-drug interactions occurring. Even physicians who may not be particularly interested in psychotropic drug use may need to be knowledgeable about this aspect of patient care since patients may suffer from toxicity due to psychotropic drugs administered by another physician or by the patients themselves. Psychotropic drugs are commonly taken by a large percentage of the population of the United States (Balter and Levine, 1971). Two hundred twenty million prescriptions are filled by patients for psychotropic drugs; 80 million for antianxiety agents; 40 million for hypnotics; 30 million for stimulants. Patients can often be taking several psychotropic drugs, sometimes administered by one physician, sometimes administered by several different physicians with the patient continuing to take one doctor's prescription as well as a second psychotropic agent added by another doctor. To this cocktail can be added proprietary medications bought without prescription. Since sedative hypnotics do reduce mental function, it is not unusual to find elderly patients who are over-medicated who may do better when they discontinue the cocktail of sedative hypnotic drugs which they are taking. For that reason, the first problem in treating the aged with psychotropic drugs is for the clinician to consider whether the patient needs the psychotropic drugs he may be on. The discontinuance of current medication to get a drug-free baseline state is a useful strategy for the treatment of many patients. It is important to evaluate the patient's medical status and use of the wide variety of drugs for treating his medical problems. This information is relevant to drug-drug interactions and side effects of possible psychotropic drugs. Having reviewed

111

the patient's baseline status and his medical problems, one may move on to consider which psychotropic drugs may be indicated for a given patient.

In the treatment by psychotropic drugs of schizophrenia, mania, and depression, in adults, there is an extensive literature of double-blind studies which provides a background of hard information on drug efficacy and side effects. Although there are a great many patients over 65 treated with psychotropic drugs in mental hospitals, nursing homes, outpatient clinic, or in private practice, it is remarkable how little evidence there is from well-controlled studies on the effectiveness of these drugs on the various psychiatric problems in the aged population. Indeed, there is so little information that for many topics one cannot find even a small number of controlled studies which may allow one to make specific statements about the use of psychotropic drugs in the aged. One must, to some extent, generalize from what is known about treating younger adults with psychotropic drugs to treating patients with essentially the same psychiatric disorders in the aged category. In many cases, drugs which are effective in patients under 65 are equally effective in patients over 65 with the same disorder. There are, however, a few exceptions. We will review the use of various psychotropic drugs in the aged, noting special clinical problems which may occur there. We will first discuss the treatment of the manic phase of manic-depressive psychosis, then the treatment of depression, then the treatment of schizophrenia and schizophrenic-like psychosis in the aged.

It is not unusual to have patients present in the aged period either with recurrent manic episodes or recurrent manic-depressive episodes. Generally, onset of this disease occurs in middle age, although in rare instances patients can have their first manic attack when they are over 65. Lithium is a very effective drug for treating both the acute manic episode and for the prevention of recurrent mania and depressions. In a patient with a severe manic attack, it is often useful to combine lithium with an antipsychotic drug such as haloperidol. The therapeutic benefits of lithium generally occur 2-3 weeks after the onset of treatment. Since there is a more rapid onset of the antipsychotic actions of haloperidol, phenothiazines, or thioxanthene derivatives, in order to get a more rapid control of the manic symptoms, it is useful to treat patients with the combination. After several weeks, when lithium has become therapeutically effective, the antipsychotic drugs can be discontinued. In treating the hypomanic patient where there is no clinical need to achieve the most rapid remission possible, lithium can be used by itself. Lithium is also useful in preventing recurrence of manic-depressive disease, and so many patients treated in the initial episode with lithium are continued on lithium for its prophylactic properties. In general, many of the same pharmacologic principles which apply to younger patients also apply to the aged. There are several important exceptions. The half-life of lithium in a middle aged adult is approximately 24 hours. In the aged the half-life of lithium is longer; e.g. 36 or 48 hours. This often means that a patient may achieve an adequate blood level on a smaller oral dose and certainly suggests that, in terms of tactics of dosage, one may start with lower doses of lithium and monitor blood lithiums more carefully in this age range. Lithium produces gastrointestinal, CNS, and neuromuscular toxicity. As with most types of drug side effects, the aged are more vulnerable than younger patients. This is particularly true with confusion. Confusion can be a common sign of lithium toxicity in the aged. It also can occur with relatively low blood levels.

In terms of comparing and contrasting the use of lithium in the elderly, lithium treatment is similar in the elderly as in the middle aged in that it is an effective treatment for mania and is used so in preventing the attacks of mania and depression. The most important difference in regard to its use in the elderly is that lower doses are required to achieve a given blood level and that patients can develop side effects on lower blood levels. These latter two points, although obviously related, should both be kept in mind. Since elderly patients excrete lithium more slowly, they can build up a higher blood level on a comparable dose, or to put the same point another way, they can build up the desired blood level with lower doses. For example, to achieve an antimanic blood level of say 1.2 to 1.5 mEq/1 one might use in a younger patient an oral dose of 1500 mg a day. In an elderly patient one might need 600-900 mg a day. A second difference is that elderly patients may develop a confusional syndrome at lower blood levels. For example, an elderly patient might develop a confusional syndrome at 1.5 mEq/1 with a good therapeutic response to 1.2 mEq/1. In evaluating lithium dose, one should put a relatively greater emphasis on the symptoms of toxicity rather than blood levels per se, although both are relevant parameters to monitor as one adjusts dosage to achieve a good therapeutic response. Increasing confusion is one of the predominant signs of lithium intoxication. This is most often troublesome clinically when a patient is being maintained in the community on maintenance lithium without close medical supervision and becomes confused. The family may attribute this to old age rather than to a drug-induced toxicity and so fail to seek medical help until the patient goes into frank coma. It is important that patients and their families be taught to recognize confusion as a possible sign of lithium toxicity. In the chronic maintenance situation, the toxicity can develop very gradually and hence be not so noticeable. It consists of a worsening of the usual fine tremor which develops into a coarse tremor, drowsiness, slurred speech, confusion, chorea, and choreoathetoid movements. There is a pitressin resistant diabetes insipidus-like syndrome characterized by a spontaneous increase in water intake and urine output, fasciculation, nystagmus, and an increase in G.I. symptoms.

Depression is a very common disorder among the aged. The depressed patient can present with symptoms of senility, and to coin a diagnostic label, one could call these cases "pseudo- senile depression." The patients can be incontinent and appear confused and disoriented, rather than overtly depressed. When they are successfully treated with antidepressants or ECT, these symptoms disappear and their mental function is adequate.In some cases, patients can be discharged home, find a job, and go back to work. It is important not to miss a treatable disease like depression because, if untreated, these patients can remain for several years in the state hospital until they die (Kent, 1963; Ayd, 1962). Both the tricyclic antidepressants and the MAO inhibitors are effective drugs for treating depression in the aged. Evidence from double-blind studies of depression in the younger age groups indicates that as a class, the tricyclic antidepressants are more effective drugs than the MAO inhibitors. They also are safer. Since the tricyclic antidepressants are discussed in another chapter in this volume, we will limit our remarks here to the fact that they can be very effective treatment for depression in the elderly. There is no indication that the elderly metabolize tricyclic antidepressants differently than younger patients in the one study so far completed (Asverg, 1971). Electroconvulsive shock treatment is probably the most effective form of treatment on a statistical basis for severe depression. It is safe to use in the elderly and is effective in the elderly (Sinsbury, 1964).

Psychosis is a common problem in the aged. It can occur in patients who have had schizophrenic-like illness for many years who live past the age of 65. It also can occur in patients who have the onset of schizophrenic-like symptoms after the age of 65. Psychosis can also occur secondary to arteriosclerotic disorders or other effects of organic impairment. There is excellent evidence from well-controlled studies that phenothiazine derivatives and other antipsychotic drugs produce a clinically substantial benefit in schizophrenic patients (Klein and Davis, 1969). Clinical evidence indicates that these antipsychotic compounds are also effective in treating organic psychoses. The question also arises whether the same indications which apply to the psychoses in patients under 65 also apply to treating psychoses in the elderly. The evidence that is available at this time indicates that in most situations the same clinical indications apply. There is excellent evidence from several double-blind studies that antipsychotic compounds are effective in treating psychoses in the aged. Haloperidol has been found to be superior to placebo (Sugerman et al., 1964; Toben et al., 1970) in a double blind study. In addition, Mellaril has been found to be useful in treating psychosis in the elderly (Lehman and Bon, 1967). In one carefully done double-blind study, Haloperidol was found to be equally effective as Mellaril in the aged population (Tsuang, Stotsky, and Cole, 1971). Mellaril produces a lower incidence of extrapyramidal side effects while Haloperidol produces a higher incidence. This study would indicate that in so far as these drugs are representative of agents which produce either low or high extrapyramidal side effects, that this property has import in suggesting differential indications since these drugs are equally efficacious. Acetophenazine has also been found in controlled studies to be an effective drug for treating the aged (Honigfeld et al., 1965). There is little doubt as a result of these studies that the antipsychotic compounds are very effective in treating psychoses in the elderly when compared to that improvement produced by placebo. The next question which arises in considering drug treatment is the matter of maintenance therapy. If the patient becomes psychotic, is treated with an antipsychotic compound, and gets better, should he be maintained on maintenance phenothiazines for several years or the rest of his life? There is a lot of literature on this in non-geriatric schizophrenic patients. Every study which has been properly controlled has found that a smaller number of patients maintained on maintenance phenothiazine relapsed than comparable patients maintained on placebo. This finding, however, may not always be true in the elderly. If one reviews the older age sub-segment of studies on maintenance phenothiazines, one finds that the evidence for a therapeutic benefit of maintenance phenothiazine is less substantial. It may be that there is a sub-population of elderly schizophrenic patients who, in some sense, have less active schizophrenic disease and are burned-out cases. Age versus therapeutic response comparisons in maintenance phenothiazine studies do indicate that such "burned-out patients" may exist. That is, when one takes patients who have been in the hospital for many years and who are over 65, one finds in controlled studies of maintenance phenothiazines that few of these patients relapse when they are taken off drugs. In a population of younger patients with more active schizophrenic disease who have been hospitalized a relatively short time, a large number of patients will relapse if their phenothiazines are discontinued and placebo is substituted. This generalization does not necessarily apply to chronic patients over 65. This represents a difference in the therapeutic indications for maintenance phenothiazines between the aged chronic patients and younger acute patients (Piren, 1969, 1970). In our opinion, the choice of whether to maintain a person on maintenance phenothiazine and how long to maintain him should be made on a clinical basis, individually making the decision for the given patient. We would require a relatively stronger indication for maintenance treatment in the elderly than in the middle-aged patient. We would be more likely to discontinue phenothiazines and not use maintenance medications on an elderly patient who has been ill for many years, particularly if he has been treated with relatively low doses. We would be more likely to maintain a patient on medication 1) if he seemed clinically to require high doses of drug when reviewing his past medication history, 2) if he seemed to have active schizophrenic illness present, and 3) if he had a history of relapsing after discontinuing drugs in the past. It would seem advisable to review medication histories of patients periodically and guard against indiscriminate use of maintenance phenothiazines for many years without review of the indications.

In the younger age range there are indications that massive doses of phenothiazines may help some patients. There is evidence which indicates that massive doses may not be particularly useful in the elderly. This evidence would suggest that although one might use massive doses in selected patients, typical elderly psychotic patients would probably not benefit more from massive doses than they would from normal doses (Piren *et al.*, 1969, 1970). This is by no means an academic question since patients maintained on phenothiazines for many years develop a terminal extrapyramidal syndrome referred to as tardive dyskinesia characterized by a wide variety of dystonic movements, particularly bizarre movements of the face and tongue which can be particularly disfiguring. This is thought to be a permanent toxicity. This would underline the necessity for avoiding excess use of antipsychotic medication. The same range of side effects of phenothiazines which affect the younger patients affect the elderly except that they may be predisposed because of factors connected with aging to have more side effects or side effects on a lower dose. There also may be interactions between disease prevalent in the aged and the pharmacologic side effects of the drugs. For example, patients who have arteriosclerotic disease such that they would be vulnerable to heart attacks and strokes may tolerate postural hypotension of psychotropic drugs more poorly than younger patients. It is, of course, important to recognize that because a certain medical complication occurs in a patient on a drug, that it may not necessarily be related to the drug. For example, hyperpyrexia does occur in patients on phenothiazines, but hyperpyrexia also occurred before phenothiazines were discovered. Hence, that particular syndrome may not necessarily be drug related (Peele, 1972).

It is not uncommon to find depressed schizophrenics. Clinical experience indicates that adding a tricyclic drug to their antipsychotic drugs may be beneficial. There are large numbers of retarded, burned-out schizophrenics in many hospitals. It would be a logical extension of this reasoning to suppose that these patients were suffering some sort of chronic depression and might be benefited by a tricyclic drug. Honigsfeld and his collaborators treated elderly schizophrenic patients with tricyclic drugs and found these to produce no therapeutic benefit. It would seem that although tricyclic drugs are useful for depressed schizophrenics, they do not reverse the social alienation syndrome or whatever else that is involved in being a chronic schizophrenic.

There is little systematic information on the use of minor tranquilizers in the elderly. In younger patients, review of double-blind studies reveals that the Librium-Valium class of minor tranquilizers produce slightly more anti-anxiety properties in most patients than do barbiturates at equal sedating doses. There is clinical evidence that these drugs are equally effective in treating anxiety in the elderly (Chersow *et al.*, 1962).

Learoyd (1972) collected clinical evidence which points to the danger of unwise psychotropic drug use in elderly patients. He reviewed the clinical records of all patients over 65 who were admitted to a medical and psychogeriatric unit over a two year period. Thirty seven out of 236 patients (16%) who had been receiving psychotropic drugs before admission and whose behavior was abnormal, improved dramatically when the drugs were withdrawn. Seven of these patients received excessive medication. Either because they were confused or for other reasons they took an excess number of tablets and became lethargic, confused, and disoriented. Sixteen suffered from such side effects as postural hypotension and some had fractures as a result of falls. The remaining 14 patients manifested restlessness, agitation, paranoid behavior, and aggression. There have been several excellent reviews of the use of psychotropic drugs in the aged (Lehmann and Ban, 1969; Kral, 1965; Kris, 1965). Treatment of the elderly with psychotropic drugs, like many other kinds of drugs, is slightly more difficult than treating middle-aged or young patients. There is a propensity in the elderly to develop side effects on lower doses. There is probably also a wider range of doses which can be therapeutically effective. Another common problem in the elderly is the fact that since these patients are more likely to suffer from concomitant physical disease, they are more likely to be placed on other medications. This makes it more likely that drug-drug interaction will occur.

We would like to discuss two side effects which can occur due to treatment with psychotropic drugs which will serve to illustrate drug-drug toxicity. The first case concerns the interaction between a drug used to treat hypotension, Ismelin (guanethidine) and psychotropic drugs. The second concerns a psychotoxic side effect which can occur as a result of the combined anticholinergic properties of phenothiazines, antiparkinsonian drugs, and tricyclic antidepressants. Guanethidine sulfate is a potent antihypertensive agent used in the treatment of hypertension. Tricyclic antidepressants, including imipramine, desipramine, and protriptyline, administered in clinically efficacious doses, reverse the hypotensive effects of guanethidine in hypertensive patients. In our laboratory, we have shown that doxepin, in doses of 200-300 mg/day, also reverses guanethidine's antihypertensive effects. Tricyclic antidepressants inhibit the neuronal uptake of norepinephrine and serotonin and, in a similar way, also inhibit the neuronal uptake of a wide variety of ring substituted bases, including guanethidine sulfate and related antihypertensive agents. Because of this inhibition, access of these substances to their intraneuronal site of action is presumably blocked and they thus fail to exert their hypotensive action. Animal studies have indicated that phenothiazines, including chlorpromazine, also block guanethidine's antihypertensive action, presumably via the same mechanism as that of the tricyclic antidepressants.

Since chlorpromazine and related antipsychotic agents are frequently used in the treatment of psychiatric patients who also have hypertension, we felt it important to evaluate whether or not chlorpromazine blocks the action of guanethidine when administered in doses used clinically, and to compare these effects with those of related antipsychotic compounds.

One male and three female chronically hospitalized adult psychiatric inpatients were admitted. They had persistent hypertension of a modefate to severe degree. On admission their standing blood pressures ranged from 230 to 172 mm. Hg. systolic and 150 to 110 mm. Hg. diastolic. They were evaluated by an internist and diagnosed as suffering from essential hypertension.

The patients were admitted to the research ward and taken off all drugs. After a clinically effective dose of guanethidine was determined, each patient's blood pressure was maintained by that dose of guanethidine sulfate for a period of at least seven days prior to the administration of the proposed antagonist. Chlorpromazine, ranging in total daily dosage from 100 mg. - 400 mg., was then added to the guanethidine regime for a period of no less than 12 days. Chlorpromazine was then discontinued and guanethidine treatment continued for a post antagonist phase of 9 days or longer, while the same dose of guanethidine was continued. In six instances, chlorpromazine was used as the antagonist. Haloperidol was used three times and thiothixene once, in a manner similar to chlorpromazine. After the patients were taken off all drugs and their blood pressure lowered with guanethidine, chlorpromazine was then administered. Analysis of the data indicated that chlorpromazine in clinically utilized doses ranging from 100 mg/day - 400 mg/day significantly reversed the antihypertensive effects of guanethidine in all 6 instances in which it was used as an antagonist. Significant but less dramatic reversals occurred when haloperidol and thiothixene were used.

The mechanism of action underlying the antagonism of guanethidine's hypotensive effects by antipsychotic agents is probably that these drugs antagonize guanethidine's access to the neurone, namely by blockade of the amine uptake pump.

The second example has to do with central anticholinergic toxicity. All psychotropic drugs, including antiparkinsonian drugs, tricyclic antidepressants, and antipsychotic agents, produce anticholinergic side effects. We have observed that, occasionally, patients placed on this combination have their clinical symptoms worsened. The hypothesis we chose to investigate was whether this worsening of the clinical picture could be anticholinergic toxicity caused by the combined anticholinergic properties of all the drugs used in combination.

Physostigmine has reversed experimentally induced anticholinergic delirium in normal volunteers and central anticholinergic poisoning in drug abusers, suicide attempters, and a few parkinsonian patients receiving anticholinergic antiparkinsonian agents. The question of whether the occasional toxic confusional state observed in psychiatric patients during administration of antiparkinsonian drugs in combination with phenothiazines and/or tricyclic antidepressants is essentially an atropine psychosis and hence can be reversed by physostigmine has not been previously studied. A study using double-blind techniques was designed to investigate whether or not the worsening of psychosis observed by us to occur after the administration of a polypharmacy of psychotropic agents was an atropine-like psychosis superimposed on the underlying schizophrenic illness, and whether this state could be alleviated by the administration of physostigmine salicylate.

Three schizophrenic female patients, receiving phenothiazines and benztropine mesylate for their parkinsonian side effects, developed an intermittently occurring toxic confusional state which was clinically consistent with an "anticholinergic syndrome." A 15-point rating scale (with 15 being the most severe) based on serial mental status exams, was designed to evaluate the confusional state. It rated symptoms consisting of visual and auditory hallucinations, disorientation, short-term memory loss, anxiety, and psychosis. The patients were given intramuscularly one or more placebo and one or more 4 mg. physostigmine salicylate injections on a double-blind basis and were evaluated for the alleviation of the confusional state by a rater who was unaware of whether a placebo or physostigmine was being administered.

All patients developed a "central anticholinergic syndrome" characterized by a marked disturbance of short-term memory, impaired attention, disorientation, anxiety, visual and auditory hallucinations, and increased psychotic thinking. The above symptoms, lasting from two to twelve hours, were associated with peripheral anticholinergic signs and were typical of the "central anticholinergic syndrome." They were not obvious in these patients because of the original psychosis and the overlap of toxic and psychotic symptomatology. In contrast to placebo, which caused no significant change in symptom complex, physostigmine dramatically reversed the toxic symptom complex for approximately three hours after injection. The five target symptoms were specific to the anticholinergic syndrome and were reversed with physostigmine, whereas the original functional (schizophrenic) symptoms were not reversed.

In contrast to easily diagnosed central anticholinergic toxicity seen in non-psychotic patients, the "central anticholinergic syndrome" presents a difficult diagnostic problem in psychiatric patients due to the fact that many of these patients are already psychotic, confused, and agitated, and the anticholinergic toxic symptomatology is in the direction of the primary psychosis, with overlap of symptoms. This overlap may lead physicians to increase psychotropic medications with a predictable subsequent worsening of symptoms. Since these drugs have anticholinergic effects, the possibility of drug toxicity is recognized and drugs are subsequently stopped. Thus, the patients are left without the benefit of antipsychotic agents. Consideration of the possibility of central anticholinergic toxicity, careful mental status exams, and thorough physicial exams focusing on the presence of peripheral anticholinergic signs may allow the correct diagnosis to be made and selective, appropriate medication reduction or discontinuation to occur. In the rare cases where the diagnosis remains uncertain or when the rapid alleviation of the anticholinergic symptoms is desirable, the use of physostigmine salicylate may prove a useful diagnostic and therapeutic tool.

However, physostigmine salicylate should be used only after medical evaluation of the patient because of the serious risk of excessive cholinergic-parasympathetic stimulation which may occur. Thus, it is important to use physostigmine with caution in patients who have no medical contraindications, starting with conservatively low test doses, and carefully observing for signs of cholinergic toxicity. Atropine sulfate is effective in reversing cholinergic toxicity and it is advisable to have this drug ready at hand when physostigmine test doses are being administered. The importance of our study is in proving that this confusional syndrome is essentially atropine toxicity. Since this question has never been studied before, one could assert that it is atropine toxicity, but there would be no direct evidence confirming this. In our study we had two types of direct evidence confirming that these confusional syndromes were essentially atropine toxicity. The memory deficit observed in the syndrome is quite typical of atropine toxicity. In all these patients there was a marked deficit of immediate memory. A convenient test for immediate memory is provided by asking the patients to remember three numbers, then waiting approximately 45 seconds and asking the patient to repeat the three numbers. These patients were completely unable to do this simple task. After the physostigmine, the patients could easily remember three numbers and some of them were able to remember three sets of two-digit or three-digit numbers. The second evidence that this was essentially atropine toxicity is provided by the fact that it can be dramatically and statistically significantly reversed by physostigmine. It is, of course, relevant to point out that there are many causes of a confusional syndrome in the aged. Based on this evidence, we feel one type of confusional syndrome that can be accounted for is essentially an atropine toxicity contributed to by the anticholinergic properties of the phenothiazine derivatives, tricyclic antidepressants, and antiparkinsonian agents. The antiparkinsonian agents may be the chief offender and may be the drug which can be most easily dispensed with. It has recently been shown that many patients do not actually need their antiparkinsonian medication. On a mg/Kg basis, the antiparkinsonian medications are more potent in producing anticholinergic changes than the phenothiazines or tricyclic antidepressants. It is important to remember, however, that phenothiazines and tricyclic antidepressants are given at a much higher mg. dosage. For example, a patient may receive 800 mg. of chlorpromazine and 4-6 mg. of cogentin. The importance of the study is to prove the etiology of the confusional state, at least in some cases. Under almost all situations the confusional state will clear fairly rapidly within a day or two if the drugs are discontinued. Many will clear just by dropping the dose or eliminating the antiparkinsonian agent. In medicine, it is a general canon that one should be as conservative as possible. Since the syndrome will clear with stopping the antiparkinsonian medication which is often not necessary anyhow, we think in a great majority of the cases that the best treatment is discontinuing the antiparkinsonian medication. We would not advocate physostigmine in any sense for routine use, either as a diagnostic agent or as a therapeutic agent. The diagnosis can generally be made by being aware that the syndrome exists and performing a mental status exam. It can be confirmed by watching the syndrome clear when the anticholinergic medication is discontinued or reduced in dosage. We would recommend that the physician watch for the syndrome, diagnose it by mental status exam, and treat it by discontinuing medication. There is no need, in a great majority of cases, to expose a patient to the risks of having a cholinergic agent administered. This should be reserved only in special circumstances when diagnosis is very cloudy or when there is some clinical reason that a rapid reversal of this "central anticholinergic syndrome" is needed. This happens rarely, for example, in a post-operative patient who is pulling out I.V.'s and tubes. In the great majority of instances, however, discontinuation of anticholinergic medication is the obvious treatment for the syndrome.

Vitamins, Hormones and Vasodilators

It is often thought that old people are often fussy eaters and may be grossly deficient on a number of vitamins such as Vitamin B and C. Lehmann and his collaborators (1969, 1970) have had an extensive experience in treating the aged and note that toxicity to Vitamin B and C is extremely low and that administration of these vitamins is usually advisable and in any case is harmless. For many years they have been administering large doses of vitamins plus 200 - 300 mg. of nicotinic acid a day. The nicotinic acid can, on occasion, cause a marked flushing of the skin which lasts for about 20 minutes, sometimes causing an unpleasant sensation of itching. The usefulness of vitamin therapy in the aged has not been verified by extensive double-blind studies utilizing random assignment of patients and appropriate placebo controls. Attempts to find a pharmacologic "fountain of youth" have often rested in the area of vitamins, hormones, and related substances. They have ranged from Royal B. Jelly to monkey glands embryocell injections. The usefulness of many of these substances has never been proven and is highly doubtful. There has at least been some suggestion that androgen therapy may improve memory function, but it also may produce liver toxicity (Silver *et al.*, 1968). Lifshitz and Klein (1961) studied 90 elderly men between the ages of 55 and 75 suffering from psychosis with cerebral arteriosclerosis or senile psychosis. About half of these received placebo and about half received estradiol valerate intramuscularly 25 mg. every two weeks. Gynecomastia was observed in every patient who received this treatment for six months or more. No therapeutic effects of the estrogens were noted whatsoever, and, indeed, the only statistically significant difference was greater mortality in the estrogen group than in the control group. No one will quarrel that elderly suffering from a hormonal imbalance should have appropriate therapy. It is certainly not unusual to see such disorders as thyrotoxic psychosis or myxedema madness cured by such specific intervention. The evidence of nonspecific hormonal effects in the elderly is quite problematical at this time. Although we would advocate specific medical investigation to diagnose any latent unrecognized imbalances in the elderly patients, we would not advocate indiscriminate treatment with any particular hormone. It is well to recognize that there is a tendency toward wishful thinking about treatment of a common disorder, namely aging. One should properly regard any uncontrolled claims for drugs which magically reverse aging with some skepticism. There have been many claims that vasodilating and related agents or CNS stimulants are useful in the elderly. There has been considerable skepticism by many clinicians that these claims are without foundation. They have generally not been supported by well-controlled studies. For example, Lucidril (A.N.P. 235) was reported in early clinical drug evaluation to be of value in reversing disturbances of memory and intellectual impairment associated with aging. Bowe and McDonald (1966) studied this drug in comparison to a matched placebo, finding no therapeutic effects. The lack of confirmation would caution against indulging in wishful thinking in terms of finding a drug which does reverse aging. Indeed, we caution against wishful thinking leading to an uncritical attitude. The converse of this may apply. One should not be such a therapeutic nihilist as to be so critical as to not even look at evidence about possible therapeutic benefits of vasodilating drugs. Lehmann and Ban (1970) have shown that 5-minute inhalation of carbon dioxide – 5% in oxygen – 95% produced improvement in patients with organic lesions. Nicotinic acid is said to be a vasodilater. However, when Smith, Hoffer, and their collaborators (1963) studied very high doses (3000 mg.) of niacin in the geriatric population they found that this drug did not produce any therapeutic benefit in comparison to a group which received 50 mg. per day.

Sourander and his collaborators (1970) reported that a combination of dixyrazine (ESUCOS) and inositol nicotinate, in a controlled study, was superior to placebo in producing improvements in the performance of geriatric patients tested on three psychological tests. Cyclandelate is a vasodilater which has been documented by indirect brachial angiography with high speed film technique to produce an accelerated arterial phase of cerebral circulation. Uncontrolled studies suggest that it may be of value in improving mental function of the aged in psychiatric hospitals. Fine and his coworkers (1971) studied cyclandelate in a double-blind, cross-over trial on 40 patients in the psychiatric hospital with symptons due to arteriosclerotic brain disease. The drug produced small, but statistically significant, improvement on a number of mental functions including changes on ratings of orientation and improved digit span. Adermand and his coworkers (1972) administered cyclandelate to 43 elderly patients in a nursing home in a double-blind, cross-over study. These workers concluded that the overall trend of their results indicated that this drug was useful in the treatment of the aged although the results were not clear cut. Although the therapeutic effects of the drugs in both these studies were small, they both agreed in finding drugs superior to placebo.

Hydergine, a combination of the hydrogenated derivatives of three alkaloids of ergotoxin, has been tried in the treatment of the elderly. Roubicek, Geiger and Apt (1972) studied 22 pairs of patients for three months on a randomized double-blind study. There were significant lessenings of a number of psychiatric symptoms such as emotional withdrawal, conceptual disorganization, depressive mood, motor retardation, blunted affect, and disorientation. The improvement in psychomotor activity is important since this is a common and troublesome symptom in the elderly. Ditch and his coworkers (1971) report a double-blind study on 40 geriatric patients where hydergine produces improvement in 19 of the 30 items rated. Triboletti and Ferri (1969) also found that hydergine produced significant improvement over placebo in 59 patients studied for 12 weeks. Similar results were found by Gerin (1969). Foster (1955) found negative results however.

Traditionally, vasomotor stimulants such as pentylenetetrazol and vasomotor dilators such as papaverine have been used to treat the elderly. Some authors report good results, others are quite skeptical of the efficacies of these drugs. The literature on this has recently been reviewed by Lu, Stotsky, and Cole (1971). These authors also performed a double-blind study on pentylenetetrazol (Metrazol), papaverine and niacin. There were only small clinical changes observed over a three month period.

It would seem to us that there is enough evidence to indicate that vasodilaters could possibly be useful in the elderly to warrant further investigation. It would be important to determine whether they do improve cerebral function as measured objectively by psychological tests, as well as determining whether they improve behavior. It would also be of interest to show objectively that they improve cerebral blood flow or otherwise have an effect on neural function. It is conceivable that these drugs could produce enough improvement so that there would be a change in behavior toward the better without a change in psychological test performance nor a change in blood flow. A drug presumably could have a behavioral effect not of such a magnitude that it could reverse intellectual function, but merely make the patient more able to use his residual function better. These drugs could also act through a mechanism different than cerebral blood flow so that alterations of this parameter are not the only variable to define in evaluating these agents. This parameter is of more interest as a possible mechanism by which these agents might act. The most definitive study would be to correlate all three so that 1) one could show that the psychological changes are real, and 2) that they correlate with vasodilation changes and hence probably are produced by them. The status of this research seems to be more at the stage of not being proven and more research is indicated.

SUMMARY

We have reviewed evidence on the therapeutic effects and side effects of drugs used to treat mental illness in the elderly. In general, roughly the same therapeutic indications and side effects occur in the elderly as in younger patients. However, there are a few differences which we have also discussed. It is particularly important in this population to keep in mind drug-drug interactions since these patients are apt to receive many drugs because they tend to suffer from multiple medical problems. We have reported data on one drug-drug interaction, namely that chlorpromazine may interfere with the hypotensive action of guanethidine. We have also presented data which suggests that certain of the worsening which occasionally occurs in patients treated with psychotropic drug combinations such as phenothiazines, antiparkinsonian drugs and tricyclic antidepressants may be essentially an atropine-like psychosis resulting from the combined anticholinergic properties of these drugs. Patients are often particularly susceptible to atropine type toxicity, and this interaction is one which would be likely to occur in the elderly.

References

1. Aderman, M., Giardina, W.J., Koreniowski, S., Effect of Cyclandelate on Perception, Memory, and Cognition in a Group of Geriatric Subjects, *J. Amer. Geriat. Soc.* 6:268-271, (1972).

2. Ananth, J.V., Sazena, B.M., Lehmann, H. and Ban, T., Combined Administration of Thioridazine and Nicotine Acid in the Treatment of Geriatric Patients, *Curr. Ther. Res.* 13:158-161, (1971).

3. Asberg, M., Price Evans, D.A., Sjoquist, F., Genetic Contrast of Nortriptylene, Kinetics in Man, *J. Med. Gen.* 8:129-135, (1971).

4. Ayd, F.J., Nialamide Therapy for the Depressed Geriatric Patient, *J. Amer. Geriat. Soc.* 19:432, (1962).

5. Balter, M., and Levine, J., Character and Extent of Psychotherapeutic Drug Usage in the U.S. Paper Presented at Fifth World Congress in Psychiatry in Mexico City on November 30, 1971.

6. Bowe, H.M. and McDonald, C., A Controlled Trial of A.W.P. 235 C "Lucidril" in Senile Dementias, *Med J. Aust.* 2:270-272, (1966).

7. Chesrow, E.J., Kaplitz, S.E., Breme, J.T., Use of a New Benzodiazepine Derivative (Valium) in Chronically Ill and Disturbed Elderly Patients, *J. Amer. Geriat. Soc.* 10:667 (1962).

8. Ditch, M., Kelly, F.J., and Resnick, O., An Ergot Preparation (Hydergine) in the Treatment of Cerebrovascular Disorders in the Geriatric Patient, Double Blind Study, *J. Amer. Geriat. Soc.* 19:208-217, (1971).

9. Fine, G.W., Lewis, D., Villa-Lande, I., and Blakemore, C.G., The Effect of Cyclandelate On Mental Function in Patients with Arteriosclerotic Brain Disease, *Brit. J. Psychiat.* 117:157-161, (1970).

10. Forster, W., Schultz, S. and Henderson, A.L., Combined Lychogenated Alkaloids of Ergot in Senile and Arteriosclerater Psychosis, *Geriatrics,* 20:26-30, (1955).

11. Gerin, J., Symptomatic Treatment of Cerebrovascular Insufficiency with Hydergine *Curr. Ther. Res.* 11:539-546, (1969).

12. Goode, P. and Damrau, F., Heterologous Sex Hormone Therapy and the Geriatric-Psychiatric Patient with an Organic Psychosis of the Senile Psychotic Type and the Cerebral Arteriosclerotic Type in a Hospital Setting, *J. Neuropsychiat.* 4:31 (1962).

13. Honigfeld, G., Rosenbaum, M., Blumenthal, I., Lambert, H., and Roberts, A., Behavioral Improvement in the Older Schizophrenic Patient, *J. Amer. Geriat. Soc.* 13:57-71, (1965).

14. Kent, E.A., and Weinsaft, P., Treatment of Depression in the Aged with Opipramol, *J. Amer. Geriat. Soc.* 11:663 (1963).

15. Klein, D.F. and Davis, J.M., Diagnosis and Drug Treatment of Psychiatric Disorders, (Ed: Kaplan), Williams & Wilkins, 1969.

16. Kral, V.A. and Papapetropoulos, D., Treatment of Geriatric Patients. In: International Psychiatry Clinics, Psychopharmacology, (Eds: N.S. Kline and H.E. Lehmann), Little Brown & Company, 1965.

17. Kris, E.B., Psychiatric Treatment of the Aged, *Curr. Ther. Res.* 7:145, (1965).

18. Learoyd, B.M., Psychotropic Drugs in the Aging Patient, *Med. J. Aust.* i, 1131, 1972.

19. Lehmann, E. and Ban, T., Comparative Pharmacotherapy of the Aging Patient, *Laval Med.* 38:588-595, (1967).

20. Lehmann, H.E. and Ban, T.A., Chemotherapy in Aged Psychiatric Patients, *Canad. Psychiat. Assoc. J.* 14:361-369, (1969).

21. Lehmann, H. and Ban, T., Psychometric Tests in Evaluation Geriatrics, 25:142-147, (1970).

22. Lehmann, H.E. and Ban, T.A., Psychometric Tests in Evaluation of Brain Pathology, Response to Drugs, *Geriatrics,* 25:142-147, (1970).

23. Lifshitz, K. and Kline, N.S., Use of an Estrogen in the Treatment of Psychosis with Cerebral Atherosclerosis, *J. Amer. Med. Assoc.* 176:501, (1961).

24. Peel, R. and Von Loetzen, I.S., Phenothiazine Deaths, Paper Presented at APA 125th Annual Meeting, Dallas, Texas, May 4, 1972.

25. Prien, R.F., Levine, J., Cole, J.O., Indications for High Dose Chlorpromazine Therapy in Chronic Schizophrenia, *Dis. Nerv. Syst.* 31:739-745, 1970.

26. Prien, R.F., Levine, J. and Cole, J.O., High Dose Trifluoperazine Therapy in Chronic Schizophrenia, *Amer. J. Psychiat.* 126:305-313, 1969.

27. Roubicek, J., Geige, C.H., and Abt, K., An Ergot Alkaloid Preparation (Hydergine) in Geriatric Therapy, *J. Amer. Geriat. Soc.* 20:222-229, 1972.

28. Sainsburg, M.J., Electroplexy in First Attacks of Depression Over the Age of Fifty, *Med. J. Aust.* 5:(1)25,950,1964.

29. Silver, D., Lehmann, H.E., Kral, V.A. and Ban, T.A., Experimental Geriatrics — Selection and Prediction of Therapeutic Responsiveness in Geriatric Patients, *Canad. Psychiat. Assoc. J.*,13:561, 1968.

30. Smith, C.M., Nicotinic Acid Therapy in Old Age. The Placebo Effect and Other Factors in the Collection of Valid Data, *J. Amer. Geriat. Soc.* 11:580, 1963.

31. Sourander, L., Ruikka, I., Rautakorpi, J., Psychological Methods Applied to Evaluation of Symptomatic Geriatric Treatment, *Geriatrics,* 1970: 124-137.

32. Sugerman, A.A., Williams, B.H., and Alderstein, A.M., Haloperidol in the Psychiatric Disorders of Old Age, *Amer. J. Psychiat.* 120:1190, 1964. 33. Tobin,J.,

33. Brousseauirr, Lorgnz, A., Clinical Evaluation of Haloperidol in Geriatric Patients, *Geriatrics,* 1970: 119-122.

34. Tribolette, F., Ferri, H., Hydergine for Treatment of Symptons of Cerebrovascular Insufficiency,*Curr. Ther. Res.* 11:609-620, 1969.

35. Tsuang, M.M., Lo, L.M., Stotsky, B., and Cole, J.O., Haloperidol Versus Thioridazine for Hospitalized Psychogeriatric Patients, *J. Amer. Geriat. Soc.* 19:593-600, 1971.

Section 3

Issues in
Clinical Management of Drugs

A Survey of Drug Effects upon Cognitive Activities of the Aged

Murray Jarvik, Ph.D., M.D.

The present paper is an attempt to review the treatment of senility over the past few decades. It will not be an exhaustive or comprehensive review, but rather will use selected illustrative examples. In order to treat a disorder, it is very useful to be able to understand its cause; that is, the physiological basis of the disease. When such knowledge is available, a rational approach can be used, but in the absence of such knowledge, a more empirical approach is necessary. Although pathologists, biochemists and physiologists are beginning to throw some light on the aging process, we still have a long way to go to understand what causes the cognitive disorders in the senium. This has not prevented the widespread use of a great variety of drugs by an expectant and sometimes gullible public for the treatment of their age-related difficulties. Some of the treatments are very far-fetched, while others have a strong element of plausibility in them. It can be fairly stated that at this stage in history, no treatment has been unequivocally shown to improve the mental status of the aged. However, the problem is so important that a continual search seems warranted. A scientist can adopt two attitudes with such drug treatments. One is destructive and highly critical of inadequate experiments with inefficient controls. This type of sceptical attitude is certainly to be encouraged, but it does not directly result in the discovery or invention of new drugs to treat senility. A somewhat complimentary attitude is a more constructive one in which the scientist takes every new discovery and examines it from all angles to see whether any new discoveries can emanate. This is, by far, the more difficult task.

The nature of cognitive disorders in the aged has been reviewed by a number of authors. In a normal aged person dementia is not a prominent feature. The major deficit seems to be one of speed. It would further appear that learning deficits do occur in aging but these are largely represented by defects in registration and retrieval (Talland, 1968). Other changes which occur as a result of aging are changed perception and motor skills

(Welford, 1959), mood (Guilford, 1962) and motivation. Where an aged individual does poorly on a particular cognitive task, one cannot be sure that the deficit is due to an intellectual factor instead of one of the others just mentioned. Within the intellectual sphere, there does seem to be an organization of functions which has never been clearly and unequivocally defined. Workers such as Guilford (19), Thurstone (19), Guttman (19) and Spearman (19) have attempted to analyze the components of intelligence and have come up with a variety of results.

The nature of cognitive disorders in the aged has been reviewed and divided into categories such as perceptual, motor, motivational, and affective factors. It would seem, however, that both aging and drugs affect what used to be called the conative functions before they do the cognitive ones, including intelligence, learning, memory, and discriminative perception.

It used to be thought that the price of living a long time was dotage and senility with its memory defects, confabulation, and disorientation. A visit to any nursing home will confirm this impression. However, although there must be an average decline in intellectual functioning in the aged, there are many extremely old people who preserve their ability to think in a high degree. And yet, even the wisest and most revered of our aged philosophers will probably be shown to suffer from a slowing down of mental functions, lengthening of reaction time, loss of muscular strength, and impairment of vision and hearing. Most readers over forty are aware of these problems in themselves. We would like to know what can be done to stem the ravages of aging upon mental function in both the most severely affected and those lucky enough to maintain a high degree of intellectual ability with advancing years.

A rational pharmacotherapy of aging would be based upon attempts to correct the pathophysiology of the aging process. Unfortunately, here we are in a situation analogous to cancer chemotherapy, where we are trying to treat an incurable condition, the cause of which is not known. The problem is an important one and it affects all of us. Thus, while we must maintain our standards of scientific criticism, we must be willing to clutch at straws. Drugs can only improve performance if old people ordinarily perform below their maximal level of capacity. The degree of spontaneous variability should tell us something about the possible upper limits, but the drugs themselves may be needed to reveal the limits. We are at a distinct disadvantage if we do not know the possible limits in advance.

This review will be mainly illustrative in nature, rather than comprehensive. One can group the types of drug treatments which have been tried into 4 categories: (a) stimulants, (b) depressants, (c) miscellaneous and (d) somatic therapy. We shall consider these in turn, being aware on the one hand of inadequacies in experimental design and, on the other hand, of potentialities for development of more effective treatments. We can say in advance that it is easy to become discouraged in reviewing the literature in this area because so little of substantive value stands out. However, over-pessimism does not seem to be completely warranted. Medical practice in general deals with a disproportionately large number of aged patients and drugs are often very effective in dealing with physical disorders. Since it is possible, if not necessary, that physical disorders underlie mental ones, the alleviation of physical disorders by drugs may even play an important role in the pharmacotherapy of intellectual dysfunction in senility.

On the somewhat pessimistic side, it appears that cognitive functions, and learning and memory in particular, are either very resistant to the effects of drugs, or else drug effects are masked by the greater susceptibility of other functions. Thus, arousal level is exquisitely sensitive to drugs and, if a drug produces severe drowsiness or sleep, obviously cognitive functions will be suppressed. Motivation and mood also appear to be much more sensitive to drugs than discriminative or cognitive functions. On the other hand, many of the studies reporting negative results with drugs used to treat cognitive disorders are really rather inadequate in terms of dosage, populations, or measurements. Proving the null hypothesis is never easy.

Stimulants

We have arbitrarily divided the centrally acting stimulants into 3 classes: sympathomimetic amines, analeptics and anti-depressants. These are all drugs which, in one way or another, increase the activity of generally inactive humans or animals.

Amphetamines and Related Drugs

The use of centrally-acting sympathomimetic stimulants has been rather wide-spread for its intellectual and emotional effects. Amphetamine and its congeners have been shown to be mild anti-depressants and they certainly are effective in increasing arousal while they also decrease appetite. One of the early reviews (Weiss and Laties, 1962) indicated that amphetamine and also caffeine might be helpful in instances where fatigue played a role. Amphetamine was capable of improving athletic activity such as swimming, particularly in fatigued subjects, but also in normal, unfatigued subjects. Since aged persons are thought to tire more easily in all kinds of situations, it might be thought that drugs of the amphetamine variety would be useful. One of the problems with these drugs is escalation of the tendency to lead to drug abuse, and also the development of tolerance which, however, is not severe. In their 1962 review, Weiss and Laties noted that a wide variety of behavior can be enhanced by amphetamine and also caffeine, but intellectual tasks seemed rather less susceptible. Few studies were done with aged individuals, perhaps because of the fear of adverse cardiovascular effects from sympathomimetic amines and caffeine.

A stimulant related functionally and structurally to the amphetamines is methylphenidate. Lehmann and Ban (1967) conducted a massive study in which this was one of several drugs given to aged patients. Thirty mg of methylphenidate given over 8 to 10 weeks to these subjects with schizophrenia or organic brain syndrome produced no facilitation in perceptual-motor performance (critical flicker fusion frequency, reaction time, tapping speed) or memory processing (digits forward, digits backwards, ideational recall, word association time). Methylphenidate, however, did cause an increase in ratings of compulsive behavior, autonomic disturbance, irritability and anxiety in this patient sample. It was rather disappointing that only 5 out of 42 different administrations of psychological tests showed significant drug effects with this variety of drugs. The problems with this study, as with most (and this was far better than most), was that there was extremely high variability both between and within subjects. (1) These rather poor results might be contrasted with good results obtained administering methylphenidate and/or dextroamphetamine to children with severe learning disorders (Weiss *et al.*, 1968; Connors *et al.*, 1967; Connors *et al.*, 1969). There seems to be a paradoxical calming effect of amphetamines upon hyperactive, brain-injured children and this has been attributed to an increase in the true arousal levels towards optimal levels in these subjects. Whether such optimization of arousal may occur in either under-aroused or hyperactive aged subjects is not yet clear.

A drug which has received a great deal of publicity and some notoriety is magnesium pemoline. The large number of studies done with this drug do not come to any unitary conclusion concerning its efficacy in facilitating learning or performance. Talland and McGuire (1967) gave young, healthy students a dose of magnesium pemoline versus a placebo in a double-blind study of learning using a number of measures. There were significant differences in favor of the drug on a maze measure of relearning. However, these results, while interesting, would demand repetition and, furthermore, their significance is not clear. Another paper by Talland *et al.* (1967) reported a study of ten Korsakoff syndrome patients receiving 25 to 50 mg of pemoline either in an acute dose or daily for three weeks, and a test battery measuring new learning and memory, attention, information uptake, and other measures of intellectual functioning showed no effects upon performance on any of these measures. Talland concluded that even though all parameters may not have been explored, the types of tests used covered a sufficiently wide range so that if any effects were there, they should have showed up. The fact that they did not and the fact that clinical observations showed no change, led him to conclude that this drug was not useful in the treatment of this group of patients. He did point out that there were no side effects or discomfort or unusual sensations. It may be that, again, the dose of drug was inadequate or that this particular group of patients was not appropriate for this type of treatment.

One of the main proponents of the use of magnesium pemoline was Cameron (1967). He gave the drug to 19 aged patients who were tested on the Wechsler Memory Scale both prior to and after medication. Comparison between pre- and post-treatment scores for all patients yielded significant differences. Unfortunately, no placebo patients were used and, therefore, practice effects were not only not ruled out but made very likely, and very likely accounted for most of these findings.

A true double-blind study of magnesium pemoline on male geriatric patients was done by Eisdorfer *et al.* (1968). They gave 25 mg per day for a month, or else a placebo. An extensive test battery included measures of intellectual functioning (Porteus Mazes, vocabulary, digit span, digit symbol substitution test, and Gottschalk Embedded Figures). New learning (serial learning), vigilance, and the Taylor Manifest Anxiety Scale (TMAS), the Stockton Geriatric Rating Scale (SGRS) were used to evaluate the general behavior of the patients. There were no significant differences on the behavioral tests between the drug and the placebo groups, or on difference scores between pre- and post-testing. The drug group did show an increase in scores on the Embedded Figures Test, but it had a much lower pre-test mean score than the placebo group. It would appear that these results should be replicated. There were some differences on the nurses' rating scale. Both the placebo and drug group showed some gains, however, the drug group showed more reduction in variance, especially in the apathy factor. The investigators concluded that any effect of pemoline was not on memory but on general alertness and interest. If pemoline is capable of improving alertness and interest, then its effects should be seen on some subtle but objective test of mental functioning.

The influence of social milieu has been stressed by Rickels and colleagues (1970). They studied the effects of pemoline (75 mg per day) versus methylphenidate (15 mg per day) and placebo, on middle aged patients given these drugs for a 4 week period. Both pemoline and methylphenidate produced significant improvement in symptoms manifested by middle class patients treated by general practitioners. Lower class psychiatric patients and the private psychiatric patients were helped less.

In 1969, Weiss and Laties wrote a rather acerbic review of studies done with magnesium pemoline and concluded that there was no basis for supporting the claims of benefit attributed to this drug. They felt that the results of too many studies were negative and that, by contrast, the positive studies were badly designed, with inadequate controls. On the other hand, Plotnikoff (1971) recently published a more sanguine review in which he described a large number of animal and human studies showing a facilitating effect of magnesium pemoline. (2). It seems to me that the preponderance of negative and poor studies were not sufficient to render a verdict of ineffective, so long as there were any good studies which show a possible beneficial effect of a drug. Here is an instance where one should clutch at straws and see whether the positive results give some clues as to how one might improve the tests measuring intellectual functioning to make them more sensitive and improve the drug so that it might be strengthened in whatever positive characteristics it has.

Analeptics

The analeptic drugs have been used for many years in the treatment of various disorders of the aged. All of these remedies contain pentylenetetrazol in combination with niacin or some other substances. The rationale for using these has not been very solidly founded until McGaugh and collaborators began a series of animal experiments (1959, 1962; Breen and McGaugh, 1961). They found that pentylenetetrazol, strychnine, and a number of other drugs were capable of facilitating performance in animals in a number of different tests of learning. However, the genetic strain of the animal is very important and it was frequently necessary to search for the optimal dose to facilitate performance. Deviance from this optimum frequently reversed the effects of the drug. LaBrecque and Goldbert (1967) gave 25 out of 50 geriatric outpatients 100 mg t.i.d.

pentylenetetrazol combined with 50 mg t.i.d. niacin for 4 weeks. They reported that this combination produced significant overall improvement in a modification of the Malamud-Sands Worcester Rating Scale. This was a double-blind study where the ratings were apparently made by individual physicians. Positive results are to be contrasted with negative findings of a number of other investigators, for example, Gabrynowicz and Dumbrill (1968) who administered 100 mg pentylenetetrazol and 50 mg nicotinic acid q.i.d. for three months. Ratings by nurses using the Crichton Geriatric Behavioral Rating Scale showed no improvement. It may be that the patients of LaBrecque and Goldberg were less impaired than those of Gabrynowicz and Dumbrill. Another study by Danto (1969) utilized somewhat higher doses of pentylenetetrazol (200 mg plus 10 mg nicotinic acid q.i.d.) and found no effect in a group of senile patients.

The enormous variability among patient populations and the use of different tests and different drug preparations may account for some of the discrepancies. The presence of even a single positive finding among a large number of negative findings certainly warrants further investigation. Animal experiments of McGaugh and collaborators provide the encouraging theoretical basis for continued investigation of analeptic drugs in humans. Unfortunately, the effective doses in animals approach the convulsive dose, whereas in humans, it is necessary to avoid convulsions at all costs.

Antidepressants

It has been known for some time that psychiatric depression impairs performance on a wide variety of tests. This may indeed be attributed to secondary effects emanating from the basic depression of mood and motivation. For example, Cronholm et al. (1957, 1961) found that electroconvulsive shock improved learning as it relieved depression in psychiatric patients. A more recent study by Sternberg and Jarvik (unpublished) found that depression relieved by imipramine or amitriptyline also resulted in significant improvement on three tests of learning and memory: paired associates learning, figure recognition, and a picture-memory test. A pre- and 26-day post-treatment comparison showed significant improvement for immediate and delayed recall measures. On the other hand, Kernohan et al. (1967) were unable to find improvement on a discrimination memory task and only a suggestion of improvement in general behavior in aged patients who were given either nortriptyline or a placebo for 12 weeks. However, these were a very heterogeneous group of patients, not all of whom were suffering from psychiatric depression. In the Lehmann and Ban study (1967), no effect was produced by amitriptyline (150 mg per day) on any of the psychological measures noted, but again, their patients were not specifically depressed but rather suffered from other symptoms. A study by Vojtechkovsky et al. (1970) suggested that an acute dose of an antidepressant drug (propazetine) might improve memory of healthy young medical students. One of the problems with the use of antidepressant drugs as tools in the study of performance is that their therapeutic effects are not that dramatic. The difference between the antidepressant medication and placebo is relatively small in the relief of depression, so that any effects secondary to depression could only be expected to be further attenuated by variability.

Depressant Drugs

Depressant drugs which depress either general activity or the activity of the central nervous system might most reasonably be expected to impair performance, and indeed there is a large literature which indicated that they do under most circumstances. However, Berger (1970) has reported evidence that meprobamate, for example, may improve performance in emotionally unstable individuals under certain circumstances. The anti-psychotic drugs, of course, can be expected to improve performance in psychotic individuals and the Lehmann and Ban study (1967) again bears this out. There was a flurry of interest in anticonvulsant drugs particularly diphenylhydantoin. Gordon *et al.*(1968) reported that this anticonvulsant drug, and also procainamide, were able to improve performance in animals, but in humans there were no positive effects. It might be expected that individuals with certain types of seizure activity in the brain might be helped by anticonvulsant drugs, but this has not yet been demonstrated with objective psychological tests.

Miscellaneous

Local Anesthetics

One of the most popular treatments for disorders of aging is a Rumanian preparation containing 2% procaine. This has been popularized by Dr. Anna Aslan (1960) of the Parhon Institute of Geriatrics, Bucharest, Rumania. Despite widespread use of this preparation there are no well controlled clinical studies to substantiate the claims. Since the treatment seems to be harmless, the chances that it will continue to be popular are very great until it is replaced by something more effective.

Hallucinogens

Hallucinogenic drugs are used widely in this country, but mainly by younger individuals. Most studies have indicated that LSD, tetrahydrocannabinol and the anticholinergic hallucinogens all produce impairment of performance. It is unlikely that these drugs will be employed in research on aged subjects in the near future. They have been used as therapeutic agents in a variety of clinical situations ranging from cancer to glaucoma and their usefulness merits further study.

Cholinergic Drugs

There is much evidence that the cholinergic system is involved in learning and memory, and again, animal studies have indicated that certain drugs which stimulate the cholinergic system might produce facilitation in animals. Anticholinergic drugs such as scopolamine have been shown to impair learning in humans and animals. It is an area worthy of further study.

Oxygen Therapy

The treatment that has perhaps created more excitement than any other among geriatric investigators is the hyperbaric oxygen therapy proposed by Jacobs and collaborators (1969). She indicated that certain aged patients suffering from senile intellectual difficulties could be improved by treatment with oxygen under pressure. Thirteen male patients, mean age 68 years, manifesting intellectual deterioration, breathed 100% oxygen at 2.5 atmospheres twice daily in 90 minute sessions, for a total of 15 consecutive days. Five control patients were exposed to the same treatment procedure, but breathed 10% oxygen in nitrogen, instead of pure oxygen. Three tests of intellectual function were administered before any treatments were given, and approximately 12 hours after the final treatment: the Wechsler Memory Scale, the Bender-Gestalt Test and the Tiens Organic Integrity Test. In this double-blind design, the results showed significant improvement between pre- and post-treatment scores for the experimental subjects, with no improvements in control subjects. When control subjects were then given an additional 15 days of hyperbaric oxygen, the pO_2 increased significantly for experimental but not control patients. Both the pCO_2 and pH values at 2.5 atmospheres did not differ between groups. Goldfarb *et al.* (in press) attempted to replicate Jacobs' study. The results were essentially negative. There were no differences between pre- and post-test scores on any measure in patients receiving hyperbaric oxygen treatments.

Somatic Therapy

Since the bodies of elderly individuals have undergone and continue to undergo readily observable deterioration, it is likely that many of the mental changes seen are secondary to physical disease conditions. The borderline between degenerative diseases and normality is, of course, rather vague and not all of these are amenable to drug therapy. However, most aged individuals are taking large numbers of medications and it is possible that some of these may influence their mental functioning directly or indirectly. I have arbitrarily divided the somatic drug therapies into 4 classes: (1) nutrition, (2) hormones, (3) cardio- and cerebrovascular and (4) miscellaneous.

Nutrition

The influence of nutrition and nutritional factors upon psychological functions associated with aging is only beginning to be realized. During the past two decades, interest in the possibility that lipids may play a role in atherosclerosis has grown to the point where milk, butter, eggs, and cheese are no longer regarded as the healthful, nutritious foods they used to be thought to be. The dairy industry is actually on the defensive. Evidence, however, that dietary fat can be influenced in such a way as to prevent or cure the effects of atherosclerosis is still not too convincing. Large scale studies with good statistical design have yet failed to reveal the relationships that one would expect. Nevertheless, drugs which reduce blood lipids, such as clofibrate, are being widely used and also being studied for effectiveness at the same time. Obviously, if cerebral atherosclerosis reaches an advanced stage, blood is not going to reach the brain in sufficient quantities. If substances could be found which would reduce these fatty deposits, then cerebral functioning with its concomitant psychological changes should be improved. The blood vessels of the coronary system of the heart are particularly vulnerable to these fatty deposits and heart disease produces a devastating toll in disability as well as death in the middle aged and aged members of the population. Whether unsaturated fats or anti-oxidants such as vitamin E are useful in the prevention of atherosclerosis is still a matter of great debate.

Carbohydrates are also a subject of controversy. It has been contended (for example, Yudkin, 1972) that sucrose is a major cause of atherosclerosis, diabetes, tooth decay and a number of other disorders, and the evidence implicating refined sugar is just about as convincing as that implicating fat in the production of disease. Protein has not yet been attacked. There has been a great deal of interest, however, in the role of protein synthesis in learning (see Jarvik, 26). Protein deficiencies in childhood and infancy have been shown to produce psychological changes in animals and there is some evidence that nutritionally deprived humans may be affected. Whether severe nutritional deprivation such as starvation affects adults the same way is a matter of controversy. However, the possibility that various amino acids might influence learning and memory has been entertained for many years. Glutamic acid, in particular, has been studied rather widely and the evidence that it may produce facilitation has been affirmed and refuted, but the story is not clear. The review by Austin and Ross (1960) indicated that negative studies tended to be well controlled while positive studies were either poorly controlled or in a few cases well controlled. The evidence seems to be growing that glutamic acid may be an important brain transmitter. The substances should be investigated further. (3)

The nucleic acids had a flurry of interest when it was reported by Cameron and collaborators (1963) that RNA preparations could facilitate learning and cognitive activities in adults. Unfortunately, these studies suffered from the same methodological and design problems that pemoline studies did. In animals, the literature is similarly controversial. A study by Talland *et al.* (1965) on tricyanoaminopropene, purported to stimulate nucleic acid synthesis, gave only negative results.

Vitamins have been a subject of interest since Casimir Funk's original discovery (1). There is no question that certain vitamin deficiencies can lead to mental changes (e.g., thiamine deficiency). Whether administration of vitamins to individuals receiving a normal diet does anything is rather questionable. In any case, there are no controlled studies of the psychological, or for that matter physical, effects of vitamin supplements in normal individuals. Nevertheless, these substances are both consumed and prescribed in huge quantities, particularly in the aged population.

Hormones

Hormones have been extensively used for the treatment of disorders of aging. Endocrine diseases of the pituitary, thyroid, and pancreas are well known and well studied and can be treated with great success. The sex hormones have been administered since the days of Brown-Sequard and Voronoff (19), primarily to improve the flagging sexual performance of aged individuals, but also to improve their general condition and feelings of well being. There seems to be some rationale for this, but the danger of cancer is apt to dissuade physicians from prescribing these substances. A study by Michael *et al.* (1970) examining the effects of estrogens upon a hospital adjustment scale, found that older women were definitely helped when they were given conjugated natural estrogens for three years. Side effects seemed to be negligible.

Cardio- and Cerebrovascular Drugs

Cardio- and cerebrovascular drugs are widely prescribed for aged individuals. There is a considerable question whether vasodilators such as nicotinic acid or meclofenoxate actually affect cerebral circulation. A study by Soukupova *et al.* (1970) reported positive effects with meclofenoxate whereas Oliver and Restell (1967) in a very well designed study could find no effect of this drug on psychological functioning.

The most exciting development in recent years is the finding by Eisdorfer *et al.* (1970) that the beta adrenergic blocking agent, propanolol, improved performance of aged individuals in a memory task. His explanation is that the drug reduces anxiety by blocking the effects of catecholamines in peripheral end organs. Excessive amounts of anxiety and excessive sympathetic activity certainly require further investigation. Propanolol obviously produces marked peripheral actions, but whether Eisdorfer's results are also due to central action remains to be seen.

Hypertension has been shown to be an important cause of intellectual decline in aging and in middle age. The advent of effective anti-hypertensive medication has begun to produce really remarkable therapeutic results. It is very likely that these drugs can preserve intellectual functioning, which might otherwise be badly impaired by hypertensive encephalopathy. Indeed, individuals suffering from hypertension should probably have their intellectual status evaluated from time to time, even though nothing is easier to measure more directly than blood pressure itself. Disturbances of the rate, rhythm, and force of contraction are quite common in aging and some of the most venerable remedies have been shown to be rather effective in some cases and not quite so effective in others. Digitalis and its derivatives are used to treat heart failure and a variety of anti-arrhythmic drugs, among which incidentally is propanolol, have been used for years, even though their effectiveness is far less. Developments in this area should be watched with great interest by gerontologists because of the proportion of individuals over 65 years of age with disturbances of the heart is exceedingly large, and probably includes most people over this age.

One drug deserves special attention because of a spate of positive well- controlled results reported in recent years; this is dihydroergotoxine (hydergine). This ergot alkaloid has been investigated for its effects on the presumed manifestations of cerebrovascular efficiency in the elderly. A number of studies have reported positive results (Danen, 1972; Rowe and Norris, 1972; Triboletti and Feri, 1969; Gerin, 1969; Ditch *et al.*, 1971; Roubicek *et al.*, 1972). It is not clear how this drug may work. Apparently it speeds the laminant electroencephalographic frequency in aged individuals (Roubicek *et al.*, 1972). It is also thought that this preparation improves ganglion cell metabolism (Emmenegger and Meierruge, 1968). Emmenegger and Meierruge feel that hydergine reduces the compression exerted by glial processes, and results in a fall in vascular resistance and an increase in blood flow in the brain. It is obvious that further investigation of this substance is warranted.

Conclusion

While most of the literature reporting the effects of drugs upon cognitive functioning in the aged is depressingly negative, there seems to be justification for optimism. Analeptic drugs probably should be further investigated because of animal experiments indicating that facilitation of learning and performance may occur. Centrally acting sympathomimetic amines certainly alleviate fatigue and can facilitate various types of performance and should be investigated further. Antidepressant medication which can restore the mood in a condition so common in the aged should certainly be investigated. Agents can be found which truly improve the cerebral circulation and they ought to be looked into, but no drug has unequivocally been shown to be a cerebral vasodilator. Hyperbaric oxygenation is worthy of further trials. The ergot alkaloid, dihydroergotoxine, shows remarkable promise and must be looked at with more objective tests and well controlled experiments. During the next decade, we may confidently expect better drugs to appear for the treatment of cognitive disorders of the aged.

References

1. Aslan, A. Procaine therapy in old age and other disorders (novocaine factor H_3). Geront. Clin., *2:* 148-76, 1960.

2. Astin, A.W. and Ross, S. Glutamic acid and human intelligence. Psychol. Bull., *57:*429-432, 1960.

3. Berger, F.M. Anxiety and discovery of the tranquilizer. In: F.J. Ayd and B. Blackwell (editors), *Discoveries in Biological Psychiatry,*Chapter 9. J.B. Lippincott, Inc., 1970.

4. Breen, R.A. and McGaugh, J.L. Facilitation of maze-learning with post-trial injections of picrotoxin. J. Comp. Physiol. Psychol., *54:*498-501, 1961.

5. Brown-Sequard, C.E. Course of lectures on the physiology and pathology of the central nervous system; Delivered at the Royal College of Surgeons, May, 1858. Philadelphia, Collins, 1960.

   Varonoff, S. Life: A study of the means of restoring vital energy and prolonging life. New York, Dutton, 1920.

6. Cameron, D.E. Evolving concepts of memory. Rec. Adv. Biol. Psychiat., *9:*1-12, 1967.

7. Cameron, D.E., Sved, S., Solyom, L., Wainrib, B., and Barik, H. Effects of ribonucleic acid on memory defect in the aged. Amer. J. Psychiat., *120,*320-324, 1963.

8. Connors, C.K., Rothschild, G., Eisenberg, L. Dextroamphetamine sulfate in children with learning disorders: Effects on perception, learning and achievement. Arch. Gen. Psychiatr. *17:*478-485, 1967.   ᛫

9. Connors, C.K., Eisenberg, L., and Barcai, A. Effect of dextroamphetamine on children: Studies on subjects with learning disabilities and school behavior problems. Arch. Gen. Psychiatr., *21:*182-190, 1969.

10. Cronholm, B. and Molander, L. Memory disturbances after electroconvulsive therapy: Conditions six hours after electroshock treatment. Acta Psychiat. Scand., *32:*280-306, 1957.

11. Cronholm, B. and Ottosson, J.O. Memory functions in endogenous depression before and after electroconvulsive therapy. Arch. Gen. Psychiat., *5,*193-199, 1961.

12. Danen, D.M. An ergot preparation, hydergine, for relief of symptoms of cerebrovascular insufficiency. J. Amer. Geriatric Soc., *20:*22-24, 1972.

13. Danto, B. Triflupromazine vs. pentylenetetrazol-nicotinic acid for treatment of chronic brain disease on a general-hospital psychiatric service. J. Amer. Ger. Soc., *17:*414-420, 1969.

14. Ditch, M., Kelly, F.J. and Resnick, O. An ergot preparation, hydergine, in the treatment of cerebrovascular disorders in the geriatric patient: Double-blind study. J. Amer. Geriat. Assn., *19:*208-217, 1971.

15. Eisdorfer, C., Connor, J.F. and Wilkie, F.L. The effect of magnesium pemoline on cognition and behavior. J. Geront., *23:*283-288, 1968.

16. Eisdorfer, C., Nowlin, J., and Wilkie, F. Improvement of learning in the aged by modification of autonomic nervous system activity. Science, *170:*1327-1329, 1970.

17. Emmenegger, H. and Meierruge, W. Reactions of hydergine on the brain: A histochemical, circulatory and neurophysiological study. Pharmacology, *1:*65-78, 1968.

18. Funk, C. *The Vitamins.* Harry E. Dubin (ed.) Baltimore, Williams and Wilkins, 1922.

19. Gabrynowicz, J.W. and Dumbrill, M. A clinical trial of leptazol with nicotinic acid in the management of psycho-geriatric patients. Med. J. Aust., *1:*799-802, 1968.

20. Gerin, J. Symptomatic treatment of cerebrovascular insufficiency with hydergine. Current Therap., Res., *11:*539-546, 1969.

21. Goldfarb, A.I., Hochstadt, N.J., Jacobson, J.H., and Weinstein, E. Hyperbaric oxygen treatment of organic mental syndrome in aged persons. J. Geront. (in press).

22. Gordon, P., Tobin, S.S., Doty, B. and Nash, M. Drug effects on behavior in aged animals and man: Diphenylhydantoin and procainamide. J. Geront., *23:*434-444, 1968.

23. Guilford J.P. Three faces of intellect. The American Psychologist, *14:*468-479, 1959.

24. Guttman, L. The basis for scalogram analysis. In: S.A. Stouffer, L. Guttman, E.A. Suchman, P.F. Lazarsfeld, A.S. Star, and J.A. Clausen, Measurement and Prediction. Princeton, N.J., Princeton, Univ. Press, 1950, pp. 60-212.

25. Jacobs, E.A., Winter, P.M., Alvis, H.J. and Small, S.M. Hyperoxygenation effect on cognitive functioning in the aged. New Eng. J. Med., *281:*753-757, 1969.

26. Jarvik, M.E. The influence of actinomycin-D on brain RNA synthesis and on memory. J. Neurochem., 1961, *11:*187-195.

27. Kernohan, W.J., Chambers, J.L., Wilson, W.T. and Daugherty, J.F. Effects of nortriptyline on the mental and social adjustment of geriatric patients in a mental hospital. J. Amer. Ger. Soc., *15:*196-202, 1967.

28. LaBrecque, D.C. and Goldberg, R.I. A double-blind study of pentylenetetrazol combined with niacin in senile patients. Curr. Ther. Res., *9:*611-617, 1967.

29. Lehmann, H.E. and Ban, T.A. Comparative pharmacotherapy of the aging psychotic patient. Laval Med., *38:*588-595, 1967.

30. McGaugh, J.L. and Petrinovich, L. The effect of strychnine sulfate on maze-learning Amer. J. Psychol., *72:*99-102, 1959.

31. McGaugh, J.L., Westbrook, W.H. and Thompson, C.W. Facilitation of maze-learning with post-trial injections of 5-7 diphenyl-1-3-diazedemantan-6-01 (1757 I.S.). J. Comp. Physiol. Psychol., *55*(5):710-713, 1962.

32. Michael, C.M., Kantor, H.I. and Shore, H. Further psychometric evaluation of older women – The effect of estrogen administration. J. Geront., *25:*337-341, 1970.

33. Oliver, J.E. and Restell, M. Serial testing in assessing the effect of meclofenoxate on patients with memory defects. Brit. J. Psychiat., *113:*219-222, 1967.

34. Plotnikoff, N. Pemoline: Review of performance. Texas Reports on Biology and Medicine, *29:*467-479, 1971.

35. Rickels, K., Gordon, P.E., Gansman, D.H., Weise, C.C., Pereria-Organ, J.A. and Hesbacher. P.T. Pemoline and methylphenidate in mildly depressed outpatients. Clin. Pharm. Therap., *11:*698-710, 1970.

36. Roubicek, J., Geiger, S.C. and Abt, K. An ergot alkaloid preparation, hydergine, in geriatric therapy. J. Amer. Geriat. Soc., *20:*222-229, 1972.

37. Rowe, D.D. and Norris, J.R. A double-blind investigation of hydergine in the treatment of cerebrovascular insufficiency in the elderly. Johns Hopkins Med. J., *130:* 317-324, 1972.

38. Soukupova, B., Vojtechovsky, M. and Safratova, V. Drugs influencing the cholinergic system and the process of learning and memory in man. Activ. Nerv. Sup (Praha), *12:*91-93, 1970.

39. Spearman, C. The Abilities of Man. New York, MacMillan, 1927.

40. Talland, G.A. and Quarton, G.C. the effects of methamphetamine and pentobarbital on running memory span. Psychopharmacologia, *7:*349-365, 1965.

41. Talland, G.A. and Quarton, G.C. The effects of methamphetamine and pentobarbital on running memory span. Psychopharmacologia, *7:*349-365, 1965.

42. Talland, G.A., Mendelson, J.H., Koz, G. and Aaron, R. Experimental studies of the effects of tricyanoaminopropene on the memory and learning capacities of geriatric patients. J. Psychiat. Res., *3:*171-179, 1965.

43. Talland, G.A. In: S.S. Chown and K.F. Riegel, *Psychological Functioning in the Normal Aging and Senile Aged.* Kargar, Basel, 1968.

44. Thurstone, L.L., Thurstone, T.G. Factorial studies of intelligence. Psychometric Monograph No. 2: Chicago, Univ. of Chicago Press, 1941.

45. Triboletti, F. and Feri, H. Hydergine for treatment of symptoms of cerebrovascular insufficiency. Curr. Therap. Res., *11:*609-620, 1969.

46. Vogel, W. The therapeutic use of 1-glutavite. Gerontologist, *6:*51-53, 1966.

47. Vojtechovsky, M., Safratova, V. and Soukupova, B. The influence of propazepine on learning and memory in healthy volunteers and in patients with slight chronic brain syndrome. Activ. Nerv. Sup., *12:*251-252, 1970.

48. Weiss, B. and Katies, V.G. Enhancement of human performance by caffeine and the amphetamines. Pharm. Rev., *14:*1-36, 1962.

49. Weiss, G.,Werry, J., Minde, K., Douglas, V., and Sykes, D. Studies on the hyperactive child: The effects of dextroamphetamine and chlorpromazine on behavior and intellectual functioning. J. Child. Psychol. & Psychiat. & Allied Disciplines, *9* (3-4) :145-156, 1968.

50. Weiss, G., Minde, K., Douglas, V., Werry, J., and Sykes D. Comparison of the effects of chlorpromazine, dextroamphetamine and methylphenidate on the behavior and intellectual functioning of hyperactive children. Canad. Med. Assoc. J., *104:*20-25, 1971.

51. Weiss, B. and Laties, V.G. Behavioral pharmacology and toxicology. In: H.W. Elliott (editor), *Annual Review of Pharmacology,* 297-326, 1969.

52. Welford, A.T. Psychomotor performance. In: J.E. Birren (editor), *Handbook of Aging and the Individual,* University of Chicago Press, Chicago, 562-613, 1959.

53. Yudkin, J. Sugar: Chemical, biological, and nutritional aspects of sucrose. J. Judkin, J. Edelman, L. Hough (eds.) London, Butterworth, 1971.

Footnotes

[1]Lehmann and Ban's study requires some additional comment. They used fairly large groups of subjects for each of the 6 groups of drugs they studied ranging from 24 patients for methylphenidate, up to 42 patients for nicotinic acid. The drugs that they used were amitriptyline (30 mg), fluoxymesterone (5 mg), meprobamate (600 mg), methylphenidate (10 mg), nicotinic acid (300 mg), thyroidazine (75 mg). All patients were given the drugs from 8 to 10 weeks. On the symptom rating scale, all the drugs except methylphenidate improved symptoms. Methylphenidate seemed to impair them; it apparently produced symptoms of irritability, anxiety, hostility, and autonomic reaction. When 12 symptoms were studied in these 6 groups of drugged patients, only 6 showed significance at the 5% level, a result which was certainly not much better than chance. In a battery of psychological tests consisting of critical flicker fusion frequency, reaction time, tapping speed, digits forward, digits backwards, ideational recall, and word association time, only 5 of these measures showed significant changes; two of these occurred with thyroidazine. This is not too surprising since this is an antipsychotic drug being given to psychotic patients. The results of this rather massive study were somewhat disappointing, but perhaps some cautious optimism is still warranted. The patients in the study were either psychotic or suffered from organic brain syndrome. Perhaps the same drugs might have been more effective if optimal, single doses were used, and this would require a dose-response curve with a large number of subjects. Furthermore, normal aged patients might be more responsive to some of the drugs than these pathological patients.

[2]Plotnikoff's review of 69 studies of animal and human performance under the influence of magnesium pemoline concluded that most of these showed enhancement. He stressed that pemoline was active in enhancing conditioning, whether positive or negatively reinforced in animals. In humans, the most promising aspect of this drug seems to be its use in the management of minimal brain dysfunction in children with learning and behavior disorders.

[3]Vogel (1966) reviewed a number of studies, some of them double-blind, investigating the therapeutic effect of L-glutavite and reported a surprising degree of therapeutic success in some controlled studies of aged hospitalized psychiatric patients. The results are so unexpected that scrutiny of the original studies plus replication seems warranted.

This paper is based largely upon: Drugs and Memory Disorders in Human Aging. *Behavioral Biology*, Vol. 7, No. 5, pp. 643-668, 1972. Jarvik, M.E., Gritz, E.R., and Schneider, N.G.

Memory Loss and Its Possible Relationship to Chromosome Changes

Lissy F. Jarvik, M.D., Ph. D.

To establish a plausible relationship between two events as far removed from each other as the microscopic elements of cellular genetics and the psychological variables of mental functioning should be a challenge sufficient in itself. That I agree to participate in a session dealing with "Drug-related Central Nervous System Changes" is a testimony to my temerity, and not an indication that we know anything about the extent to which drugs contribute either to the chromosome changes, or to the intellectual changes we so often see in elderly persons (Jarvik 1971).

We all know that far too often declining intellectual agility and failing memory reduce the older person to a pitiful caricature of his former self, but we must also remember that intellectual deterioration is neither a necessary nor an inevitable accompaniment of advancing chronological age: the vast majority of people over the age of 65 years maintains an adequate level of mental functioning. There are data from several longitudinal studies now that demonstrate the preservation of intellectual skills during senescence (Baltes *et al.*, 1971; Birren, 1964; Blum, Clark and Jarvik, in press; Eisdorfer and Wilkie, in press; Granick and Birren, 1969; Jarvik *et al.*, 1962; Kleemelier, 1962; Riegel *et al.*, 1968).

Probably the single most notable mental change in aging individuals is loss of memory. Indeed, the forgetfulness of the aged is proverbial. And yet, it is not uniform. Cicero pointed this out some 2000 years ago when he wrote: "Old people remember what interests them... besides, I never heard of an old man forgetting where he buried his money". Even though Cicero expediently dismissed in this way one of the most common concomitants of old age, the mental changes which characterize the elderly have continued to be of vital interest to us century after century.

How far have we come to understand these changes since Cicero's time? Not far at all, as most of you who heard Murray Jarvik yesterday already know. I can make that statement with even more conviction after an exhaustive review of the literature recently prepared for the Task Force of the American Psychological Association for the White House Conference on Aging under Carl Eisdorfer's chairmanship. With the help of a graduate student, Donna Cohen, we examined something like 587 publications and found few hard facts (Jarvik and Cohen, in press).

Little is known of the physio-chemical basis underlying mental functioning. Mechanisms have been postulated which are associated with the DNA-RNA-protein assembly — but they remain speculative.

Recently our own group obtained some preliminary data linking mental changes to chromosomal changes. Chromosomes, as all of you know, are the visible structures within the cell nucleus which contain the hereditary material DNA and they can be seen in nearly any type of living cell — all that is needed is for the cell to divide — to undergo mitosis. That rules out neurons since they do not divide after fetal life; but then, studying neurons would not be a very practical idea anyhow. In order to get the cells we would have to perform a brain biopsy. On how many patients, or normal persons, would we want to do so?

We need a more accessible source of cells and the most easily obtainable one is the blood. Usually a small amount of blood (10 cc or so) is taken from the antecubital vein and incubated with a nutrient medium, antibiotic and fungicidal agents, and harvested three days later after the addition of a mitotic inhibitor (cf Jarvik and Kato, 1970).

As you know, human cells characteristically have 46 chromosomes; but if you count enough cells, say 100 or more, you occasionally find a cell with either more or less than 46 chromosomes (aneuploid cell). This is the result of some defect in cell division, a mitotic error. If these cells with abnormal chromosome numbers survive and accumulate over a lifetime, then, aneuploidy should increase with age. It occurred to us that this gradual accumulation of mitotic errors might be related to the gradual mental changes we see in so many older persons (Jarvik, 1967).

In examining our data we found that in some older people the proportion of cells missing one or more chromosomes (hypodiploid cells) was indeed very high, going up to 25% or more (Jarvik and Kato, 1970). However, a high frequency of hypodiploid cells was related not to chronological age as such (our subjects ranged in age from 77 to 93 years) but to impaired mental functioning (Jarvik et al., 1971). Thus, women diagnosed as suffering from organic brain syndrome, the modern equivalent of senility, showed a significantly higher frequently of chromosome loss than did women not so diagnosed (p < 0.001). Similar results were obtained by Nielsen (1968) in Denmark when he compared women hospitalized with senile dementia and women of comparable age who were mentally intact, and found that the patients with senile dementia had a significantly higher frequency of chromosome loss than did the others.

In our own study we could further relate the proportion of cells with abnormal chromosome number to psychological test performance. The higher the frequency of such abnormal cells, the lower the scores on tests such as Vocabulary, Tapping, Digits Forward, Digits Backward, Digit Symbol Substitution, Similarities, Block Designs, Picture Arrangement and Picture Completion. By contrast, on tests where a high rather than a low score was indicative of poor performance, the correlation was positive. These tests were the Stroop Color-Word Test, the Graham-Kendall Memory-for-Designs Test and the Trailmaking Test. On the first two of these tests the correlation was statistically significant despite the relatively small number of subjects (Bettner *et al.,* 1971; Jarvik and Kato, 1969). Thus, the correlation between test performance and chromosome loss was in the predicted direction in *all* of the 15 subtests that had been administered. The greater the chromosome loss, the worse the performance. The probability that such a correlation would occur by chance 15 out of 15 times is practically zero!

It would seem then, that somehow chromosome loss is related to intellectual deterioration. This is but a first step. Next we need confirmation. I have every confidence that our results will be confirmed, since they were not discovered in a mountain of computer print-outs, but support a previously formulated hypothesis.

If we accept a relation between chromosome loss and mental decline, then the question arises as to what factors are responsible for the chromosome loss. We don't have the answer, but we know that, in general, key factors in the production of chromosome changes are radiation, viruses and chemicals. These changes range from simple breaks to complex abnormalities. The abnormalities can be produced in the laboratory but the question is always asked, and rightly so: How can you attribute what you may find in a patient to the administration of X-rays, particularly if you don't have studies before the exposure to radiation? Well, you can't be sure in any individual case and, until a few years ago, there was no good answer to the question concerning long-term effects of radiation on humans. But then, in 1966 and 1967 follow-up data for survivors in Nagasaki and Hiroshima were published (Bloom *et al.,* 1966, 1967). The increase in aneuploidy was not impressive (about 1%) but the increase in abnormal forms was very impressive – from just under 4-fold to 50-fold. So, shield your patients when you use X-rays and don't use them unless strictly indicated. That applies even more strongly to fluoroscopy.

What about drugs? When the headline stories broke about the chromosome damage caused by LSD, we undertook a series of experiments and confirmed that, indeed, in the test tube LSD will increase the number of chromosome abnormalities ordinarily observed. On the average, it doubled the spontaneous rate – and so did drugs like ergonovine maleate (a drug commonly used in obstetrics) and aspirin (Jarvik *et al.,* 1968; Kato and Jarvik, 1969). Then we went to the literature and found that a wide variety of drugs and other compounds will cause chromosome damage (Sharma and Sharma, 1960; Jarvik, 1969). Although the results are based mostly on *in vitro* experiments, usually not using human cells, and damage was caused only if the substances were added in the right amount, at the right time, under the right conditions, it is nonetheless worthwhile to consider the possible genetic consequences of drug use. We can speculate that a widespread increase in the consumption of drugs could lead to an increase in chromosome abnormalities in the population, in chromosome loss with advancing age and possibly in senile mental changes.

Should we, then, direct our efforts toward finding ways of inhibiting or retarding the chromosome loss? That would be premature. We have demonstrated that a correlation exists, but a correlation is *not* necessarily equivalent to a causal relation. We don't even know the natural history of gross chromosomal changes, something which we should determine and which could readily be done by means of longitudinal studies. There are many questions which we need to answer. For example, are there certain people more prone to chromosome loss than others? If yes, is that tendency manifested earlier in life, and, if so, when? There are indications that genetic factors play a role in the senile dementias; are then, people with a family history of senile psychosis more likely than those without such a history to show chromosome changes with advancing age? There are other questions, including the basic one of how chromosome loss, which occurs during cell division, can be related to intellectual functioning, when neurons, the cells concerned with intellectual functioning, do not undergo division post-natally. Even though neurons don't divide, glial cells do and continue to do so into old age. An increased proportion of abnormal glial cells with impaired functioning, *could* secondarily affect the functioning of neurons. It is possible also that the glial cells themselves have a greater role in intellectual functioning than the one with which they have been credited so far.

Before closing, I will bring up just two more questions. We heard in the first session this morning about the effects of cerebrovascular disturbances upon mental functioning. Why then do we need to consider another reason for mental impairment in the elderly? Those of us indoctrinated to venerate the rule of parsimony always prefer one explanation to two. There are some investigators, like Martin Roth in England, who *do* believe that all of the senile mental symptoms can be attributed to cerebrovascular changes. There are others, however, like Walter Obrist and myself, who believe that not all elderly people develop significant cerebrovascular impairment and that the mental changes they develop must be attributed to different causes. I believe that chromosomal abnormalities constitute one such cause. Finally, all of the findings I have described hold for women, but *not* all of them hold for men. For example, the frequency of cells with chromosome loss was not significantly higher in men diagnosed as having CBS than in those not so diagnosed. One of the reasons for this finding may be that in men cerebral arteriosclerosis is so common that even after careful medical evaluation it is not possible to screen out all those with cerebrovascular disease and the presence of cerebrovascular disease in itself is sufficient reason for mental impairment regardless of the presence or absence of chromosome loss. Whether this explanation is correct will have to be determined by further research, including careful pathological examination. So far, the sex difference is essentially unexplained as is the sex difference in survival itself.

I know that I have raised many more questions than I have been able to answer but I think there is value in realizing how ignorant we are when it comes to aging processes and as our conclusion we can take solace from Benjamin Disraeli who said: "To be conscious that you are ignorant is a great step to knowledge."

References

1. Baltes, P.B., Schaie, K.W. and Nardi, A.H.: Age and experimental mortality in a seven-year longitudinal study of cognitive behavior. *Developmental Psychology, 5:* 18-26, 1971.

2. Bettner, L.G., Jarvik, L.F. and Blum, J.E.: Stroop color-word test, non-psychotic organic brain syndrome, and chromosome loss in aged twins. *J. Geront, 26:* 458-469, 1971.

3. Birren, J.E.: Neural basis of personal adjustment in aging. In: P. From Hansen (Ed.), *Age with a future.* Copenhagen: Munksgaard, 48-59, 1964.

4. Bloom, A.D., Neriishi, S., Kamada, N. et al.: Cytogenetic investigation of survivors of the atomic bombings of Hiroshima and Nagasaki, *Lancet, 2:* 672-674, 1966.

5. Bloom, A.D., Neriishi, S., Awa, A.A. et al.: Chromosome aberrations in leucocytes of older survivors of the atomic bombings of Hiroshima and Nagasaki, *Lancet, 2:* 802-805, 1967.

6. Blum, J.E., Clark, E.T. and Jarvik, L.F.: The New York State Psychiatric Institute Study of Aging Twins. In: *Intellectual Functioning in Adults: Psychological and Biological Influences.* L.F. Jarvik, C. Eisdorfer, and J.E. Blum (Eds.), New York: Springer, in press.

7. Eisdorfer, C. and Wilkie, F.: The Duke Longitudinal Research Project. In: *Intellectual Functioning in Adults: Psychological and Biological Influences.* L.F. Jarvik, C. Eisdorfer, and J.E. Blum (Eds.), New York: Springer, in press.

8. Granick, S. and Birren, J.E.: Cognitive functioning of non-survivors: 12 year follow-up of healthy aged. The Eighth International Congress of Gerontology, *II:* Abstract No. 240, 67, 1969.

9. Jarvik, L.F., Kallmann, F.J., Lorge, I. and Falek, A.: Longitudinal study of intellectual changes in senescent twins. In: C. Tibbits & W. Donahue, (Eds.) *Social and Psychological Aspects of Aging.* New York: Columbia Univ. Press, 839-859, 1962.

10. Jarvik, L.F.: Survival and psychological aspects of aging in man. In: *Aspects of the Biology of Aging.* XXI Symposium of the Society for Experimental Biology, Sheffield, England, *Symp. Soc. Exp. Biol. 21:* 463-483, 1967.

11. Jarvik, L.F. Discussion of Judd, L.L., Brandkamp, W.W., and McGlothlin, W.W. Comparison of the chromosomal patterns obtained from groups of continued users, former users, and nonusers of LSD-25. *Amer. J. Psychiat., 126:* 72-81, 1969.

12. Jarvik, L.F.: Genetic aspects of aging. In: Rossman (Ed.), *Clinical Geriatrics,* Philadelphia: J.B. Lippincott, 85-105, 1971.

13. Jarvik, L.F. and Cohen, D.: A biobehavioral approach to intellectual changes with aging. C. Eisdorfer and M.P. Lawton (Eds.), *Psychological Aspects of Aging,* American Psychological Association, Washington, D.C. in press.

14. Jarvik, L.F., Kato, T., Saunders, B. and Moralishvili, E.: LSD and human chromosomes. In *Psychopharmacology,* D. Efron (Ed.), U.S. Public Health Service (No. 1836), Washington, D.E., 1968.

15. Jarvik, L.F. and Kato, T.: Chromosomes and mental changes in octogenarians: preliminary findings. *Brit. J. Psychiat. 115:* 1193-1194, 1969.

16. Jarvik, L.F. and Kato, T.: Chromosome examinations in aged twins. *Amer. J. Human Genetics, 22:* 562-573, 1970.

17. Jarvik, L.F., Altshuler, K.Z., Kato, T. and Blumner, B.: Organic brain syndrome and chromosome loss in aged twins. *Diseases of the Nervous System, 32:* 159-170, 1971.

18. Kato, T. and Jarvik, L.F.: LSD-25 and genetic damage. *Diseases of the Nervous System, 30:* 42-46, 1969.

19. Kleemeier, R.W.: Intellectual change in the senium. Proceedings of the *Social Statistics Section of the American Statistical Association, 5,* 290-295, 1962.

20. Nielsen, J.: Chromosomes in senile dementia. *Brit. J. Psychiat., 115:* 303-309, 1968.

21. Riegel, F.K., Riegel, R.M. and Meyer, G.: The prediction of retest resisters in research on aging. *J. Geront., 23:* 370-374, 1968.

22. Sharma, A.K. and Sharma, A.: "Spontaneous and Chemically Induced Breaks," In G.H. Bourne and J.F. Danielli (Eds.), *International Review of Cytology, 10:* New York Academic Press, 101-136, 1960.

Multiple System Interaction and High Bodily Concern

As Problems in the Management of Aging Patients

Eric Pfeiffer, M.D.

Introduction

Before proceeding to discuss the specific topic assigned to me, I want to make a few general observations which may place the care of the aging patient into better perspective.

It is my view that the care of aged patients is gradually but surely moving into the mainstream of American medicine. By this I mean that the care of elderly patients is no longer confined to chronic care hospitals and/or nursing homes ("warehouses for the dying," as President Nixon labeled these facilities in 1971) but is increasingly being carried out in acute care hospital facilities, in outpatient clinics, and in the offices of physicians. This is a welcome change, signalling not only a change in location but of quality of care, a change toward earlier and more active intervention in the diseases affecting the elderly.

I believe that this change has come about as a result of the removal of a number of important barriers which have previously restricted the utilization of medical services by the elderly. The barriers of which I speak have been of three varieties:
1. attitudinal barriers
2. financial barriers
3. knowledge barriers

Let us examine these barriers in some detail now. First, there has been a lessening of the attitude (both among the laity as well as among health professionals) that older persons are not worth treating or that they are not treatable. Thus it has often been falsely alleged, on the one hand, that older people had only a few years left to live; on the other hand, it has been stated that the diseases of old age should be accepted as a natural concomitant of old age. Actually, both of these assertions are wrong. A man already 65 years of age can expect to live 13 more years, on average, while a woman already 65 years of age can expect to live 16 more years, on average. Even at age 75 a man may still expect to live an additional 8 years, while a woman who has attained age 75 may expect to live an additional 10 years, on average. Nor does the myth of untreatability of older patients hold up under close examination. Elderly patients do in fact respond remarkably well to treatment (at times, they respond only too well, as we shall see below) and the occurrence of illness in old age, as in younger age, must be seen as a call not for lamentation but for intervention.

While attitudinal change has occurred, it must be admitted that this change on the part of the lay public and on the part of health professionals has thus far only been gradual and is as yet not complete.

The same can be said regarding the falling away of financial barriers. Until very recently the vast majority of the aged either could not afford adequate medical care or they at least *felt* they could not afford medical care, the result being the same in either case. Considerable progress has been made with the arrival of Medicare and Medicaid in removing financial barriers to the receipt of medical care by the elderly. However, the out-of-pocket expenses borne by the elderly are still quite large. Thus, the per capita health expenditure in fiscal year 1971 was $861 for persons 65 years and older but only $250 for persons under 65. (1) Of this $861 only between half and two thirds is paid for by programs like Medicare or Medicaid or other third party payers, such as private insurance. The rest places additional burdens on the budgets of the elderly, budgets which are already constricted to poverty or near-poverty levels. But nowhere has medical care coverage been so inadequate as in the coverage of psychiatric care for the elderly, particularly outpatient psychiatric care, the need for which is experienced by many elderly patients. So that while financial barriers have been reduced, they have not been removed, and still hinder free access by the aging population to medical services.

Also, it is only in the last decade and a half that a substantial body of knowledge regarding the aging process and the treatment of the diseases of old age has been accumulated. Several excellent and fairly comprehensive volumes are available. (2,3) But this body of knowledge is as yet not widely disseminated, as witness the infinitesimally small amounts of teaching in geriatrics and gerontology offered in present medical school or nursing school curricula. Again, this is changing gradually, but much remains to be done. Conferences like the present one attest to the growing accumulation of knowledge and interest in additional knowledge, but they also constitute signposts of how far we still have to go.

What Makes Care of the Aged So Unpopular?

In what follows I want to discuss two important factors which contribute to making the care of the aged patient so unpopular—and it is still unpopular, there can be no doubt about that. These factors are, briefly stated: multiple system interactions and high bodily concern.

Multiple System Interactions

In dealing with aged patients the clinician often finds that he has gotten more than he bargained for. An initially simple medical problem suddenly becomes complex. Treatment of one symptom or disease process not uncommonly produces, releases, or exaggerates other symptoms or disease processes. Moreover, the clinician often finds that whereas he began his treatment of a particular patient as a medical specialist, let us say as internist or as a psychiatrist, he may soon find himself functioning as a generalist, attending to both physical and psychological problems. One clinician may start out treating someone for a purely psychological complaint, let us say, for anxiety, and suddenly find himself dealing with heart failure. Or another clinician may begin by treating someone for hypertension, say with reserpine or some combination of a diuretic plus other antihypertensive drugs, and suddenly have a suicidal patient on his hands.

The situation described above stems from the fact that many of the physical and psychological adaptive systems of older persons are operating near the edge of their reserve capacity. Any additional burdens placed on these systems will result, more readily in old age than in younger years, in symptom formation, regardless of whether the burdens of which we speak are noxious external or internal environments, or whether they are well intended but nevertheless disequilibrating medical interventions.

The brief case histories which I will present below will amply illustrate the points made here. But before going on to discuss how we can cope with multiple system interactions in older persons, I want to go on to a second major factor which complicates the care of elderly patients.

High Bodily Concern

Hypochondriasis is an anxious preoccupation with one's own body or a portion of one's own body which the person believes to be either diseased or functioning improperly. Hypochondriacal concerns are relatively common among older patients, particularly among older women. Relatively few physicians, psychiatrists and non-psychiatrists, have learned how to adequately care for hypochondrical patients. In fact, many physicians have enough trouble coping with patients who present with openly admitted psychological problems; but they find particularly difficult coping with patients who present psychological complaints in the guise of physical complaints, and who will resist all attempts to retranslate these back into psychological language. In fact, hypochondriacal complaints tend to provoke extremely negative feedback from physicians and laymen alike, thus exaggerating the need for renewed symptom formation.

Without going into any great details into the dynamic origins of hypochondriasis, a very simple translation of the patient's hypochondriacal complaint would be "I want to be taken care of by a doctor." Obviously, the phrase, "There is nothing wrong with you" is not an adequate response to that person. But a response to the effect that "I will be glad to be your doctor and to take care of you" is a more adequate response. Further details of a treatment approach to hypochondriasis have been presented by Busse and Pfeiffer. (4)

The Need for Modification in Technique

Just below, I want to present several case histories, all of which make a point which I am very anxious to have clearly understood. This point is not that the treatment of older people is difficult—it is, at times—or that older people do not respond to treatment—in fact, they often respond only too well. My basic point is that the disorders arising in old age are in fact highly amenable to treatment but only if important modifications are introduced into standard techniques, modifications which take into account the special needs and limitations of older people, whether these limitations be psychological or physiological. (5)

Modifications must be made in the way a medical history is gathered; in the interpretation of the historical data obtained; and in the way instructions about a medical regimen are presented to the patient—very slowly, and one by one. Moreover, the older person's family, including one or more of his adult children, must be brought into the treatment picture, both in terms of obtaining a medical history, and in terms of explaining and supporting a treatment program designed for the older person. Obviously, this places additional demands on the busy clinician, and further decreases the popularity of the art of caring for older patients.

And now for some clinical examples:

Case Illustration No. 1

Mrs. A was a 66 year old married woman. She was referred by her internist for psychiatric evaluation because she "has had the medical group here in X at its wits' end." She was said to have "a series of mystifying symptoms," including headaches, itchiness of the skin, dryness of the mouth, and frequent urination, all of which "defy diagnosis." She had been to many specialists in X and had been worked up extensively by each of them, all with "negative" results.

In my examination of this lady I found her to be presenting her complaints in a manner typical of the hypochondriacal patient. It was a very dramatic and pained presentation of her many complaints, the reflex reaction to which could only be withdrawal and rejection of the patient. There were a number of interesting facets to her illness, however. She described how she had first come to depend on physicians when she had discovered a lump in her breast. She related how the physician had at first minimized the significance of the growth, but later the growth had proven to be malignant. She related that she underwent radical mastectomy, but that she was not told until a month after the operation that her breast had been removed because, according to her, the doctor had felt that she "wouldn't be able to take it." While the surgical intervention was actually a success (no evidence of recurrence of tumor 7 years post-operatively), the interaction around the breast lesion may have in fact established a pattern for relating to the world through physical complaints.

On detailed psychological examination in the hospital she was found to show the personality pattern typical of hypochondriacal persons, with elements of depression also present. More surprisingly, however, was the fact that she was discovered to have a very significant organic brain syndrome of which she could not permit herself to become aware. It became evident that her present hypochondriacal symptoms were in fact a plea for being taken care of for physical reasons since she could not admit the loss of intellectual functioning. This lady was treated in the hospital with anti-depressant drugs and with psychotherapy as well as with counseling being provided to her husband. Her depression lessened and her hypochondriacal complaints decreased, allowing her husband to be able to be more supportive, knowing that her intellectual decline necessitated such support.

Case Illustration No. 2

Mr. B was a 78 year old man, a retired vice-president of a large pharmaceutical firm, who had retired at age 65 and who had expected to live only four or five more years after that. But, as you all know, you can't count on dying. One day he woke up and was 78 years old and found himself having run out of a program of anything to do. He became markedly depressed and stayed in bed all day. The only activity he engaged in was the compulsive recitation of childhood verses and homilies, which of course was very disturbing to his wife, and he was subsequently admitted to the psychiatric hospital. On formal mental examination, he was intellectually entirely intact. He did, however, show signs of severe depression and of ruminative and obsessional anxiety. With hospitalization and with attention to planning for what he might do for the remainder of his life (this included plans for long postponed activities, such as undertaking to learn to type and to write his autobiography, while learning to type. His autobiography turned out to be a fascinating document of life around the turn of the century in rural Pennsylvania, Minneapolis, Minnesota, and New York City.), he improved rapidly and was discharged home.

About half a year later, he had a mild myocardial infarction for which he was hospitalized briefly and during the hospital stay, because of some mild failure, was placed on digitalis, diuretics, and a low-salt diet. He was told also to restrict his physical activity severely. The result of this was that the patient again became depressed. Since he thoroughly disliked the low-salt diet, he ate virtually nothing but continued to take his diuretics faithfully. Within a few weeks he had become lethargic, intermittently drowsy, dizzy to the point of fainting on rising from a sitting position, and finally, stumbling and confused, he was again brought to the hospital by his wife. What had happened, of course, was that as a result of his low food intake and the concomitant, perhaps unnecessarily restrictive, cardiac regimen including low-salt diet and diuretic therapy, he had developed electrolyte depletion and consequent orthostatic hypotension, with some actual, though reversable, organic brain impairment. He was hospitalized, placed on a regular diet, diuretic therapy was discontinued, and, within a week, he was functioning well again. He was no longer depressed, ate with a hearty appetite, regained weight, and was discharged home to continue on digitalis therapy regularly but on only intermittent diuretic therapy with an essentially unrestricted diet. He was also encouraged to be more physically active, avoiding only heavy work or work under extreme temperatures. (Mr. B was interviewed by the author before the conference participants for approximately seven minutes).

Case Illustration No. 3

Mrs. C was a 67 year old widow from one of the rural counties in North Carolina. She had a previous history of depressive reactions, some of which had been treated with electric shock therapy. In the two months prior to admission, she had become markedly depressed and had gone to see her family physician who had prescribed Elavil, 25 mg four times daily for her. Approximately 24 hours before admission she became grossly and acutely disturbed and combative. She began to shout and curse, using language which her seven children thought was most unbecoming for their ordinarily very religious and very pleasant mother. She expressed the fear that she would be killed, or should be killed, and tried to fend off illusional attackers. She was admitted to the psychiatric hospital on an emergency basis and the admitting resident thought she was an interesting case of *psychotic* depressive reaction or of an involutional *psychosis*. I agreed that she certainly was psychotic.

Close mental status examination, however, revealed that she was totally disoriented for time and place. She could not recognize her own children or her surroundings and at times became extremely frightened and agitated. Her mental state fluctuated from hour to hour, adding further evidence to the likely diagnosis of delirium, rather than a functional psychosis. In fact, EEG pattern at time of admission showed substantially slowed alpha wave pattern as well as some fast activity in the EEG pattern. Because of her extreme agitation, anxiety, and gross delusions that someone was going to kill her, she was given very low dosages of Thorazine, 25 mg four times daily, after an initial 50 mg I.M. dosage. Over the course of approximately seven days her psychosis and evidence of intellectual impairment all cleared and at the end of the period she had a normal EEG, normal cognitive functioning, and only some mild depressive symptomatology which, it was felt, was best handled on an out-patient basis, emphasizing increased social interaction rather than drug therapy for its treatment. The discharge diagnosis was acute organic brain syndrome, with psychosis, on the basis of drug intoxication.

Case Illustration No. 4

Miss D was a 67 year old spinster, a former schoolteacher, who lived in a church-related retirement home. She was admitted to the psychiatric service after she had sustained a series of falls over a period of time. She had bruises on both sides of her head as well as on other parts of her body. The history was that she had become depressed in the retirement home and that the doctor there had placed her on Mellaril, 50 mg two times daily, and also on Sinequan, 50 mg four times daily. On admission, she had a blood pressure of 80 over 50 and clearly staggered when she tried to walk. She was confused as to time and place, and was unable to give a history of recent events. Again, it was felt that she was suffering from a delirium caused in part by the medication (Sinequan) and in part by hypotension due to the combined drugs. Again, removal from drug therapy in the hospital caused her to gradually clear her delirium. Her EEG on admission was abnormal, and repeat EEG was improved, following seven days without drugs. The blood pressure returned to 110 over 70, and the patient was left with only a very mild depression, which again was felt could be managed best by social interaction and provision of meaningful activities, rather than through further pharmacological therapy. She was discharged back to the retirement home.

Discussion of Clinical Examples

In the case of Mrs. A we had a physical symptom (the breast lesion) and its treatment, setting the pattern for the patient's future psychological interaction. That is, being ill with a real physical illness provided her with a model of how to be taken care of by others by developing physical symptoms even though no organic disease existed.

In the case of Mr. B we saw an interesting interaction between the treatment for a physical illness, i.e. heart failure, and the recurrence of depression, which led to further physical disability, that is, to orthostatic hypotension and reversible organic brain impairment. In the case of Mrs. C we had the treatment for a psychological illness, namely depression, by a drug, namely Elavil, leading to a second psychiatric disability, namely a toxic delirium, which was treated by removal of the "therapeutic" or the "disease-causing" drug, depending on one's point of view.

In the case of Miss D we had a somewhat similar situation in which two psychotropic drugs led to a combination of hypotension and toxic delirium which led to further physical symptomatology, namely falls and bruises. Again, removal of the therapeutic or disease-inducing drug resulted in improvement.

Conclusion

From all this we can conclude that it is not simple but nevertheless rewarding to treat older people whose adaptive systems are on the edge of their reserve capacity. We must be inordinately cautious in the dosage of drugs used with older persons because such drugs frequently induce other psychological or physical symptoms or diseases. Nor are psychological or social interventions entirely without risk. But since this is a conference on the psychopharmacology of aging, I shall confine myself more narrowly. It is humbling to realize, nevertheless, that in each of the cases which I have presented, a major component in the patient's illness was medically induced in an attempt to remedy an existing medical problem.

The point to be made is not that we should or should not use drugs with our aging patients but that drug treatments must be extremely carefully tailored to the entire system of bodily and psychological systems within a given elderly patient.

References

1. U.S. President (Richard M. Nixon), *Message on Older Americans,* March 23, 1972, Washington, D.C. (press release)

2. Busse, E.W. and Pfeiffer, E., Editors. *Behavior and Adaptation in Late Life.* Little, Brown and Company, Inc., Boston, 1969.

3. Palmore, E., Editor. *Normal Aging.* Duke University Press, Durham, North Carolina, 1970.

4. Busse, E.W. and Pfeiffer, E.Functional Psychiatric Disorders in Old Age, in E.W. Busse and E. Pfeiffer (Eds.), *Behavior and Adaptation in Late Life,* Boston: Little, Brown and Company, 1969, pp. 183-235.

5. Pfeiffer, E. Psychotherapy with elderly patients. Postgraduate Medicine 50:254-258, Nov. 1971.

Responses to Psychotropic Drugs in the Normal Elderly

Carl Salzman, M.D.
Richard I. Shader, M.D.

Advancing age is often accompanied by disorders of mood and mental function. Common examples include depression that accompanies losses, anxiety over health and the future, agitation resulting from impaired perceptual processes, and impaired cognitive abilities stemming from a wide range of organic brain dysfunction. In their mild forms, these symptoms are present to varying degrees in many elderly persons. Not infrequently, as the symptoms persist or worsen, medical assistance is sought; in our "medicated" society both elderly patient and doctor may agree that drugs will be beneficial.

As psychopharmacology has advanced over the past few decades, drugs have been developed which had the potential for offering relief from many of these symptoms frequent among the elderly. Because the doctor and patient may share a sense of futility about the ultimate resolution of symptoms, there seems to be a pharmacological adventurousness that encourages the trial of all sorts of medications for the relief of symptoms which may accompany advancing age.

Unhappily, pharmaceutical progress in the development of potentially useful drugs in the elderly has not been matched by adequate research to evaluate these agents. Consequently, myriad substances appear which are dispensed by doctors to the elderly, or are purchased by the elderly for self-medicating purposes. The rationale for such drug use by both physician and patient often stems more from anecdotal evidence or bold advertising proclaiming drug efficacy, than from independent research data. Relative to psychopharmaceutical research among younger patient populations, there exist relatively few efforts to carefully study, in controlled fashion, the effects of psychotropic drugs in the elderly.

159

Our laboratory, for more than a decade, has been interested in the study of psychotropic drug effects upon mood in mild symptomatic volunteer subjects. In our past work, we have endeavored to focus attention upon those traits that exist within the subject which may interact with the pharmacology of the drug to produce a net clinical effect. More specifically, we have studied the effect of pre-existing levels of anxiety, depression, and hostility on thymoleptic properties of various psychotropic agents. Recently, we have begun to study the effect of sexual differences upon drug activity, and within women, the effect of the menstrual cycle upon mood alteration with and without drugs. Two years ago, we began to examine the possible differential interaction between age and drugs which affect mood. We quickly became aware of the lack of research documenting many claims for drug effect in the elderly. We also became aware that prescription of drugs to the elderly was rather haphazard; dosage schedules were often based on a pediatric model: start lower and increase slower, (1) while controlled efficacy studies were often lacking.

From these bases, we elected to initiate a series of studies which, with our laboratory framework of work with normal volunteers, would provide some very basic clinical information regarding the effect of commonly prescribed drugs for mood disturbances in the elderly. This paper chronicles the second study in the series. The research generally aimed at determining (1) whether outpatient volunteer studies were indeed possible, and (2) what were the effects of some commonly prescribed drugs at typical dosages on certain mood target symptoms.

Materials and Methods

Three drugs were selected for study at doses commonly prescribed to the elderly. It is interesting to note that many of our subjects actually had been prescribed some of the drugs, at the present doses we employed. The drugs and dosages were:

Diazepam (Valium)	2 mg	t.i.d.
Phenobarbital	15 mg	t.i.d.
Methylphenidate (Ritalin)	5 mg	t.i.d.

The research design called for a one week study, utilizing a shared pool of placebo subjects for multiple comparisons as illustrated in Figure 1. All subjects were randomly assigned to a treatment group; drugs were administered according to a randomized, double-blind schedule.

Figure 1
Statistical Research Design:
("Bonferroni t", Multiple Comparison)

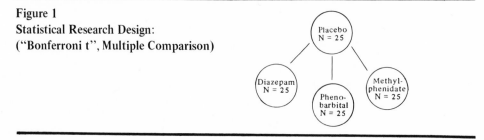

One hundred subjects over the age of 60 were recruited from advertisements in local Boston newspapers. Subjects were medically and psychiatrically screened before inclusion in the study. Subjects were paid for their participation and for transportation to and from our laboratory. It is extremely significant to note here that most of our subjects enjoyed participating in the study. Many commented that financial remuneration was of secondary importance; they participated because they wished to help scientific research particularly in the needed field of geriatrics. An identification summary of the subject population is presented in Table 1.

Table 1
Identification of Subjects

	X Age	SD	N
Total	68.86	5.635	100
Male	68.20	4.987	49
Female	69.49	6.179	51

Four paper and pencil tests which assess mood and cognitive function were employed as dependent variables. The tests and their baseline scores are displayed in Table 2.

Table 2
Dependent Variables: Mean Pre Drug Scores

	Present Study	First Geriatric Study	Young Research Volunteers
Wechsler Memory	131.65	—	—
Scheier-Cattell Anxiety Battery	5.91	—	5.99 (males and females)
Psychiatric Outpatient Mood Scale:			
Tension	5.38	5.75	11.76 (males only)
Anger	2.70	2.62	5.82 (males only)
Depression	3.81	3.30	8.02 (males only)
Vigor	10.54	9.73	9.49 (males only)
Friendliness	11.25	10.99	8.98 (males only)
Fatigue	4.09	5.16	5.06 (males only)
Confusion	3.85	4.19	4.96 (males only)
MMPI Depression (D_{60})	21.58	22.61	20.18 (males and females)
Dempsey Modification (D_{30})	5.61	6.11	6.61 (males and females)
Taylor Manifest Anxiety Scale (TMAS)	11.03	11.71	14.60 (males and females)

Prescores from the current population are shown in comparison to an earlier geriatric population (members of golden age clubs), and young (ages 21-35) normative research volunteers who participated in other studies in our laboratory. The Wechsler Memory Scale (2) is a frequently used test of memory function that has been found to be sensitive to drug effects in elderly subjects. The Scheier-Cattell Anxiety Battery (3), an 8 parallel form repeated measures self-rated instrument, has been used extensively in our laboratory, and has been found to be sensitive to psychotropic drug effects. The Psychiatric Outpatient Mood Scales (4) in its unrevised form consists of 7 subscales rating tension, anger, depression, vigor, friendliness, fatigue, and confusion. Depression was assessed chiefly through the D_{60} depression scale taken from the MMPI. The shortened Dempsey modification of the D_{60} eliminates certain items (such as those with religious or somatic content) which makes it more sensitive to depressive affect in healthy young populations. It was included here in order to learn of its sensitivity in a geriatric population who might respond to those items that were less sensitive for young adults. In addition, two self-rated scales were administered at the beginning of the study, but were not repeated as dependent variables. They were the Taylor Manifest Anxiety Scale, and the Zung Self-rated Depression Scale. It is readily apparent that the present elderly research population, as well as the previous one, reports itself as generally less symptomatic than younger subjects.

At the beginning of the study week, rating scales were filled out in our laboratory by all subjects. They were then instructed to take the capsules provided thrice daily for a one week period; at the conclusion of the research week they returned to the laboratory and completed a second set of rating scales. This format for psychopharmacological research is standard procedure in our laboratory. We feel that taking drugs for at least one week more closely approximates a clinical setting rather than administering one acute dose and observing its effect on the same day. We were pleased to note that our elderly subjects did not have difficulty in completing the research; in fact, only 2 elderly subjects left the study prior to its completion.

Results

Because of the particular research design employed utilizing three drugs compared independently against placebo, the statistical procedure used for data analysis was the Bonferroni multiple comparison t test. (5) Since our aim was not to compare active drugs with each other, this statistic was more appropriate than the one way analysis of variance (ANOVA) so often used in psychopharmacology research. ANOVA was, however, used to determine comparability of pre-treatment groups. Statistical data were computed from change scores. These scores were obtained by subtracting the pre-drug score on a given mood instrument from the post score; mean change scores were thus obtained and used for analysis. Table 3 records mean change scores for the overall study. It can be seen that the data are striking for their lack of significant results. However, because of the conservative statistical approach, and because of the hypothesis seeking nature of this study it does seem useful to highlight those changes which are suggestive of further research.

Table 3
Mean Change Scores

	Placebo	Valium	Phenobarbital	Ritalin
Wechsler	− 0.080	− 2.320	2.680	3.120
SCAB	−36.640	−45.360	−47.880	−55.960
POMS T	− 0.880	0.160	− 0.640	− 0.800
POMS A	− 0.880	− 0.880	− 0.320	− 1.240
POMS D	− 0.720	− 1.440	0.240	− 0.960
POMS V	− 0.920	− 0.040	0.040	− 1.160
POMS FR	− 0.520	0.520*	− 0.280	− 0.440
POMS FA	− 0.720	1.280**	0.400	− 0.280
POMS C	0.160	0.320	0.040	0.040
D_{60}	0.520	− 0.640	0.520	− 0.680
D_{30}	− 0.320	− 0.040	− 0.360	− 0.080

* $p < .15$ Bonferroni t, 2 tailed
**$p < .174$ Bonferroni t, 2 tailed

1. The results with diazepam reveal an overall trend toward increasing both friendliness and fatigue. These findings are consistent with the clinical impression that diazepam may be somewhat sedating in its first few days of use; positive therapeutic responses to drugs may make subjects see themselves as more friendly.

2. The lack of significant antidepressant effect of methylphenidate, which is often prescribed for mild depressions in the elderly, is noteworthy. This drug also failed to demonstrate any anti-fatigue or anti-confusion activity. Methylphenidate did reduce anxiety scores on the SCAB and POMS t subscale more effectively than either diazepam or phenobarbital, although these latter two drugs are typically used to treat mild anxiety states in the elderly.

3. Phenobarbital slightly *increased* depression as measured by the D_{60}.

Table 4
Mean Pre Scores, Males vs. Females

	Males	Females
Wechsler	134.265	129.137*
SCAB	5.95	5.87
POMS T	5.061	5.686
POMS A	2.571	2.824
POMS D	3.082	4.510
POMX V	10.694	10.392
POMS FR	11.102	11.392
POMS FA	3.184	4.000
POMS C	3.837	3.863
D_{60}	21.490	21.667
D_{30}	5.490	5.725
TMAS	10.449	11.588

* $.1 > p > .05$ t-test for independent samples

Our change score data were next subdivided according to sex. The mean pre-drug scores of subjects thus subdivided are illustrated in Table 4. With the exception of lower Wechsler Memory scores for the female cohort, the two subsamples were essentially alike prior to drug treatment. Mean change scores were next computed by drug for each sex separately. The results for males are presented in Table 5.

Table 5
Male Change Scores

	Placebo	Valium	Phenobarbital	Ritalin
Wechsler	− 0.429	− 3.786	6.182	0.0
SCAB	−55.643	−64.286	−42.455	−14.200
POMS T	− 0.929	0.286	− 1.455	− 0.700
POMS A	− 1.286	− 0.500	− 0.273	− 0.600
POMS D	− 0.857	− 1.500	− 0.364	0.0
POMS V	− 1.286	− 0.071	0.182	− 2.400
POMS FR	− 0.286	0.286	0.0	− 1.400
POMS FA	− 1.000	1.000	− 0.455	− 0.300
POMS C	− 0.071	− 0.143	− 0.091	− 0.100
D_{60}	1.286	− 1.786*	0.0	− 0.400
D_{30}	− 0.214	− 0.143	− 0.273	0.100

* $< .027$ Bonferroni t, 2 tailed

Only one significant finding emerged: diazepam had a noticeable *antidepressant* effect as recorded by the D_{60} scale. Female change scores are presented in Table 6.

Table 6
Female Change Scores

	Placebo	Valium	Phenobarbital	Ritalin
Wechsler	0.364	− 0.455	− 0.071	5.200
SCAB	−12.455	−21.273	−52.143	−83.800
POMS T	− 0.818	0.0	0.0	− 0.867
POMS A	− 0.364	− 1.364	− 0.357	− 1.667
POMS D	− 0.545	− 1.364	0.714	− 1.600
POMS V	− 0.455	0.0	− 0.071	− 0.333
POMS FR	− 0.818	0.818*	− 0.500	0.200**
POMS FA	− 0.364	1.636	1.071	− 0.267
POMS C	0.455	0.909	0.143	0.133
D_{60}	− 0.455	0.818	0.929	− 0.867
D_{30}	− 0.455	0.091	− 0.429	− 0.200

* $p< .002$ Bonferroni t, 2-tailed
**$p < .16$ Bonferroni t, 2-tailed

Two significant findings emerged on the POMS friendliness scale. Diazepam and methylphenidate both increased friendliness as compared with placebo. In Table 7, the results of a statistical comparison between male and female subjects is presented.

Table 7
Male vs. Female Change Scores

	Male Change	Female Change	Sig.
POMS V (Ritalin)	− 2.400	− 0.333	0.02
POMS FR (Ritalin)	− 1.400	0.200	0.04
D_{60} (Valium)	− 1.786	0.818	0.05

t test for independent samples, 2 tailed

It can be seen that although diazepam was a better anti-depressant for males it also decreased vigor and friendliness more than in the female subsample.

Discussion

Although positive, statistically significant findings are virtually absent from this study, we believe a number of important observations may be made.

1. Psychopharmacology research with normal geriatric volunteers on an outpatient basis is not only feasible and practical, but enjoyable and rewarding for both researcher and subject. We were most impressed with the ready cooperation and general spirit of enthusiasm evinced by many of our subjects despite the difficulties in traveling to our laboratory during New England winters, and despite apprehensions about receiving an unknown medication.

2. Although we endeavored to use common drugs at usual therapeutic doses for this population, we obtained very little positive clinical effect. Three explanations are possible. First and simplest, it may be that we used insufficient doses. While this is a likely possibility, we must wonder about the supposed clinical efficacy of these three drugs at these usual doses. Second, it may be that the essential normality of the population vitiated any psychotropic drug effect. While this, too, is possible, we note that younger populations who are essentially normal do display significant clinical effects on target symptoms of anxiety and depression. We do not see any *post hoc* reason why subjects over the age of 60 should not behave in similar fashion. Thirdly, it may be that research subjects who are grouped together simply because they are over the age of 60 are far too heterogeneous to be considered as one research sample. Large standard deviations in our statistical analysis tend to support this supposition. There may be no more of a "geriatric" research population, than there is a "pediatric" population. Careful selection of particular research samples may provide clearer and more meaningful results.

3. Although statistically significant findings were few, a number of interesting drug comparisons emerged by inspection. Table 8 summarizes the observations for diazepam, for phenobarbital, and for methylphenidate.

Table 8
Summary of Results

Diazepam
1. Increased friendliness, particularly in females
2. Increased fatigue in both males and females
3. Decreased depression in males
4. Increased confusion, more than other drugs, particularly in females
5. Best antianxiety drug for males; least useful for females

Phenobarbital
1. Improved memory scores, particularly in males
2. Slight increase in depression, particularly in females

Methylphenidate
1. Increased friendliness
2. Best improvement in memory, particularly in females (who started lower than males)
3. Best antianxiety agent for females; worst for males
4. Decreased vigor, particularly in males
5. Less useful than placebo for decreasing fatigue
6. Best antidepressant for females

---

4. Our observations lend credence to earlier comments that males and females react differentially to psychotropic drugs. Methylphenidate, for example, showed a decrement in anxiety, but only among the female subjects. Diazepam, on the other hand, demonstrated significant antidepressant activity only among the males. Two explanations seem likely. There is some suggestion that elderly males may be relatively more susceptible to the antidepressant effects of drugs than are females. In the first geriatric study in our laboratory, males receiving a geriatric elixir, Alertonic, reported greater antidepressant effects than did females. Such findings are also compatible with those of Prange, Lipton and colleagues who have noted the earlier and greater responsiveness of males to imipramine (7).

It may also be that elderly males and females differentially define dysphoric affects. In this sample, a relatively strong correlation existed between the anxiety and depression scales used for the study ($POMS_T$ x $POMS_D$, r = .63; D_{60} x $POMS_T$, r = .55; D_{30} x SCAB, r = .48). It would seem, therefore, that there is an overlap between these target symptom scales. Although the scales may measure the same affects to a certain degree, males and females may use different adjectives to describe their dysphoric affects.

5. There is another implication of the present results which we wish to share. It is likely that the rating instruments employed in this study may have less relevance for the elderly

than for younger research populations. We have commented elsewhere (8-10) on the problems attendant upon rating the elderly research subject or patient. The present results are now being examined to determine which questions on the various rating instruments were particularly relevant to our elderly research sample.

A number of future research directions are suggested by this study.
1. Dose-response studies should be undertaken in elderly volunteers to assess drug effects at different dose levels.
2. Studies should take into consideration the differential response between sexes.
3. Further work must be carried out on rating systems to assess drug effect. Rating scales developed for younger populations may have different meaning to the elderly subject, and only limited relevance.

Summary

One hundred volunteer subjects over the age of 60 were given one of three commonly prescribed mood-altering drugs or placebo. At dosages used in clinical situations, these drugs produced very little self-rated alteration in mood for the overall research sample. When drug effect was examined separately in males and females, some suggestive differential effects emerged. Diazepam was found to have some antidepressant effect in males, methylphenidate appeared to have some antianxiety effect in females. Phenobarbital had little effect in either population except to mildly increase depression, particularly in females. The implications of differential drug response according to gender were discussed, and future research directions were outlined.

References

1. Hander, M.: The use of selected phenothiazines in elderly patients: A review. *J. Mount Sinai Hosp. N.Y. 32:* 622-633, 1965.

2. Wechsler, D.: A standardized memory scale for clinical use. *J. Psychol. 19:* 87-95, 1945.

3. Scheier, I. H., Cattell, R.S., and Sullivan, W.P.: Predicting anxiety from symptoms of anxiety. *Psychiat. Quart. (suppl) 35:* 114-126, 1961.

4. McNair, D.M., and Lorr, M.: An analysis of mood in neurotics. *J. Abnorm. Psycho. 69:* 620-627, 1964.

5. Kirk, R.E.: Experimental Design: *Procedures for the behavioral sciences.* Belmont, Calif., Brooks Cole, 1969, p. 79.

6. Shader, R.I., and DiMascio, A.: Drug studies in normals: Sex differences. *Presented at the Annual Meeting of the American College of Neuropsychopharmacology,* Las Vegas, Nev., January 21, 1972.

7. Prange, A.J., Wilson, I.C., Know, A.E., McClane, T.K., Breese, G.R., Martin, B.R., Alltop, L.B., and Lipton, M.A.: Thyroid-imipramine interaction: Clinical results and basic mechanism in *Brain Chemistry and Mental Disease*. Ho, Bent T., and McIsaac, William M. (ed), New York, Plenum Press, 1971, p. 197.

8. Salzman, C., Shader, R.I., Kochansky, G.E. and Cronin, D.M.: Rating scales for research with geriatric patients. I. Behavior Ratings. *J. American Geriatrics Society 20:* 209-214, 1972.

9. Salzman, C., Kochansky, G.E., Shader, R.I., and Cronin, D.M.: Rating scales for psychotropic drug research with geriatric patients. II Mood ratings. *J. American Geriatrics Society 20:* 215-221, 1972.

10. Salzman, C., Kochansky, G.E., and Shader, R.I.: Rating scales for geriatric psychopharmacology: A review. *Psychopharmacology Bulletin 8:* 3-50, 1972.

Emotional Responses to Physical Illness

Adriaan Verwoerdt, M.D.

Determinants of Psychological or Psychopathological Responses

The psychological responses to physical illness include coping and defense mechanisms as well as emotional reactions experienced as 'feelings'. The type and intensity of these somatopsychic reactions depend on the interaction of many factors, which can be grouped into three categories: (1) stresses pertinent to the physical illness per se; (2) characteristics of the 'host' and (3) situational factors. Processes of interaction among the foregoing factors may be considered as yet another category.

A. Characteristics of the Physical Illness

Severity of the Illness:

This factor includes considerations regarding the magnitude of the actual physiological disorder, the severity of subjective symptoms, the degree of anticipated disability, and the extent to which the illness is life-threatening (1).

Time Factors:

Severity of the illness at a given point in time is not a reliable basis for accurate prediction of the psychological response. One must also take into account the time factors — that is, the duration of the illness and its rate of progression in the course of time (2). Slowly developing conditions allow more time for adaptation, both organic and psychological. A rapidly progressing illness, on the other hand, may have overwhelming psychic and somatic effects. Beigler (3) found that patients with fast-growing malignancies showed more evidence of anxiety than patients with slow-growing malignancies.

One specific measure, in which the time factor is used retrospectively, is called 'distance to death'. This is the interval between the point in time at which the investigator observes certain phenomena about the patient and the time at which death occurs. This longitudinal approach was used in a study of 30 patients thought to have a fatal illness (4), who were studied with regard to feelings of hopelessness, changes in time sense, and other variables. A follow-up study one year later revealed that 22 patients had expired, the median distance to death being two months. Those patients who had died within two months had manifested more evidence of hopelessness and had been less future-oriented than the patients who had died from two to nine months after the time of testing.

Organ System Involved:

Some organ systems (e.g., cardiopulmonary) are essential to biologic functions; others (e.g., musculoskeletal) are less important. Systemic diseases have widespread repercussions throughout the entire organism; in other conditions, the effects remain more or less localized. Some illnesses (e.g., skin disease) affect body parts accessible to the patient's sight; others, such as intestinal malignancies, are hidden. It is reasonable to assume that disease in any organ system produces specific 'signals' which originate at the site of the disturbance and are transmitted along somatic or visceral afferent pathways to the central nervous system, where they are registered as messages about the state of the 'interior' (4).

In some patients with a disease that has widespread, systemic repercussions such as carcinoma of the pancreas, careful history may reveal that the very first symptoms consisted of a vague, ill-defined depression. Thus, it would be wise to suspect and look for early systemic disease when one encounters a patient complaining of depression, especially if there have been no depressive episodes in the past.

The apperceptive capacity of the central nervous system can be defined as its capacity to evaluate the significance of afferent stimuli by comparing them with past experience. Because apperception is impaired in organic brain damage, it is important to distinguish between illnesses involving cerebral impairment and those involving extracerebral pathology. In the former, the very 'organ of adaptation' itself is affected, so that the final psychological response reflects the specific distortion caused by the mental impairment.

Characteristics of the 'Host'

Since illness and its repercussions on the patient's life situations are interpreted in terms of his characteristic life style and past experiences, the meaning of a particular disease will be quite different for different persons and the somatopsychic response pattern of every patient will have its own unique spectrum. Among the personality related variables contributing to the final psychological response is constitutional endowment (including intelligence and other 'ego apparatuses', as well as preferred response patterns) (5); experimental factors (e.g., early and later interpersonal relationships); educational level; and vocational achievements.

A person free from major intrapsychic conflict has more flexibility and resilience, and a greater repertoire of effective coping strategies. Individuals with intrapsychic conflict, however, must expend valuable energy in dealing with the internal, neurotic pressures; their coping mechanisms tend to be reduced in range and effectiveness and their overall adaptation is tenuous and rigid. As long as they do not encounter stresses too great for the narrow range of their homeostatic capacity, they may present an appearance of well-being and psychological equilibrium. Even minor stresses, however, can throw their fragile balance out of kilter.

The capacity to adapt successfully is also influenced by congenital defects or acquired disabilities, either physical or mental. The person unable to comprehend issues because of mental retardation is clearly limited in his attempts at adaptation. When illness-related stresses exceed his capacity to cope he may respond in a primitive fashion (by projection or primitive motor patterns, for example) or may decompensate, becoming agitated and confused. Likewise, patients whose range of physiological homeostasis is reduced to narrow limits may be seriously handicapped in their attempts to master stress. In the case of juvenile diabetics and youthful hemophiliacs, one may observe a cluster of highly maladaptive defenses, consisting of denial, projection, and counterphobic mechanisms.

Age and Sex:

The role of age is illustrated by the observation that, at age 7, the loss of a tooth signifies growth and is a source of pride, whereas at age 70 it signifies decline and is a cause of grief. Various mental and physical capacities develop at different rates of speed, reaching peak performance levels at different points in the life cycle. In considering the influence of age upon a particular illness, therefore, it is necessary to go beyond merely chronologic age, and to define age in terms of the maturational level of specific biologic, psychological, and social capacities. Because general homeostatic capacity, recuperative ability, resilience, and energy gradually decline with advancing years, stresses occuring late in life may have a greater impact than those occurring earlier. The stress involved in sexual involution serves to illustrate the roles played by both age and sex. Women cope with the stress of menopause during their 40's and 50's. Sexual involution in men tends to occur in the 60's and 70's, when the overall capacity for coping is not as great as during the middle years. The advantage to the male of a longer period of reproductive ability may well be offset by the advantage that women have of coping with the stress of involution while they still have many other resources (6).

The Body Image:

Sociocultural conditions being what they are, disabling illness may present a more specific threat to men; disfiguring illness, to women. In both instances, the psychological reaction depends not only on the actual impairment but also on its symbolic significance. The latter is determined by many personal and interpersonal factors, one of these being the body image. The latter is the conceptualization of the body's structure and functions and includes the ego's perceptions, thoughts, and feelings in reference to its own body (7).

As illness interferes with different physiological functions, different psychological concerns are activated. Patients with emphysema, for example, often present somatopsychic phenomena based on fears of suffocation. Less intense in the immediate agitation it produces, but profound in its disruption of body image, is disease which affects psychically significant sites. Involvement of the reproductive organs may bring loss of sexual capacities and disturbance in sexual identity; disease in the lower intestines may result in bowel incontinence and concomitant fears of losing control in general and of becoming helpless. Many of the fears and fantasies associated with diseases which gravely impair organ function are somatopsychic elaborations of the physiological disturbances. Such psychological manifestations cannot be separated from their basic physiological causes. Hence, they must be distinguished from anxieties involving body image which occur in purely psychodynamic disorders, such as cancerophobia, conversion reaction, hypochondriasis, and the somatic delusions encountered in schizophrenia and psychotic depression.

The psychological reaction to the loss of a body part (teeth, eyes, breast, limb) or the loss of a function (e.g., colostomy or hysterectomy,) includes grief and depression, shame and embarrassment, as well as apprehension about the future impact of the body alteration on interpersonal relations, occupational performance, etc. Patients with a colostomy, for example, experience a serious narcissistic injury; embarrassment can be intense, and there may be concerns about the effect of the colostomy on sexual intimacy. It may be very difficult for such a patient to reorganize the body image and to integrate the colostomy as part of it.

Another example of discomfort associated with altered body image is the painful phantom limb. Apparently, this phenomenon is frequently related to unresolved emotional conflicts concerning the loss of the limb or the circumstances in which the injury occurred.

Characteristics of Premorbid Personality:

The concept of character or personality includes the typical behavioral response patterns of the individual and his unique style of adaptation and mastery. It also reflects the nature of the individual's defense system, particularly his ego strength. Knowledge concerning the premorbid personality may enable the clinician to predict the psychological response patterns when illness occurs.

In some cases, a premorbid behavior pattern will be intensified under the impact of the illness. A passive, dependent individual may welcome illness as a means of permitting him to gratify his dependency needs. Physical illness may also be not unwelcome to guilt-ridden or masochistic personalities; since the disease satisfies their need for punishment, their emotional state may actually improve during the illness. For immature and inadequate persons, illness can provide escape from adult responsibilities.

Sometimes physical illness is the lesser of two evils. For example, an ambitious, hard-striving, middle-aged man who discovers that he has fallen short of the goals set by his ego-ideal, may find in illness an alibi that covers his shortcomings, be they real or imagined.

Individuals whose premorbid personalities showed prominent reaction-formations may react to physical illness in a surprising way. The emotionally distant personality, whose coldness is the result of reaction-formation against tender feelings, may use the illness situation for the expression of emotional warmth and intimacy. Thus, physical illness may come to be the currency that permits the exchange of emotional warmth between persons who otherwise have a distant relationship. Physical illness may be used in a similar way by patients who are overly self-reliant. They may publicly protest but secretly enjoy being sick, because the illness forces them temporarily into a position of dependency and receptivity. If, however, the illness becomes prolonged or disabling, so that the reaction-formation of excessive self-reliance is jeopardized, the patient may first fight back with an exaggeration of the very traits of self-reliance. Later, when he no longer has enough energy to sustain this behavior, this rigid line of defense may suddenly give way to regressive behavior such as excessive helplessness and dependency.

Schizoid personalities, or lonely and isolated persons, may view illness as a secure bridge leading toward another human being. They may wish to hang onto their illness — or their sick role — because the contacts with nurses and physicians provide them with a safe and predictable type of closeness. Such patients tend to develop an attachment to the hospital or clinic in general, rather than to specific members of the medical or nursing staff.

In personalities who are action-prone or tend to act out, illness interferes with the habitual pattern of activity. Anxiety, depression, and regressive behavior may be the result, especially if action had been used to ward off intrapsychic tension. Physical illness may also bring about anxiety and depression in personalities who are obsessive-compulsive, or perfectionistic. It simply becomes impossible for the patient who used to be a perfectionist to live up to his high standards.

For narcissistic personalities, physical illness is a special threat, because it represents an attack on the integrity of the body and the body image. Such individuals may have prided themselves on possessing unusual attractiveness, physical strength, or sexual prowess. The loss (either real or imagined) of these attributes leads to lowered self-esteem.

C. Situational Factors

1. The Illness Situation:

The individual with a physical illness is confronted with the necessity of assuming the sick role. For many people, this new pattern of dependent behavior is not easy to adopt, because dependency may connote inferiority and hence create feelings of guilt and hostility. Nevertheless, despite the desire to retain his independence, the patient generally responds by gradually surrendering to dependency needs. When strong denial and counterphobic mechanisms are active, however, this adaptive device is obscured and the patient tends to resist appropriate regression, — and to ignore limitations imposed by the disease and the treatment program. The physician-patient relationship is an important factor in shaping some of the patient's reactions to illness. Difficulties in the doctor-patient relationship may arise from a great variety of sources (8). Hospitalization may be refused by the patient who interprets it as confirmation of the seriousness of his illness. The patient who accepts hospitalization is usually faced with difficult adjustments, separation from home surroundings being the most consistent traumatic factor (9, 10).

2. Family Relationships:

The family may not easily accept the patient in the sick role. They may resist decisions made by medical personnel which tend to remove the patient from his usual activities, and attempt to view his symptoms within the framework of normality. When it becomes necessary to hospitalize the patient, the family may feel that they have rejected him. This feeling of guilt causes some families to make undue financial sacrifices or give the patient excessive attention.

If the patient is hospitalized for a long time, it is often necessary for the family to reorganize itself, establishing new patterns of relationships to fill the gap left by the patient. These may work out so well that problems arise when the patient returns home.

Problems of an intergenerational nature are not uncommon between elderly patients and their adult children. The latter have to recognize that they can no longer look to their parents for the support they used to receive in earlier years. It is a critical point, when a person realizes that his aging parents are no longer pillars of support but that they themselves now need the support of their children. If the relationship between adult children and their parents has been mature, the transition of roles can be made without difficulty. But when the adult child has remained immature or dependent, a crisis occurs, and he may not permit the elderly parent to become dependent. Because he continues unrealistically to regard his parent as capable and independent, the latter is subjected to the stress of having to play a role he does not want to fill and is not able to fill. In other cases, the problem originates with the parent, who may cling to an obsolete set of roles or to an outdated self-concept. In most instances, however, difficulties in the process of role reversal are due to psychological factors in both the aging parent and his adult child.

When a patient reacts to physical illness by becoming overly helpless, this regressive behavior can be a heavy burden on the family, particularly because the regressed patient frequently feels both angry and guilty about his dependency. While regression involves a withdrawal from certain adult roles and responsibilities, in true withdrawal there is a moving away from other people. The resulting isolation increases the patient's preoccupation with himself and sets the stage for the development of hypochondriasis.

Regression and withdrawal represent two types of 'moving away from'; sometimes the patient 'moves against' others, because he perceives them (on the basis of projection) to be responsible for his plight. This pattern is usually associated with feelings of hostility, ideas of being neglected, and angry accusations. The scapegoats may strike back with counter-accusations which, in turn, prove to the patient the correctness of the original ideas − all in all, a self-fulfilling prophecy.

Another type of aggressive reaction is manifested by an attempt to control others in the family. The patient may manipulate them by trying to make them feel guilty, by flattering them, by self-depreciative behavior, or other neurotic security operations. The family members may expend much time and energy in this tug-of-war, to the detriment of all concerned.

Instead of moving against others, the patient may turn against himself and become depressed. Even in such cases, one often detects an undertone of hostility beneath the facade of contrite self-accusations. The depressive symptoms may have the purpose of communicating, 'Look how much I suffer, how miserable you make me feel!' The shift from interpersonal toward intrapsychic pathology as the patient turns against himself may cause the family to become less aware of how the patient really feels and what goes on inside of him. Such problems in awareness and communication are manifestations of disturbed family interaction in general.

For some families, stress and crisis are a way of life. While a family may complain about their burdens − e.g., the presence of a sick relative in their home − it is precisely this stress that could be holding the family intact. Some families are close only during times of crisis or illness. Stressful circumstances are not always unwelcome − because the external crisis makes it unnecessary to face one's inner conflicts.

Types of Psychopathological Responses

A. Coping Behavior and Defense Mechanisms

Coping strategies include all the mechanisms, conscious as well as unconscious, used for adapting to environmental demands. The term defense mechanisms refers to the mental processes that serve to protect the individual against dangers from his impulses or affects. Adaptive coping leads to re-establishment of a dynamic equilibrium that was disturbed by stress. Maladaptive coping behavior typically leads to a vicious circle which, by depleting the patient's resources, aggravates the very problem it is supposed to solve.

In general, it may be said that an individual's coping attempts can be aimed at three types of phenomena: (a) the objective fact (the illness per se), (b) the meaning and action-implications of the illness, and (c) the person's feelings about the illness and its implications. Unless these phenomena are considered separately in exploring the spectrum of the patient's response patterns, one's formulations regarding the patient will lack clarity.

Coping strategies and defense mechanisms against the stress of physical illness can be classified into three categories, according to their goal, which may be (1) to retreat from the threat and conserve energy; (2) to exclude the threat or its significance from awareness; or (3) to master the threat. Various degrees of overlap occur in these mechanisms, and several may collaborate to achieve the same end.

Whether a defense is adaptive or maladaptive depends on its intensity as well as its appropriateness to the particular situation. Adaptive devices presuppose some cognitive awareness of illness, a willingness to seek medical help, and a realistic adjustment to the sick role. Quite often, it is the intensity of a defense — the extent to which it is being used — that makes it maladaptive. Mild degrees of denial, for example, are adaptive in many illness situations, except when the denial focuses on the very existence of illness.

(1) Defense aimed at Retreat from the Threat and at Conservation of Energy

This type of defense is represented primarily by regression — a retreat into earlier modes of adaptation and of relating to others. Its chief features are restriction of interest in the external world, self-centeredness, bodily overconcern (hypochondriasis), and increased dependency. Regression commensurate with the severity of the illness is useful, since it enables the patient to accept appropriate help. Excessive regression, however, characterized by markedly egocentric behavior, and absorbing hypochondriasis, is maladaptive, because other persons tend to view the individual as 'uncooperative'. A vicious cycle of mutual escalation of antagonistic behavior is the result.

The distinction between regression and withdrawal was discussed earlier. Withdrawal of 'psychic energy' (interest, or attention), from the affected structure or function is actually a form of regression, and insofar as it insures therapeutically useful rest, it is an adaptive response. When the patient begins to exclude the affected structure of function from his customary repertoire of anticipated activity patterns, he may reach the point where he avoids any role or any situation that calls for that particular activity. The maladaptive aspect of this type of withdrawal is that it may cause a rupture in object relations and lead eventually to disengagement, isolation, and loneliness.

(2) Defenses aimed at Excluding the Threat or its Significance from Awareness

These defenses include suppression, denial, rationalization, depersonalization, externalization (projection), and internalization (introjection).

Suppression is a conscious, willful attempt to dismiss certain thoughts or feelings from awareness. Diversionary activities become more difficult when a person is weakened by disability or illness. The increased idleness and passivity inherent in being sick, disabled, or isolated tend to put the mechanism of suppression out of commission. Nighttime may be especially difficult because of the additional lack of sensory input.

Denial is a mental mechanism by which a fact, its implications or the feeling aroused by these, are denied or not recognized. Denial may be aimed at the factual existence of an illness, at its significance and implications, or at the emotional reactions to being ill. Much more common than the denial of the illness is denial of concerns and problems associated with it. Mild forms of denial are probably conducive to good adjustment; but extreme denial, often coupled with aggressive, rebellious protest, tends to be self-destructive, since it causes the patient to neglect medical advice. Complete denial of the fact of an illness suggests serious psychopathology.

Rationalization is a process of reasoning whereby true causal relationships are ignored, minor aspects of a situation are emphasized out of proportion, or major aspects are minimized. Facts, conditions, or symptoms are ascribed to causes that are less threatening than the real ones.

Depersonalization involves a protective blurring of ego boundaries. The usual distinction between self and not-self becomes less clear, and the result is a sense of estrangement from reality. The protective quality of depersonalization lies in the individual's feeling that 'this experience is not really happening to me; it is just like a dream'.

Externalization and internalization also involve a blurring of boundaries between the self and the not-self. The former is the mechanism by which one ascribes to other people one's own undesirable condition, thoughts, or feelings; the latter is a reverse process. In externalization (or projection), the fact of the illness cannot be ascribed to others unless mental disorganization is of psychotic proportion. Frequently, however, the patient projects the cause of his condition onto somebody or something external. Projection of feelings of anger also, is very common. Internalization is the process by which a person attributes to himself something that actually came from without. A male patient in his 60's had been informed by his physician that biopsy of a lymph node in the neck revealed the presence of metastasis, probably from lung cancer. During an interview, some days later, he said: 'My internist told me something about malignancy...no, that wasn't it...I remember now, that was my own idea. It seems like I thought that myself'.

(3) Defenses aimed at Mastery and Control

These include intellectualization and isolation of feelings from thoughts, counterphobic and obsessive-compulsive mechanisms, and acceptance and sublimation.

Intellectualization and the separation of ideas from painful feelings associated with them (isolation) represent attempts at mastery by reliance on a cognitive, intellectual approach. Persons who use a counterphobic mechanism combined with intellectualization often seem to move into the area of the very danger itself. They may read extensively about their illness, follow the latest research findings, and want to be fully informed concerning the tests performed on them.

Acceptance and sublimation represent the ideal resolution of loss or disability. The mental processes involved show a similarity to the resolution of a grief reaction. After the loss has been worked through, and accepted, the patient becomes less self-centered and broadens his interests beyond the narrow scope of his own self toward the wider range of the group, the community, or even mankind as a whole.

B. Emotional Responses

Psychological reactions to illness also include a variety of emotional responses: anxiety, grief, depression, guilt, shame, and anger.

The actual loss of an object which has the qualities of something important to the psychic function of the individual results in grief or reactive depression. Toward the end of the grief reaction (which may last from 3 to 12 months) energy and interest begin to be redirected toward new people, goals, functions, or activities. This resolution of the grief reaction results in establishing new object relations. When part of the self is lost, as by amputation, the resolution may be more complex, involving a form of inner realignment, reorientation toward the self and the world, and reappraisal of previously held values. Successful adjustment is characterized by restoration of self-esteem, rooted in a framework that views personal worth on the basis of one's intrinsic value as a unique person; by acceptance of the loss and integration of the limitation into a new self-concept; and by a successful search for new ways of maintaining closeness to others and realizing remaining potentials.

Although grief usually occurs after the damage or loss has actually taken place, anticipatory reactions are not uncommon; by preparing the individual in advance, they can be beneficial in hastening post-factum adjustment periods.

A grief reaction should be distinguished from depression which, although difficult to define in exact terms, is generally considered as a pathological emotional reaction. A grief reaction involves a conscious recognition of an actual loss. Depression, on the other hand, does not necessarily follow an actual loss but can be precipitated by an imagined loss (rejection, for example). In many cases the depressed patient is not clearly aware of the nature of the loss he is responding to.

Depression is usually distinguishable on the basis of the depressive affect, the biologic concomitants, the presence of guilt feelings, and the periodicity of the depressive episodes. Sometimes, however, the depressive affect takes cover so that only its so-called 'somatic equivalents' are seen clinically (11). In these circumstances, physiologic manifestations or hypochondriacal concerns predominate. This possiblity should be borne in mind in order to differentiate between physical symptoms proper and depressive somatic equivalents.

The presence of guilt feelings may cause the patient to hold onto the more painful symptoms of his condition as a form of self-punishment. It is not uncommon in clinical practice to find depression and guilt feelings based on hostile identification with a relative who died of an illness similar to that from which the patient is suffering. In most such cases the patient has not successfully worked through and resolved his feelings about the loss — usually because the relationship with that relative was characterized by considerable ambivalence.

Guilt reactions frequently arise as a result of a patient's search for an answer to the question: 'Why did this happen to me?' When no ready answers are available, the patient may revert to a less rational kind of thinking in which explanations are sought on a magical or superstitious basis. For example, he may come to regard his illness as a form of punishment for real or imagined sins.

Feelings of guilt may also be a subtle expression of denial. The patient blames previous wrongdoings for his illness, the latter representing the retribution. If he did cause his plight, could he not also take destiny in his own hands, expiate by suffering, undo and repair the damage, and restore himself as an intact person?

Feelings of shame and embarrassment arise from the painful discovery of being exposed to the eyes of others. In illnesses that entail helplessness or profound alterations of the body image, shame is a common emotion. The patient may be ashamed of the illness itself or of the loss of face imposed by the resultant helplessness or physical disability. In patients with breast cancer, for example, reactions of shame often lead to denial, rationalization, etc. which may be responsible for delays in obtaining appropriate medical help. Following mastectomy, the patient may try to cope by covering up the cause of embarrassment. Any undue amount of shame, however, is maladaptive: not only do the cover-up attempts necessitate withdrawal from the spouse, but the patient's embarrassment is contagious and her husband begins to feel embarrassed too. Like many other maladaptive coping strategies, the attempt to cover up leads to a 'self-fulfilling prophecy' which sets up a vicious circle.

Anger and hostility represent a 'fight' reaction to a threatening obstacle in one's path. This behavior can be useful when directed against frustrating objects outside the organism; but when the source of distress lies within, as in the case of illness, it is inappropriate. Although neither fight nor flight can remove the threatening object, since it is within the self, anger may give the patient the illusion that aggressive counter-attack will succeed in doing so.

Aggressive people habitually reacting with anger to frustration tend to use projection and this tendency may become more pronounced under the stress of illness. These patients frequently deny the seriousness of their disease, suppress concerns over it and over-compensate by resorting to increased activities to 'prove' their intactness. The anger originally stemming from their physical disability is projected outward by blaming something in the environment.

Some patients resort to anger because they can tolerate aggressive feelings more easily than grief and anxiety. The anger represents a screen to cover up other painful emotions, on the premise that 'the best defense is a good offense'. Anger may also signify a protest against the blows of a cruel fate, as reflected in the bitter question, 'Why did this have to happen to me?' Any such behavior is maladaptive when, by preventing the patient from seeing the true state of affairs or by alienating others, it make conditions less optimal for obtaining medical help and less conducive to recovery.

References

1. Verwoerdt, A.: "Communication With the Fatally Ill" (Charles C. Thomas, Springfield, Illinois, 1966), p. 183.

2. Dovenmuehle, R.H. and Verwoerdt, A.: "Physical Illness and Depressive Symptomatology. II. Factors of Length and Severity of Illness and Frequency of Hospitalization," *Journal of Gerontology* 18:260-266, July 1963.

3. Beigler, J.S.: "Anxiety as an Aid in the Prognostication of Impending Death," *Archives of Neurology and Psychiatry* 77:171, Feb., 1957.

4. Verwoerdt, A. and Elmore, J.L.: "Psychological Reactions in Fatal Illness. I. The Prospect of Impending Death," *Journal of the American Geriatric Society* 15:9-19, 1967.

5. Fries, M.E. and Woolf, P.J.: "Some Hypotheses on the Role of the Congenital Activity Type in Personality Development," *The Psychoanalytic Study of the Child* 8:48-62, 1953.

6. Szalita, A.B.: "Psychodynamics of Disorders of the Involutional Age," Vol. II, Ch. 5, *American Handbook of Psychiatry*. (S. Arieti, Editor) (Basic Books, N.Y., 1966).

7. Hinsie, L.E. and Campbell, R.J.: "Psychiatric Dictionary," (4th edition) (Oxford University Press, N.Y., 1970).

8. Bogdonoff, M.D.; Nichols, C.R.; Klein, R.F.; and Eisdorfer, C. "The Doctor-Patient Relationship," *Journal of the American Medical Association* 192: 45, April 5, 1965.

9. Verwoerdt, A. and Dovenmuehle, R.H.: "Heart Disease and Depression" *Geriatrics* 19:856-864, 1964.

10. Cherkasky, M.: "Home Care of Chronic Illness," *Journal of Chronic Diseases I:346,* March, 1955.

11. Ewalt, J.R.: "Somatic Equivalents of Depression," *Texas Journal of Medicine* 60:654, Aug., 1964.

Antianxiety Agents

Samuel Gershon, M.D.

It should be stressed at the outset that this presentation will mainly point out the deficiencies in our knowledge rather than present any substantial body of scientifically significant data. There is a dearth of information on specific therapeutic efficacy of anti-anxiety agents in the geriatric population, on aspects of differential side effects, on potential differences in metabolic handling, and on drug interaction problems that may arise when anti-anxiety agents are given concurrently with drugs employed for medical management. In determining the therapeutic efficacy of these drugs we must consider such problems as a potentially high placebo response rate and the choice of psychological rating scales which are relevant and sensitive to an elderly population. Salzman and Shader have outlined the difficulties encountered by investigators in this area. We will discuss these problems in terms of each of the following categories: a) population, b) diagnosis, and c) chemotherapeutic agents.

a) The Population

The number of aged persons has increased both relatively and absolutely in recent years. The percentage of this elderly population that needs care and treatment is also expanding, but clear-cut statistics are not readily available. For instance, authorities may agree on criteria for illness, but may disagree in individual assessment of the degree of helplessness, distress, and potential danger.

The other change that has taken place is the change in the pattern of care for older family members. A three-generation family living physically or geographically together is a rarity nowadays, and with this change additional stresses on the older members have appeared. Different forms of housing and care for the elderly have been developing, though they do not necessarily represent improvements. Heightened morbidity and mortality rates have been associated with the entrance of aged into institutions. (Aldrich and Mendkoff, 1963; Blenkner, 1967; Jasnau, 1967; Lawton and Yaffee, 1967; Lieberman, 1961; Miller and Lieberman, 1965; Goldfarb and Turner, 1966).

b) Diagnosis

Even here matters are not clearly defined, unless we assume that the considerations relevant to anxiety in younger adults apply equally to the elderly subject. Otherwise the standard textbooks do not address themselves specifically to this issue. Roth (1955) has proposed a newer classification of mental disorders occuring in old age, but this also does not concentrate on anxiety symptomatology. He does, however, stress the important fact that the majority of disorders of old age are not characterized merely by profound and progressive deterioration. Geriatric psychiatry must become a discipline in its own right. The aged have different host qualities for psychiatric disorders, and the symptomatology seen in them may not fit automatically within the established systems of classification developed for a younger age group.

The typical burdens of the elderly, physical impairment, illness, and poverty, are understandable precursors of depression and anxiety. We may find that depressive features frequently accompany anxiety states in the aged. This profile may in varying degrees be superimposed upon loss of abilities and capacities and varying degrees of organic brain syndrome. Although the incidence of organic brain disease with its typical psychiatric manifestations is quite high in the older age group, it must be remembered that there are also many geriatric patients with functional psychiatric illness (Roth, 1955, and Kral, 1961). Anxiety is often encountered in the aged as a rather primitive body focused type, the result of pain, disability, dyspnoea, fragility, and failing bodily functions.

c) Chemotherapeutic Agents

Almost all the psychotropic drugs tried to date have been used in the elderly. The predicted areas of utility and target symptoms for which they are administered in the elderly are based primarily on observations made in younger persons who are in relatively good physical health. This basis for therapeutic indication may not be valid, both from the point of view of psychopathology and, even more so, because of differences in sensitivity and side effects resulting from possible metabolic differences in the aged. These issues have been considered in detail by Shader and Di Mascio (1970).

Some of the pathological changes of aging or aspects of an organic brain syndrome may substantially modify the clinical effects of these agents. Variations in absorption, circulation, metabolism, and excretion may affect the dosage needed. The half-life and toxicity as well as the clinical effect must be considered (Salzman, Shader, and Perlman, 1970). These are some of the general issues which must modify any evaluation of the data to be discussed. Discussion of the use of anti-anxiety agents in the elderly must start with a consideration of the group of so-called minor tranquilizers. This would include the barbiturates, benzodiazepines (chlordiazepoxide, diazepam, and oxazepam), and the propanediols (e.g. meprobamate and tybamate). Based on studies carried out in younger populations, all of these agents, based on pooled data, have been shown to be superior to placebo for the treatment of anxiety. Based on these considerations alone we might assume that any of these agents might also be considered as efficacious for the treatment of anxiety in the elderly.

There is enough evidence to suggest that the barbiturates are inappropriate for an elderly population. Delirium is considered to be a frequent side effect of barbiturates given to the elderly (Bender, 1964; Gibson, 1966). The data on propanediol (meprobamate) have not indicated consistent efficacy. It would appear that greater interest now resides in the benzodiazepine group for the treatment of anxiety in a geriatric population.

No double blind controlled studies of anti-anxiety agents in a geriatric population appear to have been published. Of the open studies available, no assessment instruments specifically relevant to anxiety symptoms in this population appear to have been employed. Clearly, there is serious need for developmental work in the realm of geriatric psychopharmacology.

A review of specific reports is of course pertinent to our discussion. Jones (1962) assessed the effect of chlordiazepoxide in geriatric patients. His population were residents of nursing homes admitted for nursing care, not for psychiatric reasons. Twenty-five subjects were given 30-75 mg/day, usually 30 mg/day. In this setting it was used primarily as a sedative and hypnotic. No rating scales were employed and no specific assessments of anxiety were made. However, the report does address itself to the incidence of side effects. Although most patients were receiving concomitant medication for various medical conditions, no untoward drug interactions appeared. In fact, it was felt that it was better tolerated than barbiturates.

Experience with another benzodiazepine (Valium) in the elderly patients is available from Chesrow *et al.* (1962). Fifty eight patients with various neuropsychiatric disorders were selected with an average age of 72 years. Twenty four were treated for anxiety reactions, 21 for depression with confusion, 11 for agitated depression, and 2 for paranoid reaction. Half the group received the drug at a dose of 1 mg tid, and the other half, 2 mg tid. There was no placebo. Treatment ranged from four to six months. Only global clinical assessments were made. Evaluation of these data indicate that the lower dosage was ineffective. Global assessment of response to the higher dosage was as follows: 22 of 24 patients with anxiety reaction showed a moderate or marked improvement and 2 were unchanged. Fourteen of 21 patients with depression had a marked or moderate improvement; in all 11 with agitation, a moderate or marked improvement was attained. Furthermore, no significant clinical side effects or laboratory changes were recorded. From these reports it would appear that benzodiazepines are effective and safe anxiolytics in a geriatric population. In a recent study by Feigenbaum (1971) the efficacy of chlordiazepoxide was compared with thioridazine. The design was double-blind, control with a one-week placebo and a seven-week medication period involving 20 subjects assigned to chlordiazepoxide and 24 to thioridazine. The average age for the group was 75 years, and almost all had some evidence of organic brain syndrome and secondary medical involvements. The average daily dose of chlordiazepoxide was 21.5 mg., and of thioridazine, 42 mg. The psychiatric assessments employed were a modified BPRS and a geriatric behavioral rating scale. Both drugs produced significant improvement on many of the recorded parameters, including anxiety and tension. However, at the end of the study (7 weeks on drugs) no significant difference in efficacy appeared between the drugs. The only area of difference was in the incidence of side effects, where declines of more than 20 mmHg in systolic blood pressures were noted in four thioridazine subjects and one chlordiazepoxide and 3 thioridazine subjects exhibited declines of more than 10 mmHg in diastolic blood pressure. Thus, although equivalent efficacy is established in this study, the question of placebo response is unanswered as no placebo group was included. In an uncontrolled study, thioridazine (75 mg/day) plus fluoxymesterone was effective in the treatment of anxiety (Deutsch et al., 1970).

The studies considered here lack a placebo control group in a population which has been shown to exhibit a significant degree of placebo response. This deficiency seriously mitigates any possible conclusions from such studies. Additionally, the studies reported to date do not employ rating instruments geared to assess anxiety or specifically for research in the elderly. Thus we do not have clear evidence on what is the best anxiolytic for use in a geriatric population. However, looking to the future, newer classes of agents might hold great promise. One such class of agents that should be seriously considered includes some of the active ingredients of tetrahydrocannabinol. Furthermore, it is possible that other derivatives may be able to give us compounds with a high order of anxiolytic activity together with a low incidence of side effects in this special population which is particularly susceptible to untoward effects from currently available psychoactive medications.

References

Aldrich, C.K., and Mendkoff, E. Relocation of the aged and disabled: A mortality study. *J. Am. Ger. Soc.,* 11, 185-194, 1963.

Bender, A.D.: Pharmacologic aspects of aging: A survey of the effect of increasing age on drug activity in adults. *J. Amer. Ger. Soc.* 12; 114-134, 1964.

Blenkner, M. Environmental change and the aging individual. *Gerontologist:* 7, 101-105, 1967.

Chesrow; E.J., Kaplitz, S.E., Breme, J.T., Musci, J. & Sabatini, R. Use of a new benzodiazepine derivative (VALIUM) in chronically ill and disturbed elderly patients. *J. Am. Ger. Soc.* 10, 667-670, 1962.

Deutsch, M., Saxena, B.M., Lehmann, H.E. and Ban, T.A. Combined administration of thioridazine and fluoxymesterone in the treatment of geriatric patients. *Curr. Ther. Res.* 12, 805-509, 1970.

Feigenbaum, E.M. Assessment of behavioral changes and emotional disturbances in a custodial geriatric facility. Presented as a Scientific Exhibit, 124 Annual Meeting Amer. Psychiat. Assoc. Wash. D.C. May 3-7, 1971.

Gibson, I: I.J.M.: Barbiturate delirium. *Practitioner* 197: 345-7, 1966.

Jasnau, K.E. Individual versus mass transfer of neuropsychotic geriatric patients from mental hospitals to nursing homes, with special reference to the death rate. *J. Am. Geriat. Soc.* 15, 280-284, 1967.

Jones, T.H.: Chloriazepoxide and the geriatric patient. *J. Am. Ger. Soc.* 10, 259-263, 1962.

Kral, V.A. The use of thioridazine in aged people. *Canad. Med. Ass. J.* 84, 152, 1961.

Lawton, M.P. & Jaffee, S. Mortality, morbidity, and voluntary change of residence of older people. Paper presented at Annual Meeting of American Psychological Association, Washington, Sept. 5, 1967.

Lieberman, M.A. Relationship of mortality rates to entrance to a home for the aged. *Geriatrics,* 16, 575-579, 1961.

Miller, D., and Lieberman, M.A. The relationship of affect state and adaptive capacity to reactions to stress. *J. of Geront.* 20, 492-297, 1965.

Roth, M. The natural history of mental disorder in old age. *J. Ment. Sci.* 101, 281, 1955.

Salzman, C., Gochansky, G.E., and Shader, R.I., Rating scales for geriatric psychopharmacology.

Salzman, C., Shader, R.I., and Perlman, M.: Psychopharmacology and the elderly, In Shader, R.I. and Di Mascio, A. (Eds.). *Psychotropic Drug Side Effects.* Williams and Wilkins, Baltimore, 1970, 261-279.

Shader, R.I. and DiMascio, A. *Psychotropic Drug Side Effects.* Williams and Wilkins, 1970.

Shahinian, S.F., Goldforb, A.I., and Turner, M. Death rate in relocated residents of nursing homes. Paper presented at 19th Annual Meeting of Gerontological Society. N.Y.: Nov. 4, 1966.

Management of the Patient in the Home and Community

Daniel T. Peak, M.D.

In dealing with psychopharmacology this conference is mostly concerned with the internal environment of the individual. We have heard very sophisticated discussions of neuro chemistry, synaptic transmission, enzyme transfers, etc. I would like to direct some remarks to the external environment and the interaction of it and internal functioning. I would like to make a plea for the same intensive study of the external environment when the patient presents himself in our consulting rooms. This is definitely easier said than done. However, I believe that the first rule of any good treatment is a complete understanding of the problems involved. I suggest that a comprehensive assessment of the total life situation of the elderly person is necessary before any effective treatment program can be formulated, including drug therapy.

I would briefly like to mention two projects which have been carried on at Duke University which focus on the difficulties of such comprehensive evaluation. The first is the Information and Counseling Service for Older Persons which began as a demonstration project in the Spring of 1967. The purpose was to set up an agency to assist the elderly in solving their problems whatever they were. We were interested in the types of problems the elderly were having, the types of elderly population with which we were dealing, and the uncovering of needs that were not being met. Briefly, the project revealed that most elderly were referred to us for emotional, marital, family and interactional types of problems. Some 60% of the referrals were for these reasons. Secondly, people were referred for institutional placement; thirdly, for problems related to health.

A major finding in the delivery of services was the necessity for coordination of the proper services to assure their delivery or to make the older person, in some cases, aware of them, and sometimes to lead them to help. The iceberg effect was apparent, in that the presenting problem was often only a small part of a complex of problems of family interaction, physical problems, and psychological problems. A multi-faceted approach was necessary. The population we served were people from very low income groups or from the upper income groups. People in the middle income range were not receiving services as often as the extremes. This problem of delivering of services to this middle group is now well known and is generating some attention in prepaid health plans.

Our current project is much more extensive in scope and is called the OARS Project (Older Americans Resources and Services Program). While this project focuses on a number of issues, a major one is again the accurate and objective assessment of the elderly individual. Every aspect of the person's life must be studied. In so doing we have come up with a five dimensional system which we believe can be used to give a comprehensive rating of function. The five dimensions are: physical health, mental health, social resources, economic resources, and activities of daily living. In this project we quantitatively assess these functions and arrive at an indicator which can be used as a guide to the degree of structured environment needed—the least structured being the home situation and the most a general hospital. We are attempting to itemize exact services needed and to arrive at a cost evaluation of these services so that the most efficient, effective, and least expensive way of providing needed services can be achieved. I strongly believe that such evaluation is necessary before any type of treatment plan is devised. It may be that our treatment arrows hit the bulls-eye, but we may be shooting at the wrong targets.

I would like to focus on a number of issues that relate to the elderly person and his environment. It has become evident in studying aging and elderly persons that the effects of the external environment become relatively more important with age. With the failure of internal cues and faculties, a person turns to and relies more on external supports. This phenomena has been put into practical use through the use of milieu therapy whereby an ideal environment is produced. In contrast to the use of medications, the surroundings are changed rather than the internal environment of the individual. Allied to this is a very important decision which frequently occurs at some point in the life of an elderly person and that is the question of transplanting the older person from his home environment to another setting. We have found that even in the most richly supportive environments a time may come when the individual can no longer cope and we must be aware of the traumatic effects which may result. Lieberman and others have shown that simply moving a patient from one setting to another can be related to mortality. He showed that moving a group of elderly state hospital patients from a relatively dull and lusterless environment to new and bright surroundings actually increased mortality of this group. Such a move must be carefully prepared for and the decision must include the individual to the maximum of his capability. There are cases, however, of extreme brain damage where judgment is extremely faulty and decisions must be made for him.

It is also important to understand the procedures for properly selecting the right setting. We have found that there are few guidelines for persons attempting to find an institution for an older person. In most cases this is done very haphazardly and in a non-planned way. In our present work we are attempting to devise a sliding scale of structured settings so that we may more accurately place individuals based on their present capacities and needs.

When a patient presents himself to us we must learn about his home situation. This is usually the most unstructured type of setting. Some may see it as a backward step in medical treatment but it may be necessary for the professional who deals with older people to get out of his office back into the home. Oftentimes one learns a great deal from one home visit. I realize that I am speaking about ideal situations, but I do believe that we should keep this in mind since we would like to use our limited time to the best advantage. I believe that more time and effort spent on assessment will lead to better results. This is another major focus of the current OARS Project which I previously described that is to test out this theory.

In order to give you an idea of the scope and complexity of service needs one may confront, we have come up with 22 types of basic needs which older persons have. I would like to read you this list—these include coordination of services, counseling individually and with family members, medical treatment, nursing services, physical therapy services, recreation, social interaction, personal care services, food services, hotel services, legal consultation, so called surrogate services, transportation, assistance in finding employment, vocational rehabilitation, financial assistance, checking services, day care services, respite services, and relocation and placement services, and finally psychotropic drugs. The point I am making here is that one must see the use of medications in total perspective in light of the complexity of problems older persons may have.

After a rigorous assessment medications may be considered. A number of problems are unique in the elderly. The first is the increase in side effects and the increase in idiosyncratic responses which may either be drug type or dose related. I am sure that you have heard about this during this conference. In addition, it is extremely important that the directions are followed carefully. Older persons in my experience are extremely unreliable. This is due to a number of reasons such as problems with memory, confusion, disorientation, and so forth. The easiest solution, of course, is to have a reliable person administer the drugs. This occurs in the institutional setting, but can often be arranged in the home setting. Reliable family members, visiting nurses, physician assistants, or nursing associates may be utilized. Another possibility is the development of dispensing instruments for older persons. These could be designed to compensate for failing memories. Another problem with drugs is that of poor judgment, which in some cases leads to addiction. We have seen a number of patients who, over the course of the years, have become addicted in a very insidious way. Much could be and has been said about the psychological effects of giving medications and the placebo effect. Many older persons have an increasing need to be fed, in a sense, and if given properly this aspect of the treatment can be used well.

In conclusion I would like to present several ideas from our experiences and studies in the past and from the work in which we are currently involved. A major problem is the time needed to gather information on an older person when he moves from one treatment to another. Much repetition and duplication occurs. In a small community, such as Durham, a central registry of stored information could be developed and made available while the patient is in the office. This has been developed and used in some other countries.

Another deficit is the absence of one person or agency to coordinate services for older persons. Our experience in the initial ICSOP study showed that often the community provided good services but that responsibility for correcting deficiencies or for bringing the elderly in contact with such services was often lacking. Trained, interested persons can be used for this purpose.

Specifically, the use of medications must be seen in the total complexity of the problems. We must be cognizant of failing memories, disorientation, tendencies to over indulge the use of medications. Better control of administration can be achieved. This may be done, as mentioned above, by what may seem like going back to the horse and buggy days, but with a different cast. We might consider drug clinics for the elderly where long acting drugs may be used, and, finally, we may develop the well aging clinics which have been so successful with our distant pediatric colleagues.

Psychoses in the Elderly

Bernard A. Stotsky, Ph.D., M.D.

Many studies have demonstrated the prevalence of behavioral disorders in the elderly, severe enough to be classified as psychoses. Huge numbers of aged persons, residing in mental hospitals, extended care facilities, nursing homes, rest homes, homes for the aged, in their own homes, or in the homes of their families, suffer from serious impairment due to these severe psychiatric disorders.

The symptoms may take many forms:

aggression	negativism
suicidal behavior	uncooperativeness
destructive behavior	idiosyncratic thinking
self-mutilating behavior	conceptual disorganization
noisiness	disturbances in sleeping patterns
boisterousness	bizarre rituals
bizarre delusions	delusional somatic symptoms
auditory, visual, or tactile	mannerisms
hallucinations	posturing
paranoid ideation	unpredictable giggling
hyperactivity	unpredictable crying
manic behavior	incontinence of urine
underactivity	incontinence of feces
motor retardation	inability to feed self
depression	inability to dress self
mutism	inappropriate dress
stupor	poor personal hygiene
wandering	disturbances of speech

confusion	delirium related to intake
disorientation	of medication, alcohol
extreme withdrawal	or psychoactive drugs
blunted affect	delirium related to withdrawal
	from drugs or alcohol

These disorders, observable in the community as well as in institutions, result in psychiatric hospitalization (a) when a disturbance is created, requiring intervention, either by police or by social agencies or (b) when the family is no longer able to contain the behavior at home.

The disposition of the patient with such a disorder depends on the interest, motivation, and financial resources of the interested persons, public or private, and the availability of resources for the management of these disorders. In different communities the same behavior may result in hospitalization in mental hospitals, confinement in a nursing home, temporary imprisonment, or admission to a general hospital. A crucial factor leading to admission to a general hospital is the presence of physical disease. Physical and mental disease may be so closely intertwined that they cannot be separated. Sometimes an extended period of behavioral disturbance may be followed by the acute onset of physical disease which eventuates in death of the patient after confinement in a general hospital or in a hospital for the treatment of chronic diseases.

The discussion of the psychoses of the elderly cannot be limited to patients in psychiatric facilities. Perhaps most patients with these disorders are actually being treated elsewhere—either in the community or in medical and extended care facilities. Community mental health centers have become seriously involved with the disorders of the aging patient only in the last two to three years. In the past, most psychiatric treatment of the psychotic geriatric patient has been in state mental hospitals where there are disadvantages and ultimately major risks to the patient from the standpoint of care both of his physical and his mental diseases. The elderly patient has not fared well in large mental hospitals. It is problematical whether he will do much better in smaller institutions, such as nursing homes, rest homes, and homes for the aged.

I would like to focus my discussion on the psychiatric disorders common to both diagnosed psychiatric and allegedly nonpsychiatric patients. In a series of factor analytic studies [1, 2, 3], we have identified psychotic syndromes under three basic groupings.

Organic Brain Syndrome With Psychosis

First are the organic brain syndromes associated with psychoses. We found two subgroups. In one, intellectual impairment is predominant with marked intellectual deficit, disorientation, disorganization of thought, loss of ability to perform basic self-care and social functions, withdrawal, and disturbed nocturnal behavior. These patients are usually diagnosed as suffering from senile dementias and are so disturbed in their thinking and orientation that they create concern in others. For them the outlook is grim. They almost always require institutionalization. Treatment of exacerbations of their symptoms requires tranquilizing medication, usually phenothiazines, butyrophenones, or thioxanthines. Occasionally, such patients will benefit from geriatric drugs such as cerebral stimulants (e.g. pentylenetetrazol), and vasodilators, or the ergot alkaloids (Hydergine). However, they must be carefully watched for complications and untoward side effects resulting from medication.

A second group are the more manifestly psychotic and behaviorally disturbed. In addition to intellectual impairment, particularly of recent memory, delayed recall, and time orientation, they are distinguished by auditory and visual hallucinations, ideas of reference, and paranoid ideation, either of a persecutory or grandiose nature, sometimes of an erotic nature. Their dress is often inappropriate. Speech is loud and boisterous, and they may show marked emotional lability with inappropriate giggling, sadness, and changes of mood unrelated to events which are current in their lives.

These patients are usually less regressed than those in the first group and respond well to medication and to attempts to involve them in group-oriented activity. The order of treatment usually is tranquilizing, antipsychotic medications first, to reduce excitement, agitation, and bizarre, psychotic symptoms. This is then followed by group-oriented activities. Individual psychotherapy is practically useless for such patients, though sessions which are oriented to specific, immediate, concrete goals and which often involve members of the family or other interested persons can be of great assistance. The psychosis may be a response to a specific event or trauma, such as change of residence or loss of a loved one. Sometimes it may be related to apparent provocation by another patient or a member of the staff. The behavioral disturbance is aggravated by the lack of intellectual resources enabling the patient to develop insight into the situation and to select appropriate means for coping with it.

Disorders Of Thinking

A second major grouping consists of the schizophrenic and paranoid disorders. Although schizophrenia is usually regarded as a disease of youth or early maturity, many schizophrenics grow old in the hospital and the behavioral disorder may continue into old age even in those who show some recovery or improvement following the acute phase. These people who grow old in the hospital have a hardiness as well as chronicity which makes them excellent candidates for placement in other institutionalized settings, once the more florid symptoms of their disorder are brought under control.

There are also episodic schizophrenics who become overtly psychotic in relation to some stress or traumatic series of events in their lives and improve when the external pressures decrease. As they grow older, they tend to become more paranoid and depressed so that the more obvious schizophrenic symptomology is replaced by a combination of paranoid and depressive symptoms. The residual schizophrenic symptoms emerge only on intensive interview with the observance of blunted or constricted affect, peculiarities of reasoning, and some dissociation of thinking from affect.

A third group consists of patients who appear at first glance to become paranoid in old age. A closer examination reveals that they have been sensitive, difficult persons for most of their lives, prone to grudges, resentments, extreme feelings of hostility, periods of moroseness, sullenness, and at times even negativism and uncooperativeness. They resemble the involutional paranoids and are difficult to treat because their relative intellectual intactness makes it difficult to combat their extreme suspiciousness and distrust. They, as well as paranoid schizophrenics, will be intellectually intact to a very old age and are not only suspicious of the therapist, but shrewder and more manipulative than other patients in dealing with therapists and other personnel who are involved in caring for them.

A fourth group consists of patients who seem to be on the borderline between a psychotic depression and a catatonic schizophrenia. They may either become acutely disturbed and agitated, showing a mixture of paranoid and depressive symptoms, or regress into a rigid, immobile negativistic and unresponsive state. Sometimes chronically depressed and withdrawn patients drift into a catatonic state, showing behavior reminiscent of that reported for occupants of concentration camps who gradually gave up hope of surviving, became unresponsive, refused to eat, lost weight, refused to care for themselves, and allowed themselves to die in a state of passive resignation.

I would like to delineate some of the features of these schizophrenic and paranoid disorders as obtained through factor analysis of data in our studies. The group which looked most like chronic schizophrenics we labeled hebephrenic schizophrenics, distinguished by blunted affect, emotional withdrawal, motor retardation, behavioral apathy, other motor disturbances, mannerisms, posturing, negativism, signs of inner tension, and considerable conceptual disorganization. For this group the treatment of choice was phenothiazine, butyrophenone, or thioxanthine medication combined with a vigorous program of rehabilitative and recreational activities, aggressive social work, and nursing therapy to prepare the patient for placement in the community.

We did not clearly define the group described as episodic schizophrenics, but did find patients who in some way resembled the acute episodic schizophrenics, but were also similar to paranoid schizophrenics. They were characterized by paranoid delusions, such as delusions of persecution, grandeur, and influence, occasionally erotic delusions, extreme suspiciousness, belligerence, agitation, hallucinations, mostly auditory, and unusual thought content. Intellectually, this group remained relatively intact through the most serious manifestations of the disorders. They differed from chronic paranoid schizophrenics in the acute onset of symptoms and the fluidity of their disturbed states which changed from day to day. The depressive element was more prominent in the episodic schizophrenics than in chronic paranoid schizophrenics. These patients usually responded well to phenothiazine, butyrophenone, or thioxanthine medication, combined with supportive psychotherapy and careful nursing management. Electroconvulsant therapy (ECT) was useful for patients who did not respond to the therapeutic regimen outlined above.

The third group, which we have labeled paranoid psychotics, was characterized by hostility, belligerence, grandiosity, excitement, expansiveness, suspiciousness, and delusions, but not usually by overt hallucinations. Occasionally these patients hallucinated, but quietly. They had enough insight into the unacceptability of hallucinations so that they reported them with reluctance and embarrassment. Theirs was primarily a delusional disorder, with paranoid elements most prominent. Intellectual impairment was relatively rare. Depressive symptoms and physical complaints, including difficulty with appetite, trouble going to sleep, and weight loss, were reported. These patients were highly suspicious of medication but responded excellently to phenothiazine medications which were at times given parenterally in the long-acting form. As their symptoms diminished, they became accessible to psychotherapy, which was supportive and involved brief contact (30 minutes or less).

The fourth group, which we have labeled catatonic schizophrenics, was distinguished by symptoms which bear some similarity to severe psychotic depressions, manifested by feelings of doom, death, and rotting of the body. Paranoid ideas were voiced in a verbally aggressive manner. Somatic preoccupation was often bizarre. Such patients showed negativism and sullenness and, as the disorder progressed, they became rigid and immobile. The major differences from a psychotic depression were the relative absence of suicidal symptomatology and the lesser severity of somatic symptoms. These patients sometimes had to be force-fed. In the chronic group the catatonic disturbance was more ominous because it represented an almost total withdrawal and giving up. Patients in this group were vulnerable to physical infection as they became more deteriorated and would allow themselves to die rather than accept therapeutic intervention. On the way down they became mute, unresponsive, and less and less adequate in performing the activities of daily living and self-care. In such instances, dramatic psychiatric intervention was necessary. We found it necessary to use electroconvulsant treatments, if phenothiazine, butyrophenone, or thioxanthine medications were not successful in producing improvement. Careful nursing was essential to prevent life-threatening physical diseases. Dehydration was common and required fluid supplementation by mouth or parenterally.

Affective Disorders

The third major group of psychoses is that of affective disorders.

The manic-depressive disorders continue into old age. Most are of the depressed type, characterized by depressive mood, psychomotor retardation, slowing of speech and thought, frequently associated with apprehension and agitation, sometimes with well-developed delusions, hallucinations, and paranoid ideas. In the elderly with histories of manic-depressive disorders, the depressions tend to be more of the retarded type, manifested by the loss of interest in people, inactivity, seclusiveness, withdrawal, apathy, even muteness, and, as the patients grow older, some intellectual impairment, at first in work efficiency, concentration, attention span, and ability to learn new material. Later, time disorientation, confusion, and selective memory impairment may occur. Antidepressant medications (particularly tricyclics) are useful in the milder forms of the disorder. For more severe manifestations, ECT is the treatment of choice.

A smaller group is characterized by manic episodes. These pose a serious diagnostic problem. Sometimes they can be the result of (a) toxic reactions to medication, such as steroids, cardiac glycosides, or of (b) idiosyncratic reactions to tranquilizers and sedatives. A manic reaction may be the first indicator of an organic brain syndrome. It is therefore essential when one sees a manic reaction in an elderly patient to obtain a history which reveals a previous manic episode characterized by some of the following symptoms: elation or agitation, irritability, flight of ideas, excessive talkativeness, acceleration of thought, speech, and motor activity, as well as such physical symptoms as weight loss, decreased need for sleep, and peculiar somatic symptoms and preoccupations.

Once it is determined that the patient is suffering from a manic-depressive psychosis and that this is a recurrence of an illness which has occurred earlier in life, the treatment will usually follow that prescribed for younger patients with the exception that certain precautions must be taken if complicating physical illnesses are present, such as cardiac, cerebrovascular, renal, or hepatic disorders. ECT, major tranquilizers, and lithium have to be used with due attention to the patient's present condition and with proper precautions and safeguards. Even dosage has to be adjusted with great concern for side effects as well as for the required therapeutic effect. It may be necessary to give smaller doses more frequently during the course of a day than is the case for younger adults. We have found lithium useful in the treatment of manic disorders, supplementing it with ECT or phenothiazine, butyrophenone, or thioxanthine medications during the acute phase of the disorder (the first 7 to 14 days). For therapeutic efficacy, without toxicity and annoying side effects, a blood level between 0.6 and 0.8 meq. per liter is satisfactory.

In our studies we have discovered a group whom we designated as agitated depressives. The major symptoms were overt symptoms of anxiety, tension, somatic preoccupations, worry, guilt, intrapunitiveness, hand-wringing, and depression. These patients resembled involutional melancholics. They often complained of insomnia, usually of the early morning variety, though many had difficulty falling asleep. They were usually free of marked delusions and did not ordinarily communicate feelings of doom or death until late in the disorder. These patients responded well to psychotherapy and medication, particularly the major tranquilizers (phenothiazines, butyrophenones, or thioxanthines) or combinations of tricyclic antidepressants and major tranquilizers.

The response of this group of patients to treatment was very gratifying. If psychotherapy and medication failed, ECT was almost always effective. Six to eight treatments were sufficient. Many psychiatrists prefer ECT as the treatment of choice because of the rapid relief it brings to such patients. These patients are usually intact intellectually. Such impairment as occurs is usually the result of anxiety and depression, the former producing a marked decrease in attention span and ability to concentrate and the latter a decrease in speed of response, particularly on tasks requiring psychomotor coordination or rapid verbal responses.

A third group with affective disorders consists of patients who respond to extreme stress or trauma with a combination of agitation, depression, and delusional thinking, usually of a morbid kind. These patients report feelings of doom or of impending death. Paranoid thinking may be present, without the aggressiveness and belligerence of paranoids. Vague beliefs of the existence of a conspiracy or reluctant accusations of malevolent intentions may be voiced. They will give vent to somatic concerns, ranging from reasonable physical symptoms to delusional beliefs that their bodies are rotting and that they are dying of a serious disease. Vegetative symptoms, such as poor appetite and extreme sleep disturbance, are frequent.

Psychotic depressive reaction best fits this group as a diagnosis, usually attributable to a significant event such as a loss or major change in the life situation. In many cases there will be a combination of losses—loved ones, status, possessions, money and good health. The reactions are not always immediate and may be delayed for many months. They may be triggered by a trivial-seeming event, such as a visit to the doctor or a minor physical injury.

These patients respond very well to a combination of intensive care, psychotherapy, and tranquilizing medication, usually phenothiazines, butyrophenones, or thioxanthines. Intellectually they show no serious deficit except during the acute phases of their psychoses when it is difficult to obtain a reliable assessment of intelligence. In fact, testing should not be attempted at that time if the patient's self-esteem will be threatened by a poor performance.

A more extreme form of this disorder would be a severe suicidal depression. Although suicidal depressions may occur in any of the affective reactions, they are most common in the agitated depressions described above and in the psychotic depressive reactions. These patients will verbalize suicidal threats, may in fact make suicidal attempts, and in some instances try to mutilate themselves. They generally suffer from sleep disturbances and neglect their physical appearance to an extreme degree. (All psychotic depressives to some extent neglect their hygiene, dress, and grooming). They may also become very negativistic and uncooperative though not usually to the point of rigidity and immobility. They may refuse to eat and become unresponsive to people or to stimulation. Sometimes it is hard to differentiate this kind of psychotic depression from a catatonic state. The treatment is often identical. ECT may be necessary to prevent further regression or more serious attempts at self-harm.

Special Diagnostic And Therapeutic Considerations

In concluding this discussion of affective states, it is my experience that many patients with affective disorders often show such marked underlying paranoid symptomatology that it is difficult to make a definitive diagnosis, although the choice of treatments is determined by the most severe symptoms and behaviors. The outlook for treatment is generally better when the affective elements predominate.

Another factor to consider is the intellectual state of the individual and the risk to intellectual function both from the disorder and from the treatment of the disorder.

Sometimes one may first institute a therapeutic program which is less than ideal for both speed and efficacy but less risky to the patient than the treatment of choice. For example, ECT in many cases is the treatment of choice for certain affective disorders but, in older patients showing mild signs of organic brain syndrome, may tend to increase intellectual deficit even while alleviating the emotional disorder.

Drugs are far from safe in such a group, and the administration of high doses of medication should clearly be accompanied by elaborate precautions against complications. Even psychotherapy carries some risk. There is a tendency for patients with ideas of reference to misinterpret either what the therapist says or what other therapeutic personnel may discuss with them. Memory impairment is an important factor. Some issues may be discussed over and over again by older patients, whereas a younger patient would proceed from one issue to another once the former is resolved.

Psychotic behavior may also serve as an attention-getting device. Some patients exaggerate symptoms as a way of receiving medical attention and evoking concern in nurses and members of the family. I do not mean to imply that this is malingering. It may be an unconscious mechanism utilized by the patient to evoke sympathy and to provide a face-saving reason for increased dependence on others.

Dependency is a thread which runs through all the psychiatric disorders of the aging Among some psychotic patients this may be a crucial issue. Dependency may be a life-preserver for some patients. Decreasing dependency accompanied by negativism, withdrawal, and uncooperativeness may be the first sign that the patient has given up and really wants to die. Sometimes it is a clue to slow suicide, accompanied by a refusal to eat, refusal to care for oneself, and finally mutism.

In some patients denial of dependency and assertions of independence, superiority, and grandiosity are techniques for preserving the last vestiges of self-esteem and may be unreality-oriented defenses against disillusioning insights into a present dilemma, involving loss of hope, despair, and a state of utter helplessness.

Acute Situational Disorders

In some patients episodes of aggressive behavior may occur, related to loss of intellectual control and unfavorable occurrences in the patient's life. Acute situational psychoses are not uncommon in the aged. They may take the form of psychotic depressions or agitated depressions. They may at times be manifested by manneristic behavior.

Occasionally a patient will become involved in sexual acting out which will reflect a transient disturbance but be so frightening to other people that he may be placed in a custodial institution and kept there long after the psychosis remits. There is a tendency to judge harshly sexually deviant behavior in the aged. Sometimes even relatively normal sexual behavior is regarded as inappropriate for aged persons; for example, wanting to touch other people and fondle them. In a younger person this might be considered bold but not necessarily psychotic. In the aged patient this may be interpreted as a sign of a psychosis or of senility. Inappropriate expressions of such behavior are easily treated with counseling or psychotherapy and medication.

Transient psychotic episodes may occur with forced retirement or with sudden changes in life situations, such as moving from one community to another or moving out of one's home into the home of relatives. The fear of being placed in a nursing home or of losing independence can precipitate a transient psychotic reaction. Usually these will clear up rapidly with relatively conservative treatment and sympathetic medical or nursing management. Low doses of tranquilizing medication are often sufficient.

More ominous are situational reactions of the kind described above which are associated with intellectual deterioration. These may be signs of early senile dementia or forerunners of a cerebrovascular insufficiency or cerebrovascular accident. A mental status examination should always be performed on such patients to determine the extent to which intellectual impairment exists. A neurological examination with appropriate diagnostic evaluation may be necessary to rule out an incipient cerebrovascular disorder.

The Mental Status Examination

I have always stressed the importance of a thorough mental status examination. I want to close by underlining the crucial character of such a procedure among patients who are suspected of being psychotic. Besides assisting in the differentiation of organic from "functional" disorders, a mental status examination helps assess the degree of disability and incompetence present. The onset of a psychosis inevitably raises questions regarding the ability of the patient to manage his own life and may involve litigation and legal commitment to an institution. It is the responsibility of a psychiatrist examining and treating such a patient to obtain as much information as possible so that he can render an informed opinion and see to it that the family or public and private agencies provide sufficient protection and security. Often the outcome of treatment for psychoses in the elderly may be markedly influenced by management of legal matters, as well as successful management of issues relating to the family, housing, care of physical diseases, the securing of appropriate financial and medical benefits, and long-term disposition.

Psychiatrists and family physicians must be well informed and thoroughly familiar with the therapeutic, protective, and health-care resources available in the community and with the social and environmental factors which influence the onset and course of the psychoses in elderly patients. This makes the treatment of such patients more difficult but the results, in the long run, are much more rewarding.

References

1. Stotsky, B.A. and Rhetts, J.E.: Factorial Study of Psychopathology in Psychiatric Patients Successfully Placed in Nursing Homes. *J. Am. Geriatrics Soc.* 15:437-447, 1967.

2. Stotsky, B.A.: Allegedly Nonpsychiatric Patients in Nursing Homes. *J. Am. Geriatrics Soc.* 15:535-544, 1967.

3. Stotsky, B.A.: Psychiatric Disorders Common to Psychiatric and Nonpsychiatric Patients in Nursing Homes. *J. Am. Geriatrics Soc.* 15:664-673, 1967.

Paranoid Syndromes of the Senium

Alan D. Whanger, M.D.

All of us have a tendency at times to want to blame our problems on others, but we generally temper this with reality so that it is temporary and not a major problem for us. Among elderly psychiatric patients, however, paranoid symptoms are both common and fascinating, and present a challenge in understanding and treating them.

Among geriatric patients admitted to two state hospitals in which I have worked for several years, about 8% had a primary diagnosis of a paranoid psychosis. About 11% had some form of schizophrenia, and usually were being readmitted for an exacerbation of a psychosis diagnosed long before. On close questioning, it was found that about 40% of all admissions had paranoid symptoms of varying degrees associated with their illness. It is to the patterns of these paranoid syndromes that the paper will be addressed.

The term paranoia, which literally means a mind beside itself, was used by the Greeks to refer to mental illness generally. Heinroth in 1818 was the first to introduce the present concept of paranoia and to interpret the delusions as disturbances of the intellect. Let it be made clear here that there is considerable disagreement about the definition, etiology, nosology, and clinical significance of paranoid phenomena, with the Europeans, English, and Americans often having rather different viewpoints. Without presuming to settle these differences, I will try to present a clinically useful way of looking at paranoid syndromes, borrowing observations from many. Often paranoid is used almost synonymously with persecutory, but more generally it may refer to all kinds of experience in which a person falsely, or to an exaggerated extent, believes himself to be the object of attention from others. Suspicion alone is insufficient ground for diagnosis, since there may well be justification for it. Even paranoids may have enemies! Freud hypothesized that all forms of paranoia were due to repudiation of homosexual wishes, which were then projected variously as delusions of persecution, erotomania, jealousy, or grandiosity. This has limited validity and would seem to have relevance in less than a quarter of the paranoid syndromes seen in the elderly. The official American nomenclature (1) gives little effort to the conceptualization and description of paranoid disorders, and feels them to be variants of schizophrenia or of paranoid personality. The following are the available categories:

1. Paranoid personality, which is characterized by hypersensitivity, rigidity, unwarranted suspiciousness, envy, jealousy, excessive self-importance, and a tendency to blame others and ascribe evil motives to them.

2. Paranoia, which is a rare condition characterized by a gradually developed, complex, encapsulated delusional system.

3. Involutional paranoid state, or involutional paraphrenia, which is characterized by delusion formation with the onset in the involutional period without other conspicious evidence of a thought disorder.

4. Other paranoid states, as a residual category; and

5. Schizophrenia, paranoid type, in which there are persecutory or grandiose delusions often associated with hallucinations and other significant indications of a thought disorder.

Many American psychiatrists utilize the classification generally as a mild paranoid disorder being called a paranoid personality, a moderate paranoid disorder, a paranoid state, and a severe paranoid disorder as schizophrenia, paranoid type. There is value in viewing these disorders on a spectrum, but certainly some workers tend to diagnose schizophrenia much more frequently than others. Periodic feelings of undue attention from others which are considered to be improbable or puzzling are often called ideas of reference. Post (2) calls more persistent experiences of self-reference "over-valued ideas." The person doubts the reality of these, but cannot rid himself of them. These may not necessarily be paranoid, but may be hypochondriacal in content. A delusion is a false belief which resists logical argument, and is not shared by the person's fellows or culture.

In order to better evaluate the significance of paranoid symptoms, it is of help to understand the paranoid mode of thinking as indicated by Swanson (3). No single characteristic is either essential or sufficient in determining the presence or absence of a clinically important paranoid stance, but it is rather on the basis of the relative amounts and influence of all the characteristics. They are as follows: projective thinking, hostility, suspiciousness, centrality or great focus of attention on the self, delusions, fear of loss of autonomy, and grandiosity.

Incidence:

The incidence of paranoid syndromes in the elderly is not known with any certainty, but the few studies done have indicated a probable 15% prevalence of significant psychiatric disorder among the community elderly. Extrapolation might mean that 1 to 2% have major paranoid syndromes. In the studies in San Francisco, Lowenthal (4) and her group noted a frequency of paranoid symptoms among the elderly who were hospitalized there of about 40%, but only 6 of their 52 patients were predominantly characterized as suspicious. Their incidence of major paranoid disorders seems much lower than ours, for reasons I do not fully understand. Suspiciousness itself never was the precipitant for the hospitalization, and was considered a predisposing factor in only 10 cases. It seems that the rather common paranoid syndromes in the elderly apparently were considered by the population at large to be relatively normal concomitants of aging, or at least traits supported by the community and the family. Violence, suicide attempts, excessive drinking, and confusion were much more likely to cause or explain hospitalization than were hallucinations, delusions, hazardous acts, verbal abuse, or paranoid symptoms. Of their 14 patients with a primary diagnosis of a functional paranoid psychosis, only one was admitted for harmful behavior, 6 for potential harmful behavior, and half for environmental factors. In half their patients, the symptoms had been present for less than two years.

Etiology:

The dynamics of paranoid syndromes certainly go back to earliest childhood and the primitive defense mechanisms. Cameron (5) speculates that persons who develop functional paranoid psychoses are those who were unsuccessful in early childhood in developing basic trust, so that they view the world and people as essentially unfriendly and hostile. He feels that there is a prolonged prodromal phase in paranoid reactions, whether recognized or not, in which the person responds to threat, loss, or frustration by withdrawing his interest from his environment. Like any isolated person, he undergoes regression, and then tries to understand what uncomfortable things are happening to him. Because of the rigidity of his delusional beliefs, he must reconstruct the world around him in such a way as to confirm his delusions that this is indeed a dangerous place. This apparent confirmation increases his anxiety, and things seem changed to him, and he even feels estranged. Projection, or the symbolic spitting out of bad things, is a mechanism readily available, and he perceives his growing anxiety as a growing danger from his surroundings. Like anyone in danger, he becomes uncertain, watchful, and hyperalert, and begins to examine his environment in a minute way, so that many small things seem to have a special meaning. Everything around him seems to confirm his distrust, and he seeks some explanation of what is going on. A mistaken conclusion seems to be more comforting to people than no conclusion at all, and the paranoid person typically has little ability for communication and for objectively evaluating situations. As he cannot give up his denials and projections because of their defensive nature, he begins to feel part of some scheme in which others may be watching him. The final step in a paranoid reaction is to find an answer to who "they" are and what they are doing, which is the formation of a "pseudocommunity" of real or imagined persons intent on harming the person's reputation or being. This replaces his confusion, fear, and suspicion with a delusional reality, in the light of which he interprets everything else. Most of his actions worsen his situation, and tend to drive other people away, or else stimulate counteraggression, confirming his fears of being attacked.

Of course there are many factors which tend to make a person's outer world seem more threatening or less comprehensible, or else raise within oneself painful or unacceptable feelings which may be projected. The older person may find the world harder to cope with, and his own more complex and sophisticated coping mechanism less effective. As Busse (6) points out, the elderly constitute a minority group who are often excluded from positions of power and authority, and may be actively discriminated against. Age factors alone may move a person rather suddenly from his secure and familiar position and relationships into loneliness and insecurity. It is of interest that while the delusional systems of younger people often involve strange people and exotic mechanisms and forces, those of older people often involve their families and neighbors in supposed schemes of spying, stealing, poisoning, or sexual intrigue. There is often hostility in the paranoid expression which is directed toward those upon whom the older person depends, which tends to alienate them. In addition the aged person may have excessive time to spend in introspection and brooding about his real or imagined slights and rejections. Perhaps as compensation, many older people develop rather grandiose religious ideas.

Clinical Features:

Paranoid syndromes of the senium differ widely in clinical features and in diagnostic significance, and may be purely psychogenic or may be associated with a variety of organic states of either an acute or chronic nature.

Paranoid Personality:

The suspicious, hostile, or cantankerous person who has lived many years with his jaundiced view of people and the world seldom reaches the psychiatrist. He often gradually withdraws from society and lives as an eccentric.

Acute Functional Paranoid Reactions:

These may occur as a result of social stresses in predisposed personalities in which the hyper-sensitive individuals may view others from a standpoint of inferiority, while the litigious personalities adopt a position of strength from which they fight against their imagined adversaries. Their symptoms are not bizarre, and are generally understandable in the reality of the context in which they occur. The symptoms may abate as soon as the stress is relieved or they are placed in a secure situation.

Paranoid Syndromes Associated with Sensory Defects:

Loss of the ability to perceive stimuli from the outer world seems to disrupt human thought process so much that the person will use a variety of mechanisms to fill in this void. We know that experimental sensory deprivation will result in hallucinations within a few hours in an otherwise normal person. Severely impaired vision is often associated with visual illusions or hallucinations. Most will recognize their illusory nature, but they may be involved by some in their paranoid ideation. Deafness is much more frequently involved in paranoid tendencies, with incapacitating hearing loss being found in about a quarter of those with paranoid states, as compared with a similar loss being present in only about 10% of older depressives. Post (2) reports that about 75% of deaf senile paranoid individuals had auditory hallucinations compared to only 60% in those with adequate hearing. Auditory illusions and hallucinations are experienced by probably the majority of all deaf people, but most recognize them as imaginary, and do not become paranoid. Older people do frequently have diminution of the senses of taste, smell, and touch, and this may contribute in a vague way to their difficulty in perceiving the world accurately.

Paranoid Symptoms Associated With Other Functional Psychiatric Disorders:

Vague or fleeting paranoid symptoms may be found in conjunction with other psychiatric disorders, such as ideas of reference in neurotic disturbances. In conditions with anxious or depressive affect, they may be of depreciatory nature, while in elated states, they may be of wishfulfilling or self-aggrandizing content. There is a considerable group of patients with admixtures of depressive and paranoid elements, often in fluctuating degrees, and I feel that a number of these are basically affective disorders, especially if the delusions are consonant with and directly related to the mood content. Occasionally severe persecutory delusions may be associated with manic-depressive psychosis in the elderly.

Paranoid Syndromes in Acute Brain Syndromes:

Acute, and often rapidly fluctuating paranoid symptoms are often found in many toxic states, and the person's basic personality undoubtedly has much more to do with the symptoms than does the nature of the organic disease. Intoxications are a fairly common cause, with bromides, amphetamines, antiparkinson compounds, and alcohol, being among the most frequent offenders. In some infections, a paranoid syndrome may be the first symptom. After such infections as influenza and infectious hepatitis, paranoid symptoms are probably as common as depressive ones; and it has been observed by Davidson (7) that typhus, typhoid fever, and trypanosomiasis are especially likely to produce paranoid states. Occasionally the paranoid syndrome may outlast the physical disease, and even when the delirium is lifted the patient may be left with residual delusions, often with a belief in the reality of hallucinations which may have occurred during the acute brain syndrome. Some of the hallucinogenic drugs frequently produce paranoid reactions, but these are rarely used by the older citizens yet.

Other Organic Paranoid Syndromes:

Paranoid syndromes are fairly frequently seen in other systemic conditions. They may follow a state of exhaustion and are probably precipitated by sleep deprivation, as they can often be cured by sleep. An elderly patient kept awake by dyspnea or pain may suffer in this way. Endocrine and metabolic disorders are important causes, especially myxedema, and occasionally hyperthyroidism and porphyria. Uremia, congestive heart failure, lupus erythematosus, malaria, encephalitides, and occasionally brain tumors, especially in the frontal lobe, may all give rise to paranoid complaints. General paresis, which used to be very prevalent in state hospitals, frequently has expansive types of delusions. Tuberculosis has a significant relationship with mental illness, and there is a proclivity for paranoid syndromes. Epileptics, especially in the post ictal phase, may demonstrate paranoid delusions and an excited state, which may result in marked aggression. Occasionally psychomotor epilepsy presents marked paranoid ideation, as well as sometimes anxiety and depression. Paranoid psychoses have occasionally developed during treatment with anticonvulsant drugs, especially Phenurone. Two vitamin deficiencies have a definite correlation with paranoid symptoms, namely pellagra and pernicious anemia, which in these days are much more likely to be found among the elderly.

Paranoid Syndromes with Senile Dementia:

About 50% of people with senile dementia have associated symptoms which are far more disabling than the brain syndrome itself, and about 20% of those with senile dementia manifest paranoid reactions. Abstract reasoning is diminished, as are the capacities for insight and self evaluation. The paranoid tends to retain his memory surprisingly well for a time, which may mask the organic nature of his paranoid syndrome, which develops because of the person's feeling that the world is getting overwhelming. There is occasionally a paranoid-hallucinatory syndrome in the early stage of Alzheimer's disease before the onset of the obvious organic symptoms.

Cerebral Arteriosclerotic Paranoid Psychoses:

The person with cerebral arteriosclerosis generally develops symptoms earlier than those with senile dementia. Corsellis (8) noted again a 20% incidence of paranoid symptoms in those with this condition. They frequently have insight into the dementia, which tends to fluctuate and manifest emotional lability. This combined with a diminution of the physiological inhibiting mechanisms tends to make them vulnerable and sensitive to many threats. Their delusions may be transient or are often rather simple. Paranoid syndromes were found in about 35% of those cases with both cerebral arteriosclerosis and senile dementia present.

Paranoid States:

This group of psychogenic disorders is found more frequently in women, and as mentioned before, falls into controversial categorizations. The majority of these people experience hallucinations, but they are generally alert and in good contact with their surroundings. There is often no deterioration in habits. Many have affective symptoms, most frequently those of depression. Post (9) subdivided patients with these reactions into three categories: one with hallucinations only; one with "schizophreniform" phenomena, but which were easily understandable; and the schizophrenic group in which there were intrusions of thought, bizarre delusions, ideas of influence and passivity, and often a hallucinated running commentary on actions and thoughts. Kay and Roth (10) subdivided these into three groups as well, but one group was those without hallucinations, the second was paraphrenias arising under unusual circumstances or after prolonged isolation, and the third was endogenous paraphrenias. Davidson (7) divided the paranoid states into three groups, namely, 1) paranoid moods without delusion formation, 2) paranoid states with unsystematized delusions, and 3) paranoid states with systematized delusions. He observed the frequent presence of paranoid syndromes and depressive moods. With these the depressive complaints and paranoid symptoms may change inversely, but the basic stance seems to be a belligerent attitude toward the environment. Retterstol (11) in Norway made a distinction between paranoid states which he considered basically reactive and paranoiac disorders which are similar to true paranoia. He observed that the paranoid states frequently resolved spontaneously upon admission to the hospital, whereas the paranoiac disorders remained.

Paranoid Schizophrenia of Late Life:

Only about 5% of cases of schizophrenia begin after age 60. There is some evidence for a hereditary predisposition to late life schizophrenia, which is different from that occuring in early life. The clinical picture is frequently similar. These people often seem to be singularly healthy physically, with considerable resistance to dementia. Without treatment, however, late life schizophrenia tends to run a prolonged course.

Treatment:

Until recently the outlook in the functional paranoid states was rather bleak. The use of the phenothiazine type of psychotropic drugs has markedly changed the response, however. Actually, paranoid states in the elderly and late life schizophrenia respond generally more satisfactorily than the similar conditions in the young. I myself have generally used either trifluoperazine (Stelazine) or haloperidol (Haldol) for treatment, with about 80% remission rate. Relapses occur in many, however, if they do not continue to take the antipsychotic drugs in a maintenance dose for long periods of time. As indicated, paranoid symptoms which are a part of other psychiatric disorders frequently disappear on hospitalization when the person's environment is structured and protected, or when the person is removed from the frightening or hostile surroundings. Many times the person remains aware of his delusion and remains convinced of its reality, although it often has lost its urgency and the person develops various rationalizations for no longer acting out on it. The effects of the minor tranquilizers are erratic and generally temporary, and may simply represent a clouding of consciousness. Among those with organic brain disease and paranoid symptoms which may be troublesome because of the person's emotional lability and loss of inhibitions, the use of small dosages of phenothiazines or other major tranquilizers may reduce the frequency and severity of the problem. I have found frequently that very low dosages of the drugs, such as 2 mg. of Stelazine or 0.5 mg. of Haldol twice a day, may help clear the psychosis and maintain the person as well. This low dosage may also help reduce the frequency of extrapyramidal side effects. Occasionally much higher dosages may be needed initially, however. The drugs may not only suppress psychotic symptoms, but may also reduce the physiological arousal level of the person to problems and threats in his environment.

Electroshock may occasionally improve a state which is resistant to phenothiazines, although the results may be only temporary due to the resultant confusion. I have noted at times that the symptoms may get temporarily worse about the third ECT when the patient's memory and defenses begin slipping. It is a clinical observation that the patient often seems to respond to phenothiazines better after several ECT when there was initial refractoriness.

When there is a mixed depressive and paranoid syndrome, I have noticed that treating either with antidepressant or antipsychotic drugs will often clear the disorder. Generally, however, I treat with both, beginning with small doses initially, and titrating them upward. Where a paranoid syndrome is present, there is frequently a marked strain on those caring for the patient which may destroy an interpersonal relationship that will later be valuable to the patient. I feel that it is important to minimize the paranoid symptoms rather rapidly. The therapeutic relationship with the patient is difficult to establish but is important in maintaining the patient's health. The therapist must try not to develop a hostile attitude toward the patient in response to the patient's aggression and suspiciousness. Often an initial attitude toward the patient of making a few demands on him but of offering services to him when he wants them gives the patient some structure to the environment, but does not threaten him with a closeness or supposed loss of control he cannot handle at this point.

Prognosis:

Formerly the patient with paranoid symptoms was generally given a rather gloomy prognosis. As indicated, since the advent of the antipsychotic drugs, this has improved considerably. Certain features have been found to be indicative of a favorable long term course by Retterstol in Norway. (12)These are ideas of reference, marked by depression of mood, and good emotional contact during the hospitalization. In addition, there were found to be definite beneficial effects of psychotherapy, prolonged psychotropic medication, adequate follow up treatment, improvement in general circumstances, and a positive attitude on the part of the caretakers. It was noted as well that those with the onset of the paranoid illness after age 30 had a better prognosis. Many may have complete remission of symptoms although some may relapse again as much as ten or more years later. Fortunately, they may respond to the drug therapy again, and thus the lives of many older people marred by paranoid syndromes, and the lives of their families, have been made considerably happier and more productive.

Bibliography

1. American Psychiatric Association: Diagnostic and Statistical Manual of Mental Disorders, Second Edition. Washington, D.C., American Psychiatric Association, 1968.

2. Post F.: The Clinical Psychiatry of Late Life. Oxford Pergamon Press, 1965.

3. Swanson D.W., Bohnert P.J., and Smith J.A.: The Paranoid. Boston, Little Brown and Company, 1970.

4. Lowenthal M.F.: Lives in Distress. New York, Basic Books, 1964.

5. Cameron N.A.: Paranoid reactions, in Comprehensive Textbook of Psychiatry. Edited by Freedman A.M. and Kaplan H.G. Baltimore, Williams & Wilkins Co., 1967.

6. Busse E. and Pfeiffer E. (eds): Behavior and Adaptation in Late Life. Boston, Little, Brown and Company, 1969.

7. Davidson R.: Paranoid symptoms in organic disease. Geront. Clin. 6:93-100, 1964.

8. Corsellis J.A.N.: Mental Illness and the Aging Brain. London, Oxford University Press, 1962.

9. Post F.: Persistent Persecutory States of the Elderly. Oxford, Pergamon Press, 1966.

10. Kay D.W.K. and Roth N.J.: Environmental and hereditary factors in the schizophrenias of old age ("late paraphrenia") and their bearings on the general problem of causation in schizophrenia. J. Ment. Sci. 107:649-686, 1961.

11. Retterstol N.: Paranoid and Paranoiac Psychoses. Oslo, Universitetsforlaget, 1966.

12. Retterstol N.: Prognosis in Paranoid Psychoses. Springfield, Charles C. Thomas, 1970.

Detection of Affective Disorders in the Aged

William W. K. Zung, M.D.
Robert L. Green, Jr., M.D.

One of the tasks of the physician when examining an emotionally disturbed patient is to determine whether the patient's condition is a normal reaction to the vicissitudes of life, or whether it is an illness which requires skilled medical attention. In order to perform an evaluation for the presence or absence of an affective disorder in any patient, clear-cut diagnostic criteria must be kept in mind for each of the disorders which the clinician is considering. In addition, he must know and understand the effect of variables, such as age, and their influence on the emotional "baseline" of the normal persons. Specifically, in assessing the elderly patient, we must ask ourselves: How much anxiety and how much depressive symptomatology are usually present in the normal aged? Understanding the status of the normal elderly person would help us in the evaluation of the disturbed elderly person.

In this presentation, we will report data from several studies which attempt to measure anxiety and depression in normal subjects 65 years of age and older, and compare them with data from other age groups, and from patients with affective disorders.

Methods

Measurement of Depression

In order to obtain baseline values on normal subjects, we must first ascertain that there is an operationally defined set of signs and symptoms that can be demonstrated in patients diagnosed as having depressive disorders, with some high degree of universal agreement and validity. In the present study we used the Self-rating Depression Scale or SDS (1) for such a purpose. The SDS in summary is as follows: It contains 20 items which are constructed on the basis of the clinical diagnostic criteria most commonly used to characterize depressive disorders in terms of the presence of a pervasive affective disturbance with its concomitant physiological and psychological signs and symptoms (see Table 1). In using the SDS, the subject is asked to rate each of the items as to how it applies to him at the time of testing in four quantitative terms (none OR a little of the time, some of the time, a good part of the time, most OR all of the time), which have numerical values of 1 to 4. The SDS Index is derived from the responses on the 20 items and ranges from 25 to 100. In addition to the U.S.A. studies, we have also been able to demonstrate the validity of the diagnostic criteria used in the SDS (2) in a cross-cultural study of depressive symptomatology in Japan, Australia, Czechoslovakia, England, Germany, and Switzerland.

Table 1.
Diagnostic criteria for depressive disorder

1. PERVASIVE AFFECTIVE DISTURBANCE
    1. Depressed: sad, blue, down-hearted
    2. Tearful: have crying spells, feel like it

2. PHYSIOLOGICAL SIGNS
    1. Diurnal variation
    2. Insomnia, middle & late
    3. Decreased appetite
    4. Decreased weight
    5. Decreased libido
    6. GI: constipation
    7. CV: tachycardia
    8. MS: fatigue

3. PSYCHOMOTOR DISTURBANCES
    1. Agitation
    2. Retardation

4. PSYCHOLOGICAL SYMPTOMS
    1. Confusion
    2. Emptiness
    3. Hopelessness
    4. Indecisiveness
    5. Irritability
    6. Dissatisfaction
    7. Personal devaluation
    8. Suicidal rumination

Measurement of Anxiety

As in the measurement of depression, in order to obtain baseline values on normal subjects, we must first ascertain that there is an operationally defined set of signs and symptoms that can be demonstrated in patients diagnosed as having anxiety disorders, with some high degree of universal agreement and validity. In the present study, we used the Self-rating Anxiety Scale or SAS (3) for such a purpose. The SAS in summary is as follows: It contains 20 items which are constructed on the basis of the clinical diagnostic criteria most commonly used to characterize anxiety disorders in terms of the presence of anxiety as an affect and associated somatic symptoms (see Table 2).

Table 2.
Diagnostic criteria for anxiety disorder

AFFECTIVE SYMPTOMS
1. Anxiousness: anxious, nervous
2. Fear: afraid for no reason
3. Panic: easily upset, panic spells
4. Mental disintegration: falling apart, going to pieces
5. Apprehension: uneasy, anticipation of danger

SOMATIC SIGNS

MS:	1. Tremors		GI:	10.	Nausea and vomiting
	2. Body aches and pains				
	3. Fatigue		GU:	11.	Urinary frequency
	4. Restlessness				
			SKIN:	12.	Sweating
CV:	5. Palpitation			13.	Face flushing
RESP:	6. Dizziness				
	7. Faintness		CNS:	14.	Insomnia, initial
	8. Dyspnea			15.	Nightmares
	9. Paresthesias				

In using the SAS, the subject is asked to rate each of the items as to how it applies to him at the time of testing in four quantitative terms (none OR a little of the time, some of the time, a good part of the time, most OR all of the time) which have numerical values of 1 to 4. The SAS Index is derived from the responses on the 20 items and ranges from 25 to 100.

Subject Population

Patient data are from previous studies (1, 3-7), while normal control data are from previous studies (1, 3, 8-10) and new data collected from this report. The criterion for normalcy in these studies was that the subjects were carrying out age appropriate activities. Thus, subjects 19 years-old-and-under were tested while attending school at the junior high and high school levels. Subjects 20 to 64 years of age were tested while at school or at work at their jobs, and subjects 65 years-old-and-over were participants in club and community activities.

Results

Measurement of Depression

The total number of patients tested with a diagnosis of depressive disorder was 360, and the total number of normal subjects tested was 1,108. Data reported for patients represents those whose ages ranged from 20 to 64 years old (see Table 3). Data for all normal subjects tested with respect to their age distribution and SDS indices are also found in Table 3.

Table 3.
A comparison of SDS indices of normal subjects grouped by age: 19 years old and under, 20–64, 65 years old and over) with patients with depressive disorders (ages 20–64 years old).

GROUP	N	SDS INDEX M ± S.D.	SDS INDEX 49 & UNDER		SDS INDEX 50 & OVER	
			N	(%)	N	(%)
Controls:						
19 & Under	576	49 ± 9	299	(52)	277	(48)
20–64 Y/O	363	39 ± 9	316	(88)	47	(12)
65 & Over	169	48 ± 10	94	(56)	75	(44)
	1108					
Patients: Depressed (20–64 Y/O)	360	64 ± 12	54	(12)	315	(88)

If we use the SDS index of 50 as the morbidity cut-off score, we can see that this would include 88% of the depressed patients, and miss 12% of them (see Figure 1). Now applying the same cut-off score to the normal subjects, we get the following picture. If we age match the depressed patients with the normal subjects (20-64 years old), we see that 12% of the normal subjects would be considered "depressed" and the rest (88%) would be considered as not depressed (see Figure 2). The accuracy of this procedure using the SDS is comparable to that achieved in other studies on the accuracy of diagnostic procedures using other rating scales (11, 12). Statistical analysis using the t-test showed the mean SDS of the normal (m = 39±9) and depressed subjects (m = 64 ± 12) to be significantly different (P = < 0.01). Statistical analysis using chi-square comparing the distribution of SDS indices of the normal and depressed groups and using the SDS index of 50 as the morbidity cut-off scores (see Table 3), showed the groupings to be significantly different, with P = < 0.01.

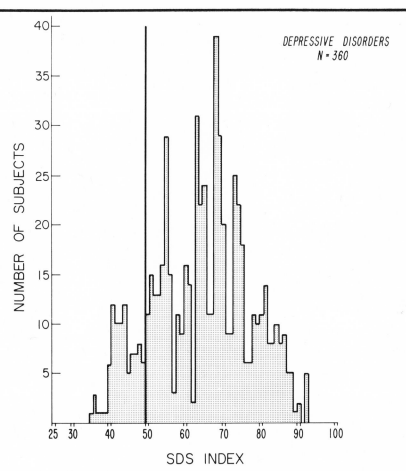

Figure 1.
Distribution of SDS indices of 360 patients with diagnoses of depressive disorders, ages 20 to 64 years old.

If we look at the results obtained from the younger and older normal subjects, we see a different picture. Using the t-test, statistical analyses of the mean SDS indices of these two extreme age groups were both significantly different from the mean index of the depressed patient group. However, using the morbidity cut-off score of 50 on the SDS, 48% of the 19 years-old-and-under normal subjects would be considered "clinically depressed," and so would 44% of the 65 years-old-and-over group. However, chi-square tests comparing the younger normal subjects with the depressed patients, and older normal subjects with depressed patients showed significant differences between the normal and depressed groups (P = < 0.01). Thus, although normal subjects at the two extreme age groups have baseline depressive symptoms which are significantly lower than those depressed patients, they nevertheless have higher baseline values than normal

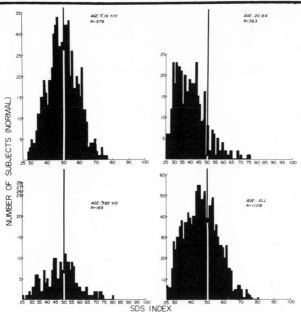

Figure 2.
Distribution of SDS indices of 1,108 normal subjects by various age groups.

subjects in the age range between them (20-64 years old). Thus, the number of "hits" on the "depressed" side is impressive enough to make us aware of the trend toward higher SDS values in the young and elderly normal population.

In addition to looking for quantitative differences between normal and depressed subjects as studied by using the SDS, we were also interested in looking for possible qualitative differences. Data for normal subjects 65 years old and over were factor independent dimensions needed to account for most of the variance in the original set of variables. There were 4 factors extracted with latent roots greater than 1. Factor 1 could be identified as "loss of self-esteem" since the most important saturations are in those items which measure personal devaluation, emptiness, indecisiveness, dissatisfaction, and hopelessness. A comparison of this with results of a previous factor analysis on data obtained from patients with depressive disorders points to a notable qualitative difference (7). Factor 1 of the depressed patients included in addition to the above psychological items, biological items which measure diurnal variation, decreased appetite and decreased libido.

Measurement of Anxiety

The total number of patients tested with a diagnosis of anxiety disorder was 56, and the number of normal subjects tested was 343. Data reported for patients represents those whose ages ranged from 20 to 64 years old. Data for all normal subjects tested are grouped by age and their SAS results are found in Table 4.

Table 4.
A Comparison of Self-rating Anxiety Scale (SAS) indices of normal subjects (grouped by age) with patients with anxiety disorders.

GROUP	N	SAS INDEX M ± SD	SAS INDEX 45 & UNDER		SAS INDEX 50 & OVER	
			N	(%)	N	(%)
Anxiety Disorder						
(20–64Y/O)	56	58 ± 13	12	(12)	44	(79)
Normal Controls:						
19 & Under	200	45 ± 8	144	(72)	56	(28)
20–64 Y/O	96	34 ± 8	96	(100)	0	(0)
65 & Over	47	40 ± 7	38	(81)	9	(19)

A statistical test using analysis of variance showed the mean SAS indices from patients with anxiety disorders and normal subjects to be significantly different ($P = <0.01$).

Figure 3 shows the distribution of SAS results of normal subjects grouped by age, as well as results of patients with anxiety disorders.

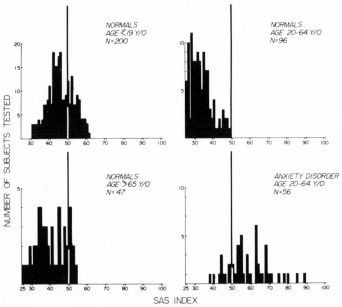

Figure 3.
Distribution of SAS indices of normal subjects by age, and patients with diagnoses of anxiety disorder.

Using the SAS index of 50 as the morbidity cut-off score to indicate the presence of anxiety of clinical significance, we can see differences between patients and normal subjects. While 79% of patients scored 50 or higher, no age-matched normal subject scored 50 or above (see Table 4). Looking at the data from the two extreme age groups of the normal subjects, we see that 28% of the 19 year-old-and-under scored 50 and above and only 19% of the 65 year-old-and-over. Again, as we found with the depression scale results, the two extreme age groups have a higher baseline than those in between. The difference here being that the 65 years-and-over group did not score as high on anxiety as they did in depression, relative to the 19 year-old-and-under group.

Discussion

The emotions and emotional problems in the aging and aged are the same as those encountered in the younger years (13). Thus, a rational approach to the detection of affective disorders in the aged have similarities to the detection of affective disorders in the younger years. First, we must keep in mind that mood or affective states are internal experiences. This is both its strength and its weakness, when we are dealing with its detection and recognition. It is a strength because whatever information we elicit from a patient about his mood has to come from him as a self-reporting of his subjective experience. It is also its weakness, because the accuracy of the assessment of mood is dependent upon a responsive and cooperative subject. Therefore, there are times when it is appropriate to use a self- and an observer-rating scale in the measurement of psychopathology. In order to be able to correlate self- with observable-ratings, scales using the same diagnostic criteria must be used, since the deficiency of one scale may not be necessarily corrected by the other if they don't measure the same thing. For this purpose, depression and anxiety can be observer-rated by using the Depression Status Inventory (14) and Anxiety Status Inventory (3), which use the same diagnostic criteria as their self-rating counterparts.

A rational approach to the detection of affective disorders in the aged has, in addition, several unique problems. In the aged, the central nervous system may be marginally operational and thus there is an increasing potential for perceptual distortion of external stimuli. If one misperceives the stimulus, then the response will be inappropriate, and the environment reacts negatively to the inappropriate response. We may see either an overt negative reaction or the more passive isolationism. Both will increase feelings of insecurity which lead to anxiety, anger, or agitation. We all tend to resort to or rely on patterns of behavior that we have found to be successful in earlier life; but such a pattern becomes a more dominant characteristic of their psychological adjustment. The more rigid the behavior pattern the less successful it tends to be in getting one's needs met, and the resultant anxiety and depression tend to further compromise the rather tenuous physiological and psychological functions. At this time the previous subtle signs of organic deficit now become more blatant and the physician is confronted with the problem of differentiation between organicity and affective disorder. In the aged patient the following symptoms — labile affect, decreased libido, constipation, psychomotor retardation and/or agitation, feelings of pessimism, confusion and withdrawal — are all characteristic of an organic brain syndrome, as well as depression and anxiety. The labile affect, characteristic of an organic brain syndrome, is most frequently misinterpreted as a symptom of severe depression. Not infrequently the manifest affect in an organic patient is inappropriate to the thought content and inappropriate in quantity. Perhaps an oversimplified means of differentiating the organic components is the demonstration of impairment of recent memory, fluctuating orientation, and impaired judgment, as manifested by inappropriate behavior, deterioration of personal habits and hygiene, in addition to the labile affect. In addition to the CNS changes, there are the changes associated with aging of other parts of the body. Justifiably, the elderly are preoccupied with the resultant physical impairments such as decreased hearing, decreased eye-sight, presence of crippling arthritis, and residual losses from vascular diseases. Unrecognized, untreated, or inadequately treated physical illness with its secondary effect on the psyche will take its toll in emotional disorders.

Though there may be little or no clinical difference in the manifestation of depression between the younger patient and the geriatric patient, we believe that there are some significant differences in the etiologic or dynamic factors. Several authors have commented that depression in the aged tends to take a form which is different from that usually found in younger individuals (15-17). The elderly depressed patients are characterized by their states of apathy, inertia and gloominess, appearing disinterested in their surroundings, lacking drive. This may be a pathological extension of Factor 1 found in this study, where apathy and disinterest are other dimensions of the feeling of worthlessness, emptiness, hopelessness, psychomotor retardation and suicidal rumination. The importance of this factor in the etiology of depression in the aged was underscored by one report (18). They found in their experience that guilt and introjection of hostility or introjection of unacceptable impulses were relatively unimportant factors with elderly people, and not the major cause of feelings of depression. Instead, depression was more related to feelings of inferiority and the loss of self-esteem. We are very much aware that in the aged population the possible development of an affective disorder is increasingly more influenced by predictive but changing environmental circumstances. The aged population are more subject to social pressure over which they have little or no control, such as forced retirement, decreased financial resources, loss of emotional support by death of friends and relatives, and a relative degree of isolationism secondary to decreasing efficiency of physiological functions. Each of these factors tends to decrease one's self-esteem, increase feelings of insecurity and facilitate feelings of anxiety and depression characterized by pessimism. Pessimism is so common in the aging population it is frequently considered the normal neurosis of the aged. Though a certain degree of pessimism may be considered a normal or predictive response to aging, the gloomy outlook may be magnified and distorted to such a degree that the individual develops nihilistic ideas leading to severe depression and even suicide.

According to Freudian theory, a characteristic anxiety reaction is the fact that something in the present is precipitating a response pattern that revives unconscious memories of unresolved anxiety or revives unconscious memories of a time when the individual was really helpless. More and more we have come to believe and understand that the fears, resentments and anxieties felt as a child have a lasting effect on the individual and a replication of circumstances may very easily revive those feelings even in late life. Anxiety is an exceedingly unpleasant feeling and to put it in simple terms — anxiety is an affective state characterized by feelings of apprehension, uncertainty and helplessnes which are not attached to a real external danger and frequently associated with somatic symptoms, as measured by the rating scale used in the study. One must remember that all ages of man are now characterized by some form of anxiety, not all of which is inappropriate (19). As one ages, one's intellectual and emotional resources are somewhat compromised and therefore one is less adaptable and less capable of dealing with stressful situations.

We have thus found in this study higher basline values for anxiety and depressive symptomatology in the normal elderly population. We have discussed a number of factors which we believe are contributory to this observation and have stressed the need for understanding the total patient when evaluating him for the possible presence of an emotional disorder.

Summary

Using operational definitions of anxiety and depression as distinct psychiatric entities in the form of the Self-rating Depression Scale or SDS, the Self-rating Anxiety Scale or SAS, patients diagnosed with affective disorders and groups of normal subjects were tested for quality and quantity of psychopathology present.

Results of the measurement of depression showed that depressed patients scored significantly higher (P = $<$ 0.01) than the normal subjects tested. However, when data from normals were grouped by age — 19 and under, 20-64, 65 and over — there appeared to be definite age-related differences. Using 50 as a morbidity cut-off score on the SDS, only 12% of the 20-64 years old control subjects fell above it, but included 48% and 44% respectively of the 19 and under and 65 and over subjects. Factor analysis of the SDS results of the 65 and over group resulted in four factors, the first of which was identified as "loss of self-esteem." Factor analysis of data from depressed patients indicated a qualitative difference in Factor 1 of patient data included in addition to the psychological items, items which measured biological complaints.

Results of the measurement of anxiety showed that anxious patients scored significantly higher (P = $<$ 0.01) than the normal subjects tested. Again, when data from normals were divided by age as above, age-related differences were apparent. Using 50 as a morbidity score on the SAS, all subjects between 20-64 scored below it, but included 28% and 19%, respectively, of the 19 and under and 65 and over subjects.

The unique problems of detection of affective disorders in the aged were discussed. These included factors contributed by aging of the central nervous system manifested by organic brain syndromes, by aging of the body as manifested by multiple somatic disturbances, and lastly, by aging of the psyche as manifested by pessimism and loss of self-esteem.

References

1. Zung, W.W.K.: A Self-rating Depression Scale, *Arch. Gen. Psychiat. 12:*63-70, 1965.

2. Zung, W.W.K.: A cross-cultural survey of symptoms in depression, *Amer. J. Psychiat. 126:*116-121, 1969.

3. Zung, W.W.K.: A rating instrument for anxiety disorders, *Psychosom. 12:*371-379, 1971.

4. Zung, W.W.K., Richards, C. and Short, M.J.: Self-rating Depression Scale in an outpatient clinic, *Arch. Gen. Psychiat. 13:*508-515, 1965.

5. Zung, W.W.K.: Factors influencing the Self-rating Depression Scale, *Arch. Gen. Psychiat. 16:*543-547, 1967.

6. Zung, W.W.K.: Evaluating treatment methods for depressive disorders, *Amer. J. Psychiat. 124* (suppl.): 40-48, 1968.

7. Zung, W.W.K. and Wonnacott, T.H.: Treatment prediction in depression using a self-rating scale, *Biol. Psychiat. 2:*321-329, 1970.

8. Zung, W.W.K.: Depression in the normal aged, *Psychosom. 8:*287-292, 1967.

9. Zung, W.W.K.: Depression in the normal adult population, *Psychosom. 12:*164-167, 1971.

10. Zung, W.W.K.: How normal is depression? *Psychosom, 13:*174-178, 1972.

11. Spitzer, R.L., Cohen, J., Fleiss, J.L. and Endicott, J.: Qualification of agreement in psychiatric diagnosis, *Arch. Gen. Psychiat. 17:*83-87, 1967.

12. Spitzer, R.L. and Endicott, J.: Diagno: A computer program for psychiatric diagnosis utilizing the differential diagnostic procedure, *Arch. Gen. Psychiat. 18:*746-755, 1968.

13. Kern, Richard A.: Emotional problems in relation to aging and old age, *Geriatrics 26:*82-94, 1971.

14. Zung, W.W.K.: The Depression Status Inventory: an adjunct to the Self-rating Depression Scale, *J. Clin. Psycho.,* in press.

15. Levin, S.: Depression in the aged: A study of the salient external factors, *Geriatrics 18:*302-307, 1963.

16. Mayer-Gross, W., Slater, E. and Roth, M.: *Clinical Psychiatry,* London: Cassell and Co., Ltd., 1960.

17. Foulds, G.: Psychotic depression and age, *J. Ment. Sci. 106:*1394-1397, 1960.

18. Busse, E. and Reckless, J.: Psychiatric management of the aged, *J.A.M.A. 175:*645-648, 1961.

19. Claghorn, J.: The many faces of anxiety in different age groups, *N.Y. State J. Med. 71:*331-334, 1971.

The Use of Antidepressant Drugs in the Elderly Patient

Arthur J. Prange, Jr., M.D.

Depression is a common syndrome in the general population, and the elderly are not spared. Silverman (1), in her work on the epidemiology of this condition, wrote: ". . . depression . . . reaches it greatest frequency in the middle years, and may decline somewhat in the later years of life." Even the slight decline, I think, may be more apparent than real because of misdiagnosis. In any case, Roth (2) found that about half the elderly patients admitted to a mental hospital suffered from this syndrome.

Drugs should not be viewed as an exclusive treatment for the depressed elderly patient any more than they should be viewed as an exclusive remedy for any mental disorder at any time of life. Nevertheless, they have contributed so substantially to management and their numbers and complexity have increased so rapidly that another review of this field, though brief, might be a profitable exercise. I conceive my task as having two parts: to paint in broad strokes what seems to be a consensus about antidepressant drugs, and then to state what may be peculiar about drugs, or peculiar about elderly people, to cause us to prescribe the former for the latter in a special way.

In trying to present a consensus I have drawn heavily on recent reviews, especially the excellent general reviews by Klein and Davis (3) and by Ban (4) and the reviews of geriatric psychopharmacology by Lifshitz and Kline (5) and by Kral and Papetropoulos (6). The number of conceivable opinions is staggering, and only a few are missing in the psychotropic drug literature. For every statement I shall make, therefore, a host of qualifications would be appropriate. For such refinements the reader should consult the work already cited.

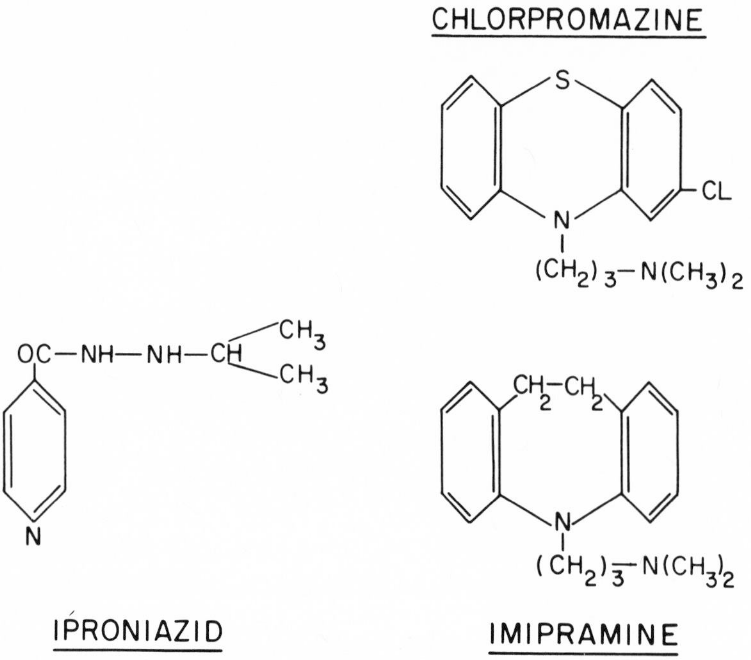

CHLORPROMAZINE

IPRONIAZID

IMIPRAMINE

Figure 1

A Brief Review of Antidepressant Drugs

Figure 1 shows some molecular relationships. Imipramine is an old substance but a relatively new drug. It was tested clinically in the hope that its virtues would excede those of chlorpromazine. It failed in all respects except as an antidepressant (7). By comparing molecular structures one might expect imipramine to share some properties with chlorpromazine and also to show some differences, as it does. Figure 1 also depicts the structure of iproniazid, the first important monoamine oxidase inhibitor, which happens to be of the hydrazine type. Its molecule is quite dissimilar from the other two.

Table 1 shows examples of substances which are used for their antidepressant properties. Some of them, such as chlorpromazine and lithium, are used mainly for other disorders, but do have antidepressant action. In addition, there are substances which, strictly speaking, are not drugs, but which may have antidepressant value. I refer to the amino acid precursors of biogenic amines, DOPA, tryptophan, and 5-hydroxytryptophan.

Table 1.

I.   Mood-Active Substances
    A. MAO INHIBITORS
        1. Hydrazines
           e.g. phenelzine (Nardil)
        2. Non-hydrazines
           e.g. tranylcypromine (Parnate)

    B. TRICYCLICS
        1. Non-sedating
          a. Methylated
            e.g. imipramine (Tofranil)
          b. Demethylated
            e.g. desipramine (Pertofran, Norpramin)
        2. Sedating
          a. C = C, ring to side-chain
            e.g. amitriptyline (Elavil)
          b. C = C, ring to side-chain; oxygen in ring
            e.g. doxepin (Sinequan)

    C. STIMULANTS
        1. Potent but addicting
           e.g. d-amphetamine (Dexedrine)
        2. Non-addicting but impotent
           e.g. methylphenidate (Ritalin)

    D. LITHIUM SALTS

    E. AMINO ACIDS
        e.g. L-DOPA, L-tryptophan

    F. PHENOTHIAZINES
        e.g. chlorpromazine (Thorazine)

There is no present purpose in detailing chemical differences between MAO inhibitors, as I shall set the MAO inhibitors aside as a class. These drugs have no special virtues but do have special drawbacks. They are inherently toxic (8); they predispose to interactive toxicity both with other drugs (8) and with certain foodstuffs (8). There is no reason, in my view, to commence treatment with an MAO inhibitor unless the patient gives a clear history of prior excellent response to one, coupled with a history of poor response to other antidepressants. After a week delay, however, MAO inhibitors may reasonably be used when other drugs have failed. It is worth remembering, because of interactive toxicity, that pargyline, a drug commonly used to treat hypertension, is a potent MAO inhibitor.

Another set of drugs that can quickly be set aside is the stimulants. They are rather impotent, as are deanol and methylphenidate, or rather addicting, as in amphetamine, and prone to produce a brief "high" followed by a low that is just as profound. Moreover, in depressed patients amphetamine may produce an ego-dystonic motor agitation more than a mood elevation. Since lithium salts are used chiefly in mania and since amino acids are mainly experimental, we can disregard them for present purposes as well. It will be necessary, however, to return to the phenothiazines, particularly chlorpromazine.

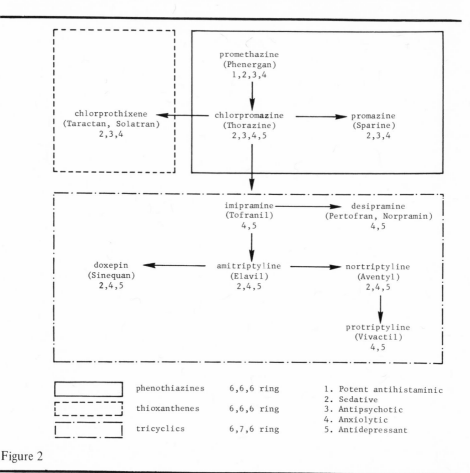

Figure 2

We are left finally with an enormously important class of drugs, the tricyclics. Imipramine is the prototype in this series, and Figure 2 shows its family tree. Promethazine is an excellent sedative and antihistaminic. It also potentiates barbiturate anesthesia, and it was hoped that this property would be extended by a minor change in the side-chain. The drug molecule that resulted was named chlorpromazine, and as I have already stated, the efficacy of chlorpromazine led directly to the investigation of the molecule that came to be known as imipramine.

The notion was widely held that imipramine, the side-chain of which contains two terminal methyl groups, and is therefore a tertiary amine, had to be partly demethylated in the body to become an active antidepressant. Because slow onset of action was a drawback of imipramine, the demethylated product, desipramine, was synthesized, in the belief that it would be a faster acting drug. The data, however, that have been adduced to show that desipramine acts faster than imipramine or that nortriptyline acts faster than amitriptyline are slender indeed (9).

Nevertheless, a notable difference was produced when a carbon atom replaced the nitrogen atom in the central ring of imipramine and when its link to the first side-chain carbon was double-bonded. The result was amitriptyline. Amitriptyline is distinctly more sedating than imipramine or desipramine and so is its congener, doxepin. Amitriptyline, doxepin, and nortriptyline also demonstrate anxiolytic properties but so do imipramine and, for that matter, desipramine. Perhaps the original proponents of imipramine were so delighted (and rightly so) to possess the first reasonably non-toxic antidepressant that they neglected to draw attention to its beneficial effects on anxiety. This oversight, if it was one, left a fertile field for the development of a substance that could be claimed both antidepressant and anxiolytic. In fact, our group has performed many studies with imipramine and we have never found it wanting in anxiolytic properties when anxiety was coextensive with depression. What distinguishes certain of the newer tricyclic drugs, then, is first, their sedative properties and only secondly, their anxiolytic properties. Doxepin may be an exception, for its tranquilizing effect has been found to compare favorably with that of chlordiazepoxide (10). Protriptyline, on the other hand, is a stimulating drug.

It is remarkable that all tricyclics, with the exception of protriptyline and the partial exception of nortriptyline, are about equally potent on a milligram basis, and that their dose range is so narrow — barely three-fold — compared to other psychotropic drugs. Nortriptyline is somewhat more potent than the others and protriptyline markedly so. This is sometimes called an advantage but I have never understood the advantage of taking drugs in very small amounts so long as needed quantities were not likely to satiate the appetite.

If one asks experienced practitioners how they choose between tricyclics, one will find that it is almost always on the basis of like or dislike based on personal experience. While this may seem capricious, it is a practice difficult to fault. If differences between drugs are slight, one might be well-advised to learn one or two in depth and to disregard the remainder. But my task is to draw some distinctions between these agents, even where those distinctions are not profound.

Table 2 contains more art than science. But choosing between drugs of the same class *is*, in part, the art of pharmacotherapy. The goal, of course, is to strike the most favorable balance for each patient between the good and the bad that a drug is apt to do.

Once the decision has been made that a tricyclic is to be prescribed, I believe this chart could be examined with profit whatever the age of the patient. Our focus, however, is the elderly patient and I should like to preface an examination of this chart with some general remarks.

Table 2

	Inherent toxicity	Guanethidine blocking	Anticholinergic effects	Sedation	Potency	Speed of action	Antianxiety effect	Antidepressant effect (Under 60)	Antidepressant effect (Over 60)
imipramine (Tofranil)	2	1	2	2	3	2	2	1	2
desipramine (Pertofran, Norpramin)	2	1	2	2	3	2	2	1	2
amitriptyline (Elavil)	2	1	2	1	3	2	1	2	1
nortriptyline (Aventyl)	2	1	2	1	2	2	1	1	2
protriptyline (Vivactil)	1	1	2	3	1	2	2	1	2
doxepin (Sinequan)	3	2	3	1	3	2	1	2	1

Toxcity   Therapy

1. most
2. intermediate
3. least

Antidepressants for the Elderly

What is special about the elderly patient? For the pharmacotherapist the answer is quite simple. In the elderly patient the margin for error is reduced. Whether or not he has frank organic disease of the brain, the cardiovascular system, or the endocrine systems, the compensatory capacities of these systems are sure to be reduced. "Potent drugs produce toxic reactions more readily" (11). When we consider tricyclic drugs for the elderly we are most concerned about a lowered threshold for toxic confusion, for glaucoma, for urinary retention, for constipation, for cardiovascular embarrassment, and for Parkinson's disease.

The first four side-effects of tricyclics and to some extent the fifth — cardiovascular embarrassment — are related to the anticholinergic properties of these drugs. So is the side-effect, dry mouth, but this is generally a mere nuisance. These matters could be discussed at great length, but here I only wish to point out that in the elderly patient toxic confusion from a drug may readily mimic an aspect of the syndrome for which it was prescribed. In the elderly, depression is often accompanied by an element of confusion. This may lead to the prescription of more drug, and the establishment of a vicious circle.

Cardiovascular side-effects probably are partly owing to the anticholinergic action of tricyclics and partly owing to their potentiation of biogenic amines. I will write more about this later.

The Parkinson syndrome that these drugs produce, especially in large doses, escapes my understanding but not my interest. The drugs are anticholinergic and can produce Parkinson's syndrome; but anticholinergics are commonly used to treat this syndrome. The tricyclics enhance the action of biogenic amines, but enhancement of one biogenic amine, dopamine, is thought to account at least in part for the efficacy of L-DOPA in spontaneous Parkinson's disease (12). Furthermore, both imipramine (13) and desipramine (14) have been used in the treatment of Parkinson's disease. Perhaps a study by our group offers a way out of this quandary. We showed that enhancing indoleamines, the presumable effect of giving L-tryptophan and pyridoxine, aggravates spontaneous Parkinson's disease dramatically (15). Perhaps in the elderly depressed patient, who is predisposed to Parkinsonism, one should use a tricyclic that potentiates catecholamines more than indoleamines. On the basis of animal work (16) one would expect tertiary amines (imipramine, amitriptyline, and doxepin) to be most offensive in the patient predisposed to Parkinsonism, and secondary amines (desipramine, nortriptyline, and protriptyline) to be least offensive. In line with this, Pohlmeier and Matussek (17) believe that desipramine is superior to imipramine in treating Parkinson's disease.

When Parkinson's syndrome does occur during the course of tricyclic treatment, another trap has been set for the physician. He is likely to treat this tricyclic side-effect with an anticholinergic drug such as benztropine (Cogentin). Such drugs, like the tricyclics themselves, are likely to produce toxic confusion. Recently El-Yousef *et al.* (18) have shown that toxic delirium due to anti-Parkinsonian agents can be identified by a single dose of physostigmine, but they would agree, I am sure, that the situation is best avoided, especially in the elderly. Reducing tricyclic dosage is the safest course.

Table 2 can now be examined for its applicability to the elderly depressed patient. Briefly, it appears to me that the relatively new drug, doxepin, has much to recommend its use. Its latency is no longer than that of other tricyclics, it has anxiolytic properties, and it has been shown, in fact, to have excellent antidepressant action (19). All this is by way of saying that doxepin has many valuable properties. We should now examine the possibility that it may also be "less bad" than its competitors.

I have mentioned the potential dangers of anticholinergic effects in the aged. Doxepin, according to Ayd (20), is the least offensive tricyclic in this regard. It may have another advantage as well. Early work suggested that doxepin, compared to other tricyclics, is only weakly capable of blocking the mechanism by which guanethidine is taken into the nerve end. The same pumping mechanism presumably is responsible for the reuptake inactivation of released biogenic amines, and this would have several implications. First, doxepin could conveniently be used with antihypertensive drugs of the guanethidine type. Second, since the storage-inactivation of biogenic amines is little affected, cardiovascular side-effects should be slight. However, definitive work by the same group (21) indicates that in man doxepin, when given in full doses, blocks guanethidine about as effectively as do other tricyclics. Whether in a given patient a dose can be found that is antidepressant and yet lacks this blocking property is uncertain. Indeed, it is the blocking of reuptake inactivation of biogenic amines that is thought to account for their antidepressant action (22). The cardiovascular toxicity of doxepin, of course, is finally an empirical question. It does seem low (23), whatever the explanation may be.

Is doxepin antidepressant in part by virtue of a sedative-tranquilizing action? In this connection, it should be recalled that the sedative action of doxepin, like the sedative action of any drug, is a therapeutic effect or a toxic effect according to whether it is desired. In the elderly patient, especially if he is not actively employed and if he is troubled by insomnia, sedation may be a boon.

In suggesting doxepin for the treatment of geriatric depression I have only one reservation, but it is important and comprehensive. It is a new drug, and the history of new psychotropic drugs is that with time they tend more and more to resemble other members of their class. Comments about the clinical use of doxepin are based on only a few reports and all of them are recent. Fann and his colleagues (21) have offered a valuable tabular summary.

In this regard, it is important to note that we were far from being pharmacologically helpless with the depressed geriatric patient before doxepin was introduced. In 1960 Abse and Dahlstrom (24) reported treating a series of patients from age 60 to 90 who showed depression, agitation, paranoid ideation, and confusion. A variety of substances were used, including placebo, and one group received no medication. In outcome there was little difference among chlorpromazine, reserpine-pipradol, and deodorized tincture of opium, or between drugs and placebo. However, the patients who received regular medication (including the placebo group) improved, while the no medication group worsened. The active concern attendant upon giving medication is obviously an important ingredient in managing the disturbed geriatric patient. It would be difficult to overestimate the importance of this point.

More recently Hordern et al. (25) compared imipramine and amitriptyline in a double-blind study of depressed women between the ages of 30 and 70. They found amitriptyline to be the more effective drug, especially in patients over 50. Sandifer et al. (26) compared the drugs in a series of depressed women but found only a trend for the superiority of amitriptyline. Their patients were younger than those of the Hordern group, and an advantage for amitriptyline in the elderly is a sufficient explanation for the discrepancy between the two studies (3).

Phenothiazines have been used successfully in agitated depression (27) and their use with imipramine in the aged when anxiety is prominent has been advocated (4). Thioridazine might be the choice because of its low toxicity. My own belief is that drug combinations should always be approached with caution, especially in the elderly, since benefits may only add while side-effects may multiply. If a second drug must be used, I consider it a sound practice to give the initial medication alone long enough to allow assessment of its wanted and unwanted effects.

Two more principles of drug administration in the elderly need mention. Klein and Davis (3) recommend that the entire daily dose of a tricyclic be given at bedtime. Side-effects are partly avoided, sedation becomes a virtue, and the patient is freed from repetitive drug ingestion during the day. The elderly, however, should be exempt from this practice (28); the peaking of drug blood levels may be poorly tolerated. Moreover, taking medicine, whatever its pharmacologic activity, always conveys suggestion – the placebo effect – and this is generally useful. To the patient, taking medicine regularly may mean regularly, "I am doing something to relieve my illness."

Finally, it is generally said that elderly patients require smaller doses of antidepressants than younger patients. I believe that this is sometimes, but not invariably, true. When this principle is rigidly followed some patients will be deprived of the dosage that they require. I believe it is sounder practice to regard the ideal dose as unknown in a given geriatric patient and to approach its attainment with gradual increments, while watching for side-effects.

The Context of Drug Treatment

I repeat, this time in full, the previously cited quotation from Silverman (1): "The generalization can be made at this time that depression is reported to be rare in infancy and childhood, makes its clinical appearance in adolescence, increases in young adulthood, reaches is greatest frequency in the middle years, and may decline somewhat in the later years of life." Since we remain uncertain of the causes of depression, we are in a weak position to discuss the causes of its variations in incidence by age. There is ample reason, however, to believe that biogenic amine activity is deficient in this disorder (22,29,30,31,32,33), and in this connection the recent report by Robison *et al.* (34) is of interest. These authors chemically examined 55 human brains obtained at autopsy. They found that monoamine oxidase steadily increased and norepinephrine levels steadily decreased with age. They suggested that "this relation of age to enzyme activity might be a predisposing factor to depression which accentuates changes in brain amines precipitated by other events." With increasing age there is hardly a paucity of "other events" which could lower the threshold for depression. After a long plateau endocrine function diminishes, and this is not limited to gonadal function (35). Nutrition may fail.

Diminishing cardio-renal function may lead to the accumulation of toxic products. Meanwhile, object loss proceeds *pari passu*. Busse *et al.* (36) has offered a systematic description of these events.

The point is quite simple. In the elderly patient measures of general care must be taken, and it is my firm belief that pharmacotherapy of depression will succeed to the extent that they *are* taken. In a pharmacologic treatise this will sound like lip service. I do not mean it as such. I refer the reader to the full discussions by Goshorn (37) and by Dovenmuehle (11).

There is another general point worthy of mention. It has to do with how the elderly may instruct us. Depression remains common in the aged but mania becomes rare. Roth (2) was astonished to find mania accounting for only 0.6% of the total cases of affective disorder. We think that both depression and mania are predisposed by heredity factors, often the same ones (38), and we think that genes do not change with age, though, of course, their expression may. Apparently, then, with advanced years the patient becomes less able to "choose" mania as a response to a basic brain malfunction. Perhaps increasing monoamine oxidase activity limits the choice, but one suspects the determination is more complex. These considerations deserve the attention of other scholars of depression-mania relationships (39, 40).

The context of pharmacotherapy needs one more extension. Just as pharmacotherapy requires attention to general measures of physical care and to supportive psychotherapy, its wise application also requires consideration of non-drug, primary treatments, principally electric shock. Although there is now less reason to commence treatment with this modality, there is still occasion to do so. I refer to the late middle-aged or elderly patient, usually a man, with severe agitation and frank suicidal ideation. I consider him the most severe suicidal risk in psychiatric practice. At our clinic we have no hesitation to administer electric shock to such a patient as soon as essential studies of physiologic state can be accomplished. Furthermore, we may use daily shock until temporary mental confusion has reduced the ability to accomplish suicide. Whether shock alleviates depression per se faster than drugs is moot, but I have no doubt that when used in this fashion it reduces the ability to accomplish suicide much faster.

Summary

Drugs are valuable additions to the management of depression in the aged, just as they are in depression in younger age groups. In the elderly they must, however, be used with care, with regard for the peculiarities of the patient who confronts us, particularly with regard to his increased susceptibility to side-effects, and with attention to other therapeutic modalities. I close by paraphrasing Dovenmuehle (11): In the elderly patient there are no specific treatments for symptoms, only specific programs for management.

References

1. Silverman C.: *The Epidemiology of Depression.* Baltimore, Johns Hopkins University Press, 1968.

2. Roth M: The natural history of mental disorders in old age. J Ment Sci 101: 281-301, 1955.

3. Klein DF, Davis JM: *Diagnosis and Drug Treatment of Psychiatric Disorders.* Baltimore, the Williams and Wilkins Company, 1969.

4. Bann TA: *Psychopharmacology.* Baltimore, the Williams and Wilkins Company, 1969.

5. Lifshitz K, Kline N: Psychopharmacology of the aged. In: *Clinical Principles and Drugs in the Aging,* (ed) JT Freeman, Springfield, Charles C Thomas, 1963.

6. Kral VA, Papetropoulos D: Treatment of geriatric patients. In: *Psychopharmacology,* (eds) NS Kline, HE Lehmann, Boston, Little, Brown, 1965.

7. Kuhn R: Über die Behandlung depressiver Zustände mit einem Iminodibenzyl-derivat (G-22355). Schweiz Med Wschr 87:1135, 1957.

8. Goldberg LI: Monoamine oxidase inhibitors. JAMA 190: 456-462, 1964.

9. Hollister LE et al: Evaluation of desipramine in depressive states. J New Drugs 3: 161-166, 1963.

10. Sterlin C et al: A comparative evaluation of doxepin and chlordiazepoxide in the treatment of psychoneurotic outpatients. Curr Ther Res 12: 195-200, 1970.

11. Dovenmuehle RH: Psychiatry: Implementation. In: *Clinical Features of the Older Patient,* (ed) JT Freeman, Springfield, Charles C Thomas, 1965.

12. Barbeau A: L-DOPA therapy in Parkinson's disease: A critical review of nine years' experience. Canad Med Assoc J 101: 791, 1969.

13. Strang RR: Imipramine in treatment of parkinsonism, a double-blind placebo study. Brit Med J 2:33-34, 1965.

14. Laitinen L: Desipramine in treatment of parkinson's disease. Acta Neurol Scandinav 45: 109-113, 1969.

15. Hall CD, Weiss EA, Morris CE, Prange AJ: Rapid deterioration in patients with parkinsonism following tryptophan-pyridoxine administration. Neurol 22: 231-237, 1972.

16. Lidbrink P, Jonsson G, Fuxe K: The effect of imipramine-like drugs and antihistamine drugs on uptake mechanisms in the central noradrenaline and 5-hydroxytryptamine neurons. Neuropharmacol 10: 521-536, 1971.

17. Pohlmeier H, Matussek N: Untersuchungen uber den Einfluss von Desmethyl-Impramine = Pertofran auf den Parkinsonismus beim Menschen. Arch Psychiat Nervenkr 207: 175-185, 1965.

18. El-Yousef MK, et al: Reversal by physostigmine of cogentin toxicity. Presented at the annual meeting of the American Psychiatric Association, Dallas, Texas, May 2, 1972.

19. Goldstein BJ, Pinosky DC: Clinical evaluation of doxepin in anxious depressed outpatients. Curr Ther Res 11: 169-177, 1969.

20. Ayd FJ: Recognizing and treating depressed patients. Mod Med, Nov 29, 1971, pp. 80-86.

21. Fann WE, et al: Doxepin: Effect on biogenic amine transport in man. Psychopharmacologia 22: 111-125, 1971.

22. Schildkraut JJ: The catecholamine hypothesis of affective disorders: a review of supporting evidence. American J Psychiat 122: 509-522, 1965.

23. Ayd FJ: Long-term administration of doxepin (Sinequan). Dis Nerv Sys 32: 617-622, 1971.

24. Abse DW, Dahlstrom WG: The value of chemotherapy in senile mental disturbances. JAMA 174: 2036-2042, 1960.

25. Hordern A, Holt NF, Burt CG, Gordon WF: Amitriptyline in depressive states: Phenomenology and prognostic considerations. Brit J Psychiat 109: 815-825, 1963.

26. Sandifer MG, Wilson IC, Gambill JM: The influence of case selection and dosage in antidepressant drug trial. Brit J Psychiat 111: 142-148, 1965.

27. Fink M, Klein DF, Kramer JC: Clinical efficacy of chlorpromazine-procyclidine combination, imipramine and placebo in depressive disorders. Psychopharmacologia 7: 27-36, 1965.

28. Davis JM: Personal communication.

29. Prange AJ: The pharmacology and biochemistry of depression. Dis Nerv Sys 25: 217-221, 1964.

30. Bunney WE, Davis JM: Norepinephrine in depressive reactions. Arch Gen Psychiat 13:483-494, 1965.

31. Coppen A: The biochemistry of affective disorders. Brit J Psychiat 113: 1237-1264, 1967.

32. Lapin IP, Oxenkrug GF: Intensification of the central serotoninergic processes as a possible determinant of the thymoleptic effect. The Lancet 1: 132-136, 1969.

33. Glassman A: Indoleamines and affect disorders. Psychosom Med 31: 107-114, 1969.

34. Robison DS, et al: Aging, monamines, and monoamine-oxidase levels. The Lancet 1: 290-291, 1972.

35. Perloff WH: Geriatric endocrinology. In: *Clinical Features of the Older Patient,* (ed) JT Freeman, Springfield, Charles C Thomas, 1965.

36. Busse EW, et al: Studies in the processes of aging. The strengths and weaknesses of psychic functioning in the aged. Amer J Psychiat 111: 896-901, 1955.

37. Goshorn RW: Psychiatry: Orientation. In: *Clinical Features of the Older Patient,* (ed) JT Freeman, Springfield, Charles C Thomas, 1965.

38. Winokur G, Cadoret R, Dorzab J, Baker M: Depressive disease: a genetic study. Arch Gen Psychiat 24:135-144, 1971.

39. Whybrow, PC, Mendels J: Toward a biology of depression: some suggestions from neurophysiology. Amer J Psychiat 125: 1491-1500, 1969.

40. Court JH: Manic-depressive psychosis: an alternative conceptual model. Brit J Psychiat 114: 1523-1530, 1968.

Electroshock and The Aged Patient

William P. Wilson, M.D.
L. Frank Major, M.D.

The subject of physical trauma to the brain may at first glance seem unrelated to psychopharmacology. Still, to consider the use of the largest number of pharmacological agents in the treatment of mental problems in the aged, it is necessary that we include electroshock. This is true because we must know how to use anesthetic agents and other drugs in this treatment modality.

In the history of psychiatry, we have observed the phenomenon that when a new treatment is introduced, it almost always is most beneficial to patients with affective disorders. Metrazol, electroshock, insulin, psychosurgery, psychotropic drugs and lithium treatment have all produced better overall results in affective disorders than in schizophrenia or neurosis. Indeed, electroshock has proved to be a specific treatment for depression and mania. The extraordinarily dramatic response to electroshock, the *restitutio ad integrum* that it produces, and the unusual safety of the procedures all combine to earn it a place in the armamentarium of 90% of the psychiatrists in this country. Still, there exists a basic fear of the procedure by the patient as well as a reticence to use it by the psychiatrist except when all other treatment possibilities have been exhausted. In spite of its obvious efficacy, it is interesting that we are still overwhelmed by the patient's mystical fear of being unconscious, of losing control. It is likely that this "primal" fear accounts for the attitude of reluctance to use electroshock that we find among many psychiatrists.

In the recent past when psychopharmacologic agents were first introduced, it was not uncommon for us to hear that these agents would soon replace electroshock. One came to believe after listening to some "prophets" that electroshock should immediately be done away with, that it should be used only as a lifesaving procedure, if at all, and that with enough drugs it soon would be dropped from our armamentarium. This, of course, has not happened. It still is in widespread use. We must then occasionally reappraise its value. It is the purpose of this essay to do just that, especially its usefulness as a treatment technique in the aged.

We can begin by asking the questions, how useful is electroshock, when is it indicated, and are there special precautions that have to be taken with aged patients.

Electroshock was introduced by Cerletti and Bini in 1933 (1). Its use quickly spread throughout the world so that by 1939 it was beginning to be widely used in this country and by the start of WW II it was in general use. The major problem of its use in the early days was the high incidence of fractures, especially of the spine (2, 3, 4). A figure as high as 30% was reported in some series. That this complication was a problem is attested to by the vivid memories of actually having heard bones break during a seizure. Most psychiatrists with this experience were, therefore, reticent to treat the aged patient because of their brittle bones, and even though they might have had a treatable disorder, they were often left to suffer because of x-ray reports that indicated an increased risk of fractures. Numerous efforts were made to reduce this danger but most were, to say the least, ineffective. The use of Glissando techniques and unidirectional currents (5, 6, 7) did little to eliminate the dangers of fracture and other complications.

In the meantime, (8) because of this problem, curare was used to modify the seizure and although its use did allow treatment to be administered to more high-risk patients, it still was used only when absolutely necessary. (9, 10). Its dangers, pulmonary bronchospasm, blood pressure drops, a prolonged period of paralysis (20 minutes average) still left electroshock a risky procedure, even in the healthier aged patient. Deaths from curare itself did occur! Because there was a need for a good muscle-relaxing drug, much research was being done and, after a few abortive introductions, succinylcholine was introduced in 1949 (11). Because of its unique short action and lack of side effects, it quickly came into widespread use. Nevertheless, it still had the disadvantage of requiring the services of persons with some training in resuscitative techniques to support the patient during treatment. At first it was given without sedation but since patients objected strongly to the respiratory paralysis, it gradually became a standard practice to give a small dose of barbiturate before giving the muscle relaxant. The short duration of action, where the mean respiratory paralysis is 1.9 minutes, and the lack of other side effects only minimally increases the risk of shock treatment even when resuscitative assistance is not available.

Though succinylcholine had solved the problem of fractures, there was still the problem of the patient with other disease, especially with heart disease. What was to be done about these complicating factors?

This problem had been to some extent investigated by Bankhead, Torrens, and Harris (12) but Nowill et al (13) were the first to extensively investigate the effects of shock on the heart and to attempt to develop methods to minimize these effects. In their studies they observed a high incidence of arhythmias but were able to control these with large doses of atropine and/or digitalis and quinidine. As a result of their work and that of others, electroshock could be safely given to the high-risk, aged patient with almost any complicating problem except for pulmonary cardiae, renal or hepatic failure. That the procedure was safe was documented by studies of metabolic activity (13). In these it was demonstrated that the effort expended during a modified seizure was no greater than that expended lying quietly in bed. Electroshock could obviously be a relatively minor stress to the physically compromised patient. The statistics accumulated on the dangers of electroshock since 1950 indicate that when all precautions are taken electroshock is a remarkably safe procedure (14, 15, 16).

Unfortunately the age-old problem of the induced memory defect has not been solved. This troublesome side effect of electroshock may be quite severe and may create real management problems. A very confused patient behaves, of course, as an organic patient and he can say and do things which cause serious emotional anguish in his relatives. This undesirable effect of electroshock also can be quite disturbing to the attending physician as it limits his ability to communicate effectively with the patient. In others, guilt can be engendered because the patient's organic state is sometimes pointed to as evidence of permanent damage to the brain even though there is no evidence in any of the many studies performed that psychological and neurophysiological changes do not revert to the pre-treatment levels of function. It is unlikely that we will ever be able to control our feelings about these complications.

In what disease is electroshock indicated and under what circumstances?

The answer is, of course, quite straightforward. Electroshock has its greatest use in the treatment of affective disorders, but it can be to a lesser extent useful in treating other problems. Let us concentrate then on its use in patients with disturbances of emotion.

The affective disorder diagnoses available to us in DSM II are as follows: 1) Depressive reaction; 2) Manic depressive reaction; depressed, manic and circular types; 3) Involutional melancholia; 4) Involutional paranoid state; and 5) finally, Psychotic depressive reaction. Every one of these entities can be seen in the aged patient but they frequently present diagnostic problems even though the criteria in both our manual and in the standard textbooks may seem quite clear. The primary difficulty is the occurrence of affective confusional states (17), and the occurrence of organic confusional states in which severe disturbances of affect are seen. It is not within the scope of this essay to go into this subject in detail, but it does seem worthwhile to point out that affective confusion is a primary disturbance in many aged patients and that such an illness may on examination seem organic. Even the psychological examination may not help us here. It is only by observation that one comes to recognize that the patient's confusion is primarily a complaint. We can know this when we observe that he can find his way around the environment and above all he knows where to seek help in an effort to obtain relief from his suffering. The evidences that are provided by our inspection of the activity of his various biological functions are found to be typical of affective disorder. These help us recognize and differentiate the affective disturbances from the more clearly organic ones. To further support the diagnosis of organicity, an abnormal EEG, clear evidence of retention and recall, as well as memory disturbances (which are evidence that awareness of the self and the environment is reduced) is good evidence of organicity if there is only minimal pervasive disturbance of affect.

Now, what about indications? Here our dilemma is not so great. Electroshock is indicated in all of these disorders. Most psychiatrists prefer to use drugs first, but if challenged, their arguments are likely to be that drugs are less expensive and more innocuous. But is that really the case? One cannot be sure, for to pay for drugs 3 to 6 months, to be only improved (and still suffering), to develop dyskinesia tardive, be chained by Parkinson symptoms, or to have recurrent problems with cardiovascular complications are matters that cannot be taken lightly. In contrast, one can predict that the memory loss that occurs with electroshock is on occasion going to be a troublesome complication but that it is only transitory. Thus it appears that electroshock may on many occasions be equally or more useful than drugs. As an added advantage, the patient treated with electroshock is also usually completely recovered and requires no further treatment. Admittedly, electroshock must be given in a hospital environment and requires 4 to 6 weeks hospitalization, but because of its now well-demonstrated safety, there is no reason to withhold this treatment in the aged if indicated.

Finally, we come to the results of the treatment. The evidence here can be summed up in a few sentences. The response of affective disorders treated with electroshock is far better than what can be expected with drugs. If we take the best statistics afforded us with various drugs, we can get only a rate of 60% moderately to markedly improved (18). With electroshock we can expect a recovery from an attack of depression in 65 to 85% of the patients. Follow-up of 5 years reveals that 85% of these have remained well without further symptoms. Manics respond less well with only 65% recovering, and in these there is an appreciable relapse rate (19, 20, 21).

With paranoid psychoses occurring in late life and in patients with evidences of cerebral degenerative or vascular disease, the best we can hope to do is improve an affective disturbance. Electroshock cannot restore dead brain cells. Finally, neurotic disorders of long-standing and disorders of affect secondary to problems of living cannot be expected to respond to electroshock.

Conclusion:

We can summarize our discussion by saying that the efficacy of electroshock in treating the presenium and senium is well-documented. Affective disorders respond most readily to treatment. Well circumscribed illnesses respond to treatment more readily than with drugs. In other disorders such as paranoia and organic disease, as well as neurosis, response is poor. As electroshock is quite safe, it can be considered the treatment of choice in severe affective disorders or in cases where good control of symptoms cannot be achieved with drugs.

Electroshock should not be considered barbaric or damaging to the psyche or intellect, as there is no evidence to document these at times irrational points of view.

References

1. Cerletti, U. and Bini, L. "L'Electtroshock." *Arch. Gen. Neurol. Psichiat. Psicoanal.* 19:266, 1936.

2. Janis, Irving L. "Psychologic effects of electric convulsive treatments (II. Changes in word association reductions). *J. Nerv. Ment. Dis.* 111:383-397, 1950.

3. Flordh, P. "Curareprofylax vid elektroshock." (Experiences in the use of curare in electroshock). *Nordisk Medicin* 43:250-253, 1950.

4. Barrett, J.E., Funkhouser, J.B. and Barker, W.A. "Spinal injuries in shock and epileptic convulsions." *Am. J. Psychiat.* 99:386-390, 1942.

5. Bayles, S., Busse, E.W., and Edbaugh, F.G. "Square waves (BST) versus sine waves in electroconvulsive therapy." *Am. J. Psychiat.* 107:34-41, 1950.

6. Epstein, J. and Wender, L. "Alternating current versus unidirectional current for electroconvulsive therapy—comparative studies." *Confinia Neurologica* 16:137-146, 1956.

7. Friedman, E. "Unidirectional electro-stimulated convulsive therapy. II Therapeutic results in 536 patients." *J. Nerv. Ment. Dis.* 109:540-549, 1949.

8. Bennett, A.E. "Preventing traumatic complications in convulsive shock therapy by curare." *JAMA* 114:322-324, 1940.

9. Duncan, C.P. "The effect of electroshock convulsions on the maze habit in the white rat." *J. Exp. Psycho.* 35:267-278, 1945.

10. Margolis, L.H., Simon A., and Bowman, K.M. "Effects of decamethonium bromide (C 10) and d-tubocurarine on electroconvulsions." *A.M.A. Arch. Neurol. Psychiat.* 65: 174-180, 1951.

11. Bovet, D., Bovet-Nitti, F., Guarino, S., Longo, V.G. and Marotta, M. "Pharmaco-dynamical property of certain derivatives of succinylcholine with curare-like action — Esters of trialkylethanolamine of dicarboxylic aliphatic acids." *Rendic. Ist.* super. san. 12:106, 1949.

12. Bankhead, A.J., Torrens, J.K., and Harris, T.H. "The anticipation and prevention of cardiac complications in electroconvulsive therapy." *Am. J. Psychiat.* 106: 911-917, 1950.

13. Nowill, W.K., Wilson, W.P., and Borders, R. "Succinylcholine chloride in electroshock therapy, II. Cardiovascular reactions." *Arch. Neurol. Psychiat.* 71:189-197, 1954.

14. Wilson, W.P. and Nowill, W.K. "Succinylcholine chloride in electroshock therapy, I. Clinical use." *Arch. Neurol. Psychiat.* 71:122-127, 1954.

15 Kalinowski, L. "Convulsive therapies." IN: *Comprehensive textbook of psychiatry.* A.M. Freedman and H.I. Kaplan (Eds.) Williams & Wilkins Co.: Baltimore, 1947. Pp. 1279-1285.

16. Elithorn, A. "The treatment of depression." IN: *Aspects of Psychiatric research.* D. Richter, J.M. Tanner, Lord Taylor, and O.L. Zangwith. (Eds.) Oxford University Press: London, 1962. Pp. 420-439.

17. Hohman, L.B., and Wilson, W.P. "Variety of Affects: Affective confusion." *Dis. Nerv. Syst.* 23:706-708, 1962.

18. Caffey, E.M., et al. V.A. Bulletin IB 11-2. "Drug treatment in psychiatry." U.S. Government Printing Office, Washington, D.C. 1970.

19. Abrams, R. "Recent clinical studies of ECT." *Seminars in Psychiatry* 4:3-12, 1972.

20. Lippincott, R.C. "Depressive illness: Identification and treatment in the elderly." *Geriatrics* 23:149-152, 1968.

21. Tait, Jr., C.D. and Burns, G.C. "Involutional illnesses. A survey of 379 patients, including follow-up study of 114." *Am. J. Psychiat.* 108:27-36, 1951.

22. Bennett, A.E. "An evaluation of the shock therapies." *Dis. Nerv. Syst.* 6:20-23, 1945.

Index